THE
JOURNEY
OF THE SOUL

THE JOURNEY OF THE SOUL

Traditional Sources on *Teshuvah*

translated and edited by

Leonard S. Kravitz and Kerry M. Olitzky

JASON ARONSON INC.
Northvale, New Jersey
London

This book was set in 12 pt. Electra.

10 9 8 7 6 5 4 3 2 1

Library of Congress Cataloging-in-Publication Data

The journey of the soul : traditional sources on Teshuvah / translated and edited by Leonard S. Kravitz and Kerry M. Olitzky.
    p. cm.
   Includes index.
   ISBN 1-56821-424-3
   1. Repentance—Judaism. 2. Self-actualization (Psychology)—Religious aspects—Judaism. 3. Rabbinical literature—Translations into English. I. Kravitz, Leonard S. II. Olitzky, Kerry M. III. Title: Self-discovery.
   BM645.R45S68 1995
   296.7'4—dc20   94-49000

Manufactured in the United States of America. Jason Aronson Inc. offers books and cassettes. For information and catalog write to Jason Aronson Inc., 230 Livingston Street, Northvale, New Jersey 07647.

Contents

Preface

Some may just see this volume as a collection of Hebrew sources translated into English, thus making a small body of classic Jewish literature more readily accessible to the general public. While that is true, there is much more to this book. This volume—as the title suggests—is dedicated to the process of self-discovery through *teshuvah*. *Teshuvah* is the method, described by our tradition, through which one literally turns or returns (as the term suggests) to the correct path in life and to God. In the complete works from which selections were made for this collection, individual authors suggest that their writing is designed to assist one's search of the inner life. In keeping with the tradition of this literature, this collection is a culmination of the efforts of these individual authors and is dedicated to the same purpose. By bringing these sources together—and including only the section of the author's work that focuses on *teshuvah*—we are helping the reader to redirect his or her life by indeed "making *teshuvah*." This effort at *teshuvah* requires constant attention through study, prayer, and good acts. This book is only the beginning. By sharing with you these classic Jewish sources, we hope to get you on your way.

According to the Rabbis, the Torah was used by God as a blueprint to create the world. Like a blueprint that both describes the structure of a machine and suggests its function, in the rabbinic mind the Torah describes the origins of the universe and suggests its function: to produce good. This is the meaning of the verse "And God saw all that had been made and behold: it was very good" (Genesis 1:31). However, we may yet not have experienced that good. It will become manifest according to God's timetable. In the meantime, the universe—and everyone in it—must follow the divine blueprint that stretched through time and space from creation to redemption.

But how do we as individuals—once created—move through that chasm from creation to redemption? Through *teshuvah*, repentance, the redemptive process that actually accompanied the creation of the world (or existed before it, according to the Rabbis), we can actually bring the messianic era for ourselves and the world. Thus, the very foundation of Torah is inextricably linked to *teshuvah*.

Were we unable to control our actions, there would be no purpose for Torah. We would be unable to respond to its instructions for holy living. If we were unable to change, ultimate redemption would be elusive to us. *Teshuvah* allows us to move from what is to what ought to be. In fact, *teshuvah* makes the entire system of *mitzvot* possible. Suppose one had the ability to take only one free action, and having done so, one had sinned. Whether small or great, a sin is a sin: it is a rejection of divine guidance. The sinner might feel that it made no sense to attempt to fulfill other *mitzvot*, having failed in the one. Repentance makes it possible for the sinner to try again. One's intention to change and one's attempt at change bring the individual back on the path to God. And God wants us to change.

Repentance is certainly important to the modern world. It unabashedly proclaims the possibility of change for individuals. As is suggested in many of the texts included in this volume, what those in the past did can be replicated only if we approach the task of *teshuvah* properly with complete devotion, with the intention to forsake sin and return to God and the way of Torah.

A note about the translation: Recognizing the fact that these men wrote at times in Jewish history that were not necessarily gender-sensitive, we have sought to make the texts as inclusive as possible, generally transcending the gender specificity of the text when the context allowed for such liberties.

How to Use This Book

The Jewish calendar provides numerous opportunities for the individual to take a good, hard look at one's life so that he or she may make the necessary changes to realign it, to set oneself back on the proper course. Jewish tradition calls this process of self-analysis and self-discovery *cheshbon hanefesh*. Most instructive is the text from *Pirkei Avot*, which teaches us to "repent on the day before death" (2:10). Since none of us is aware of the moment we are destined to leave this fragile earthly life, we must be in a constant posture of *teshuvah* — ever ready to evaluate who and what we are as human beings and where we are going.

Some people thus attempt to follow the rhythm of the Hebrew calendar, bringing their lives in sync with its melody. In general, the individual authors cited in this collection considered their writing to be guided instructions or study materials to be studied and followed during the introspective periods of the Jewish holiday calendar, particularly during the Ten Days of Repentance, beginning with Rosh Hashanah and culminating in Yom Kippur. Others take their cues from Rosh Chodesh, the first day of the new month, using it as a prism through which to view the entire year. Find the pattern that works for you; then make sure you allow it to work through you.

❧ 1 ❧

Menorat Hamoar
(Lamp of Light)

Isaac Aboav

Isaac Aboav lived in the latter part of the fourteenth century, probably in Spain. He spent much of his adult life as a
rabbinic author and preacher. His *Menorat Hamoar* became
one of the most popular works of religious reading from the
Middle Ages. It has been printed in over seventy editions and
translated into various languages including Spanish, Ladino,
Yiddish, and German. In addition, numerous authors have
added their own commentaries. One of the best known was
issued as *Nefesh Yehudah*, a Yiddish translation and commentary by Moses ben Simeon Frankfurt of Amsterdam. Aboav's
work has also appeared in abbreviated form taking names such
as *Sheva Petilot*.

Aboav prepared *Menorat Hamoar* "for the ignorant and the
learned, the foolish and the wise, the young and the old, for
men and for women." He prepared it to return *aggadah* (nonlegal material) to what he considered its rightful place in the
Jewish community. Just as Maimonides compiled a standard
edition of law in his *Mishneh Torah*, Aboav sought to prepare
Menorat Hamoar as a standard reference for *aggadah*. As a result, it quickly became a handbook for *divrei Torah* (words of
Torah, sermons) and often served as public reading material
when no rabbi or teacher was available.

Like the biblical lamp stand (Exodus 25:31–35:14) that
provided its name, the complete work is divided into seven

major branches (sections), which are then further subdivided. As headings, the author takes his themes from Psalm 34:15, in which the individual is taught how to "depart from evil." As part of that process, this section focuses specifically on the subject of *teshuvah*.

—•—

The Fifth Lamp: the ways of *teshuvah*. It is divided into three sections [*klalim*]. The first section is the matter of repentance. The second section deals with the days of repentance. And the third [section] deals with those elements of suffering that purge [scour away] sin.

INTRODUCTION

Teshuvah is what keeps people alive. Were it not for repentance, no one could withstand the force of the [divine] Attribute of Justice. We learn in the third chapter of the *Pirkei deRabbi Eliezer* that before the Holy One created the world, God was all alone. Thinking to create the world, God first made a model. The model did not last. This might be compared to a sovereign ruler planning to build a palace, who first made a model of its foundations, its entrances [and its exits] before he started building. Thus the Holy One first made a model of the entire world [before creating it]. It would not stand until God had created repentance.

This *mitzvah* [of repentance] is easier for those who are possessors of the Torah than it would be for those other people who imitate the Jewish people by their laws. We have seen that Christians require excessive self-affliction for the sake of repentance—such as the making of pilgrimages across the sea and to far-off places. That is not the case for us. Our Torah does not instruct us to engage in these afflictions. Only our mouths and our hearts are to be afflicted as it says, "For this commandment which I command you this day, it is not too hard for you, neither is it far off" (Deuteronomy 30:10). This is what is meant by "and [you] should turn to Adonai your God" (Deuteronomy 30:2). The Torah is telling us that to repent we need not go "beyond the sea" or go up to high places that are compared "to heaven." Rather the Torah is telling us that ultimately "the word is very close to you in your mouth and in your heart, that you may do it" (Deuteronomy 30:14). We learn thereby that one should confess with one's mouth, repent with one's heart, and resolve never again to do what one has done. Even though the Sages related this verse to the Torah in its totality, this verse also relates to repentance. We note that the verse equates the action of mouth and heart in repenting from sin.

Even though there is nothing that can withstand repentance, there are minor sins that repentance alone can heal. In addition, there are transgressions that require the Days of Atonement to make atonement. There are major transgressions that require suffering to purge. Here are the classifications of Rabbi Ishmael given in the chapter on the Day of Atonement (Babylonian Talmud, *Yoma* 86a) [already noted in the first Lamp]: He divided all sins except those of desecrating the Divine Name, into three categories: (1) those related to [the nonperformance of] positive commandments for which repentance alone suffices [for atonement]; (2) those related to [the doing of things prohibited by the] negative commandments for which the Day of Atonement, that specific day of atonement, suffices; and (3) those sins punishable by excision and death at the hands of the court, which are purged by suffering.

All of the three require *teshuvah*. Were it not so, when the Ten Days of Penitence arrive or suffering befalls a person, were that person not to motivate oneself to repent, then one's sins would last until one's dying day and bring eternal punishment. However, were that person to motivate oneself and repent, God would receive that repentance, for God's right hand is stretched forth to receive penitents, as the verse teaches, "Return, you mortal children" (Psalm 90:3). We learn in the chapter dealing with the Eve of Passover (Babylonian Talmud, *Pesachim* 119a) that Rav Kahana said in the name of Rabbi Ishmael, son of Rabbi Yose, and Rabbi Simon ben Lakish said in the name of Rabbi Judah the Prince: "What is the meaning of 'And they had the hands (*yadav*) of a person under their wings' (Ezekiel 1:8)?" *Yadav* can be read as *yado* "His hand!" It is the hand of the Holy One that is outstretched beneath the wings of the celestial beasts (*chayot*) to receive penitents and save them from the Attribute of Justice.

We learn in the *Sifre* that "O Adonai, God, You have begun" (Deuteronomy 3:24) means "You forgave even against a Divine Oath" [a play suggesting that the root *chul* may mean "begin" or "nullify"]. "Your greatness" (Deuteronomy 3:24) refers to the Attribute of Your goodness, as the verse has it, "And now, I pray, let the power of Adonai be great" (Numbers 14:17). "Your strong hand" (Deuteronomy 3:24) refers to Your right hand, which is stretched out to receive all who come into the world, as it is written, "Your right hand, O Adonai, glorious in power" (Exodus 15:6). Another verse says, "But Your right hand, and Your arm, and the light of Your countenance, because you are favorable to them" (Psalm 44:4). And yet another verse says, "By Myself have I sworn, the word is gone forth from My mouth in righteousness and shall not come back. That to Me every knee shall bow, every tongue shall swear" (Isaiah 45:23).

[The strength of] "Your strong hand" (Deuteronomy 3:23) means that using mercy You conquer your Attribute of Justice, as it is written, "Who is a God like You, who pardons the iniquity, and passes by the transgression of the remnant of Your heritage?" (Micah 7:18). "Were one to repent, God would have compassion." [This is the interpretation required for the *midrash* on Micah 8:19; otherwise, the verse is translated as "You will again have compassion upon us."] Yet a verse says, "You will show faithfulness to Jacob, mercy to Abraham" (Micah 8:20). "For what God is there in heaven or on earth that can do according to Your works?" (Deuteronomy 3:23). God's qualities are different from those of flesh and blood. Among mortals, one who is powerful can impose his will upon one who is not. God is different! Though it can be said of God, "Who can stay Your hand?" as shown by the verse "But God is at one with Godself, and who can turn You" (Job 23:13), [God will forgive if we repent]. Rabbi Judah ben Abba compared it to a person who was placed under a royal order. Even were that person to give a great sum of money, he could not delay the decree. But You, Adonai, have said, "Repent and I will receive your repentance," as it says, "I have blotted out, as a thick cloud, Your transgressions" (Isaiah 44:22).

We learn in the *Pesikta* about "Good and upright is Adonai" (Psalm 25:8). Rabbi Pinchas said, "Why is God good? Because God is upright! And why is God upright? Because God is good!" "Therefore does God instruct sinners in the way" (Psalm 25:8), that is, God teaches sinners the way that they may repent.

We learn too that the Holy One does not desire the death of sinners; moreover, God desires their repentance, as it is said, "For I have no pleasure in the death of the one who dies, says Adonai, God. Therefore, turn yourselves, and live" (Ezekiel 18:32).

In God's unique mercy toward Israel, God has revealed

God's secret to God's servants, the Prophets, that they might announce to Israel the decree enacted against them because of their sins, that they might turn toward the good, and that God would be patient if they would repent. [Alas,] they deafened their ears and they hardened their hearts. They were not willing to repent. God then removed God's presence and steadfast love from them that they might be exiled among the nations. Even though the decree came into force, the Divine Presence remained for a while deep in the wilderness waiting for their repentance. We learn this in the tractate *Rosh Hashanah*, (Babylonian Talmud, *Rosh Hashanah* 31a): Rabbi Yochanan said, "For six months the Divine Presence waited for Israel in the wilderness, hoping that they might repent. However, they did not. When they did not, God said, 'May their bones dry up as it says, "But the eyes of the wicked will fail, and they will have no way to flee and their hope will be the drooping of the soul" (Job 11:20).'"

In God's mercy for Israel in general, and on those among them who are righteous in particular, they are punished in this world so that they may go purified to receive their reward in the world to come, a world that is eternal. God does not do this to the peoples of the earth in general or the wicked among them in particular. God does not punish them in this world. Rather, God uses up their merit that they may go to everlasting destruction. We learn this at the end of the first chapter of *Kiddushin* (Babylonian Talmud, *Kiddushin* 40b): Rabbi Elezar bar Zadok said: "To what can the righteous be compared in this world? To a tree that stands totally in a pure place but whose foliage leans toward a place of impurity. Should those branches be lopped off, then the entire tree would exist in purity. Thus the Holy One brings suffering upon the righteous in this world that they may inherit the world to come, as it is said, 'And though your beginning was small, yet your end should greatly increase' (Job 8:7). To what can the wicked be compared in this world? To a tree all of which stands in a place of uncleanliness and yet whose foliage leans toward a pure place. Should the foliage be lopped off, then all the tree would exist in impurity. Thus the Holy One provides benefits to the wicked in this life that they may inherit the lowest level, as it is written, 'There is a way which seems right for a human, but the end are the ways of death' (Proverbs 14:12)."

We learn in the tractate *Horayot* (Babylonian Talmud, *Horayot* 10b) that Rabbi Nachman bar Rabbi Hisda interpreted the verse "There is a vanity which is done upon the earth. There are righteous people who gain as a result of the work of the wicked, and there are wicked people who gain from the work of the righteous" (Kohelet 8:14) in this manner: "Happy are the righteous who gain as a result of the wicked" in this world and woe to the "wicked people who gain from the work of the righteous" in this world. Rabba said to him, "Would the righteous hate possessing both worlds?" Rather Rabba stated, "Happy are the righteous 'who gain as a result of the wicked' in this world [i.e., that the righteous enjoy what the wicked enjoy in this world while the righteous *are* in this world] and woe to the wicked 'who gain as a result of the work of the righteous' in this world [i.e., that the wicked should experience in this life the kind of life that the righteous have in this life]." Rav Papa and Rav Huna, the son of Rabbi Joshua, once went before Rabba. He said to them, "Have you mastered such and such a tractate?" They answered, "Yes." He asked, "Have you gotten richer as a result?" They answered, "Yes." He asked again, "Have you bought a portion of land?" They said that they had. He then applied to them the phrase "Happy are the righteous, when what happens to the wicked in this world happens to them!"

We also learn in the first chapter of *Taanit* (11a) that the meaning of the phrase "A God of faithfulness and without iniquity" (Deuteronomy 32:4) is that the Holy Blessed One will grant a good reward to the righteous (as was indicated in the introduction to the First Candle).

Thus we learn that the Judge of all the earth does justly when God punishes those with few transgressions in this world, a world of vanity and striving for wind, one whose days are like a passing shadow, so that God may reward them for the multitude of their merits in the world to come, a world that is totally good and enduring. God does the reverse to those whose transgressions are many and whose merits are few. One, therefore, should bestir oneself to repent at every moment. How much the more [shall one repent] during those days designated for judgment and atonement! Let no one reject reproaches and pain. Such things subdue the body while delighting the soul. In so doing, they scour away all transgressions as it says, "Return and be healed" (Isaiah 6:10).

The First Principle: Concerning *Teshuvah*

This is divided into four sections. The first section deals with remorse. The second section deals with forsaking [evil]. The third section deals with fasts. The fourth deals with the reward of *teshuvah*.

Section One: Remorse. It is divided into four chapters.

CHAPTER ONE

Were one to be physically ill and yet not be aware of one's illness and think oneself well or were one to be aware of one's illness and yet not be willing to seek medical attention, but rather distract oneself with pleasure, that illness would worsen and would without doubt cause death. The same is true with illnesses of the soul. There are people who are not aware of their illness and imagine that they are healthy, even though they cannot distinguish between right and wrong. Scripture speaks of them, when it says, "The way of the wicked is as darkness. There is a way which seems right for a person but its end is the ways of death" (Proverbs 14:12).

One may be aware of one's illness. One may be aware of being enmeshed in desire. Yet one may not be willing to be healed. Instead, one may wish to indulge one's desire [literally quench one's thirst]. About such persons, Scripture says, "I shall have peace, though I walk in the stubbornness of my heart" (Deuteronomy 29:18). Just as with sickness of the body, one may imagine the sweet to be sour and the sour to be sweet, and reject the kind of food and drink that will preserve health and pursue the kind of food and drink that will cause further illness. Likewise, it is so with sickness of the soul. One may imagine what is evil to be good and what is good to be evil. One may reject what would do good for one's soul and choose what would work evil to the soul. About such cases, Scripture teaches, "Woe to them who call evil good and good evil" (Isaiah 5:20).

One might be aware of one's physical illness and regret the pattern of life that engendered it. Now wishing to be healed, such a person must seek a physician who will properly advise him [or her] how to avoid those things that in his [or her] mind had brought on his [or her] illness by changing his [or her] prior healthy condition. In a similar manner, one who has proceeded on an evil path and, now aware of the sickness of the soul, regrets transgressions, should seek healing for the illness and go to the Sages, who are the physicians of the soul, that they may advise him [or her] in the matter.

We find that regret that touches the heart may move one

from the evil path upon which one has been moving. One may then recognize the evil of one's deeds and be sorry for having done them. All of this motivates one to *teshuvah*. As with physical illness, one who is aware of a small mistake or some small change in one's physical constitution may immediately turn from that dangerous path and immediately be healed because the dangerous behavior has not yet been set into the body. Similarly, one who has habitually moved on a proper path, but who has inadvertently sinned or who has been tempted by sudden desire, will immediately become aware of the problem and will regret it. That person will find repentance to be an easy matter. Because the person did not become used to mischief, that person will have no difficulty in returning to the proper path.

We learn in the third chapter of *Berachot* (Babylonian Talmud, *Berachot* 19a) about a scholar. It was taught in the School of Rabbi Ishmael: should you see a scholar sin and commit a transgression at night, do not think badly of this scholar, for perhaps that person has already repented. "Perhaps," you say? Certainly that person has repented! The person became aware immediately that he or she erred and repented because he or she did not get used to mischief.

One who is used to doing wrong will find *teshuvah* difficult. Such a person will think that what is forbidden is permissible. The Sages said it: "One who sins and sins again will think that the act is permitted." Permitted? You have to say that for such a person the transgression *seems* permitted.

On the other hand, one who immediately regrets the sin committed and completely repents will have the sin treated as if it had been done inadvertently. That person will receive immediate remission. Such repentance is described in the verse "Return, you backsliding children. I will heal your backsliding"

(Jeremiah 3:23). [This matter was treated above in the question of Rabbi Mattiah ben Heresh.]

It is also stated, "Return, O Israel, to Adonai your God" (Hosea 14:2). This was discussed in the [Babylonian] Talmud in the eighth chapter of *Yoma* (86b): Rabbi Simon ben Lakish said, "Great is the power of *teshuvah*. Through it, intentional sins become inadvertent sins, as the verse has it, 'Return, O Israel, to Adonai your God, for you have stumbled in your iniquity.'" "Stumbled" suggests that the sins were inadvertent.

We learn too in the *Pesikta*: Rabbi Yudan bar Simon said the verse "Return, O Israel, to Adonai your God" means even if one has denied God [and thus the phrase "to Adonai your God"]. Rabbi Eliezer said, "It is usual in the world that if one insulted another in public and then wished to apologize in private, the one insulted would say, 'You insulted me in public and now you want to apologize in private! Go get those people who were there when you insulted me and then apologize to me before them!'"

God is different. One can mock and blaspheme God in the marketplace. Yet the Holy One says to such a person, "Repent just between the two of us, and I will immediately accept you."

We also learn in the *Pesikta* that the verse "Return, O Israel, to Adonai your God" may be compared to a city occupied by gangs. There was an old person there who tried to warn all the people of the city and said to them, "Watch out!" Those who paid attention to the older person were saved. Those who did not pay attention were attacked and murdered. In the same way, the prophet cried out to the people, "Return, O Israel, to Adonai your God!"

It was taught in the name of Rabbi Eliezer, "You are the hope [*mikveh*] of Israel, Adonai" (Jeremiah 17:13) may be interpreted thus: Just as a ritual bath [*mikveh*] purifies those who are ritually impure, the Holy One purifies Israel through *teshuvah*. For that reason, the prophet Hosea warns Israel, "Return, O Israel, to Adonai your God."

We learn in *Bereishit Rabbah* in the section "*Vayeshev*" that the verse "And Reuben returned to the pit" (Genesis 37:29) raises the question, from where was he returning? Rabbi Eliezer and Rabbi Joshua sought to answer it. Rabbi Eliezer said, "Reuben had been occupied with sackcloth and fasting [repenting of the sin which he had committed with Bilhah, his father's concubine, Genesis 35:22]. When he was finished [with his *teshuvah*] he went up to the pit and looked into it, as the verse has it, "And Reuben returned to the pit." The Holy One said to Reuben, "No one has sinned before Me and then repented. You have started the process of *teshuvah*. By your life, your grandson will arise and he too will begin with repentance." Who was that grandson? It was Hosea, who said, "Return, O Israel, to Adonai your God."

Concerning such an act of *teshuvah*, the Sages said that it would reach the very Throne of Glory, as the verse has it, "to Adonai your God."

CHAPTER TWO

At the moment that one regrets one's sins and repents, one's repentance is acceptable to the Holy One, particularly when one departs from this world having repented completely.

There are, however, seven degrees of *teshuvah*, one greater than the other. The highest and best is the act of repentance that is performed immediately after the sin, which was spoken of above and which is accepted immediately. Rabbi Abahu spoke about such repentance when he said, "In a place where

[such] penitents stand, not even completely righteous persons can" (Babylonian Talmud, *Berachot* 34b). He meant that the completely righteous person may never have sinned because that person's [*Yetzer Hara*, the Evil] Inclination had never desired anything. Had that person's nature been so warm as to move the person to lust, that person might not have been able to escape it. The one, however, whose nature is warm, which causes sexual desire, is in great pain when one refrains [from sexual intercourse]. This is what the Sages mean by "According to the pain is the reward" (*Pirkei Avot* 5:23). It was because of this [the individual's nature] that one might be called "great" as the Sages said, "The one is great whose inclination is greater than one's fellow" (Babylonian Talmud, *Sukkah* 52a). Such a person, even though sin befalls that person in thought or in deed due to the compulsion of one's nature, because of the greatness of the intellect, that person regrets it immediately and repents. That person is called "great" because of one's power. Because of this person's fear of sin, that person is able to conquer the inclination [to evil]. Rabbi Abahu was speaking of such a person and of similar cases. He was speaking of matters of Torah that had they not been decreed [by the Torah] would not have been required by reason, like sexual prohibitions and similar matters. However, with regard to intellectual matters, even though they were not decreed, they would still have to be maintained. That is what reason requires. The soul that yearns for them [i.e., things that are immoral] attests that it has become deficient and evil and indicates that it possesses an evil quality in as much as it desires things that are contrary to reason. About such a soul it is said, "The soul of the wicked desires evil" (Proverbs 21:10).

About the pious person who does not desire such things, Scripture says, "To do justly is joy to the righteous" (Proverbs 21:15). Even so, were a person to regret immediately one's sin and repent, that person would immediately be forgiven. This is the highest of the seven levels of repentance because there was no delay between sinning and repenting.

The second level [of *teshuvah*] relates to one who has been enmired in sin for many days or years but still repents while still young and in full possession of bodily faculties. That person now regrets the path taken and conquers the [evil] inclination and completely repents. Scripture says about such a person, "Remember your Creator in the days of your youth" (Kohelet 12:1). The verse means that you should remember your Creator while you are in possession of your physical capacities and you are still able to sin as once you did. Thus, the only thing that keeps you from sinning is your fear of sin. The Sages spoke of this in the last chapter of *Yoma* (Babylonian Talmud, *Yoma* 86b): "Who is really a penitent? The one who comes upon the opportunity to sin and does not!" Rabbi Judah added, "The same time, the same woman, the same place, that is, one has one's youth, the same woman is available, and there is nothing standing in the way—[and one does not sin!]."

The third level of repentance: Although one is still young, the opportunity for sin is no longer there. Or perhaps [it is there but] one is [now] embarrassed to pursue one's [evil] inclination. Little by little, one has turned from the way of evil [and repented]. Even though it came about because of something preventing further sin, since the sinner is still young, such repentance is acceptable. About such repentance Scripture says, "And I will take away the blood out of your mouth, the detestable things from between your teeth" (Zechariah 9:7). The verse "Happy is the one who fears Adonai" (Psalm 112:1) was interpreted in the first chapter of *Avodah Zarah* (Babylonian Talmud, *Avodah Zarah* 19a) thus: "Happy is the man"—why a "man" and not a woman? Rabbi Amram in the name of Rav said [the verse means] "Happy is he who repents while he is a [young] man." Rabbi Joshua ben Levi said, "Happy is he who controls his inclination like a man."

The fourth level of repentance: This is the one who repents because of fear of troubles or a divine decree. We find such cases in the people of Nineveh. They were not moved to repentance by the stirring heart but rather by the reproaches of Jonah the prophet who said to them, "In forty days, Nineveh will be overthrown" (Jonah 3:4). Immediately, "the people of Nineveh believed God" (Jonah 3:5). The repentance of these people was accepted, even though it was due to their fear of the divine decree. They had felt remorse. They did turn from their transgression, as it says, "And God saw their works, that they had turned from their evil way and God repented of the evil, which God said God would do to them and God did not do it" (Jonah 3:10). We read about this in the fourth chapter of *Taanit* (Babylonian Talmud, *Taanit* 16a): "My brethren, it is neither sackcloth nor fasting that are factors. It is repentance and good deeds that are factors." We find this too in the people of Nineveh, for it is not written that "God saw their sackcloth and their fasts" but rather it is written, "And God saw their works, that they turned from their evil way."

The fifth level of repentance concerns one who regrets one's sins after getting into lots of trouble. Then that person repents. Even though people will not accept that kind of repentance, as shown by Jephthah, who said, ". . . why have you now come to me when you're in distress?" (Judges 11:7), the Holy One, because of great divine mercy over God's creatures, will, as it is written, "In your distress, when all these things have happened to you in the end of your days, you will return to Adonai your God . . . for Adonai your God is a merciful God" (Deuteronomy 4:30, 31). The Sages spoke about this in the tractate

Pirkei Avot (4:11) when they said that "repentance and good works are as a shield against retribution."

The sixth level: repentance in one's old age, when one is too feeble to be able to proceed along the path of sin. Nonetheless, if one regrets the evil done in one's youth and repents completely with all one's heart, that repentance will be accepted. About this the Psalmist said, "You turn humans to contrition (*dakah*)" (Psalm 90:3). That refers to contrition when one is crushed (*nidkah*) and weakened [by age]. Still, the verse continues, "Return, you mortal children." We learn at the end of the first chapter of *Kiddushin* (Babylonian Talmud, *Kiddushin* 40b), "Rabbi Simon ben Yochai said, 'Were a person to be completely righteous all one's life and yet rebel at the end, that person would lose all the merit gained by one's previous life, as the verse teaches, "The righteousness of the righteous will not deliver one on the day of one's transgression" [Ezekiel 33:12]. On the other hand, were a person completely wicked all one's life and yet repent at the end, no evil would be imputed to that person, as the verse continues, ". . . and as for the wickedness of the wicked, that one will not stumble as a result on the day that one turns from one's wickedness." Let the life of the righteous person who rebelled be regarded as half-filled with merits and half-filled with transgressions! Shall that person lose the merit of one's previous life? ["No"] Rabbi Simon ben Lakish said, "because that person has regretted doing good deeds in the past!"'"

The seventh level, the lowest of all: The person who never having regretted what had been done continues sinning even though it will prove fatal, and repents only when that person sees that death is approaching. We read about such a person in *Pirkei Avot* (2:10): "Repent one day before your death."

We also learn in the second chapter of *Shabbat* (Babylonian Talmud, *Shabbat* 32a): "They say to a person who has become critically ill, 'Confess all your sins, for those about to be executed confess.' When one goes out into the marketplace, let that person think of oneself as being arraigned before a magistrate. If one has a headache, let that person think of oneself as having a chain around one's neck. If one falls getting into bed, let that person think of oneself as being placed on the scaffold. Were that person to have great supporters, that person might still be saved. But if not, not! The supporters that might save such a person are repentance and good deeds. Even were there to be 999 accusers and but one defender, the individual would be saved, as the verse teaches, 'If there be for the individual an angel, an intercessor, one among a thousand, to vouch for a person's uprightness, then God is gracious to the person and says: "Deliver that person from going down to the pit, I have found a ransom"' (Job 33:23, 24). Rabbi Eliezer, the son of Rabbi Jose the Galilean, said, 'Even were there to be 999 joined with that angel to condemn and one angel there to defend, that person would be saved, as the verse has it, "An intercessor, one among a thousand."'"

Elihu said the same thing: "Yea one's soul draws near to the pit, and one's life to the destroyers. . . . Pray to God, and God will show favor to you" (Job 33:22, 26). The verse means that even if one's time had come to die, were one to repent and entreat God, God would be favorable and would be forgiving of sins. We learn this in the case of Eliezer ben Dardia in the first chapter of *Avodah Zarah* (Babylonian Talmud, *Avodah Zarah* 17a). [This was discussed at the end of the First Lamp.]

Even though the aforementioned kinds of repentance were relatively different, each one of them was acceptable. However, the person who keeps sinning even to the day of death and who would die without repentance is considered to be a heretic. Such a person does not believe in the day of judgment and destroys one's body and soul merely to provoke God. That person will suffer in punishment in Gehenna for generations. Therefore wise Solomon warned, "Whatever you can do by virtue of your own ability, do so, for there is no work, no device, no knowledge, no wisdom, in the grave, where you are going" (Kohelet 9:10). He meant, "Do all that you can do in this world." In other words, repent every moment that you can as soon as you can. It is best to repent while you have the power to do so, for when one dies without repenting [it is too late]. In the grave to which you go, there is neither repentance nor repair. The Sages alluded to this when they said, "Prepare yourself in the foyer so that you can enter the banquet hall" (*Pirkei Avot* 4:16). They meant that in "the banquet hall [the life to come]" no improvement is possible! About this the prophet proclaimed, "Turn, turn from your evil ways, for why will you die, O house of Israel?" (Ezekiel 33:11). Another verse says, "And make you a new heart and a new spirit; for why will you die, O house of Israel?" (Ezekiel 18:31). The meaning is clear. Why will you die without repenting? However, if they repent, even though they have been recalcitrant for a very long time, there is healing for their affliction, as it says, "Return, you backsliding children. I will heal your backslidings" (Jeremiah 3:22).

CHAPTER THREE

People might understand the case of one who has never sinned (and three matters that are different than the seven aforementioned levels of repentance) and the case of the one who had never repented (comprising five distinct though related matters), and what might occur to them. The *Midrash* compared them to five groups of people who came on board a ship. These people went on a voyage and got on a ship. They traveled for many days, but they had not reached their destination. One day a strong wind arose and carried the ship and the people on it to an island in the midst of the sea. On that island there were many tall trees bearing all manner of marvelous fruits, each of which was too beautiful to look at and delightful to eat. On that island there were many wells of water sweeter than honey. These wells continually watered the entire island so that the grasses and the herbs grew in abundance, the fruits and the roses blossomed, and the branches of the trees sent forth their shoots and were covered with foliage. Upon these branches every kind of bird burst forth with song. The entire island was a delightful place to be, with wells of water shaded by trees.

On the ship were five groups of people. The first group did not wish to leave the ship and venture out on the island because they said, "Were we to leave the ship, another wind might arise and move the ship and we would be left on the island. Why should we stay on the island for temporary enjoyment? Should we lose ourselves merely for the pleasure of the fruits? If the ship should leave, we would be stuck on the island and die there!"

A second group left the ship and went to the island but quickly ate some of the fruits, speedily walked around the island, and returned to the ship. They found their places on it and relaxed, having lost nothing for having gone on the island.

A third group left the ship, came to the island, ate the fruits, walked around the island, and remained there until the wind arose. The sailors worked to get the ship ready for departure and when they finished, they blew trumpets, which was the customary way of getting the passengers back to the ship. When those on the island heard the trumpets, they feared for their lives and came aboard and found that their seats had been taken by other travelers. They could not find seats as easily as had the first group.

A fourth group, who had landed, were eating the fruits and had been wandering all around the island. When they heard the sound of the trumpets, they said to themselves, "Even though the trumpets have sounded, the ship will not move until they set up the mast." When the mast was set up, they said, "The ship won't leave until the sails are set." When the sails were set, they said, "The ship won't leave until the sailors eat." All the while, these people were still sitting on the island, eating fruit and drinking wine. The sailors finished eating and prepared the ship for departure. Only when the ship began to move did these people say, "If we wait one more minute, the ship will leave and we will be lost." Immediately they ran down to the water's edge and jumped in, putting themselves at risk but finally getting to the ship. Getting on, they found scant room for themselves on it and only with great difficulty could they sit down. They did not have the ease that those who hadn't waited around on the island had.

The fifth group stayed on the island, eating and drinking and rejoicing. They did not think of the ship until it had already gone. Now they were stuck, and they wandered up and down the island. Warm weather passed and cooler weather came. The leaves dried up on the trees; no more fruit could be found. Sometimes there was scorching heat by day and frost by night. Wild animals began attacking them, injuring some and devouring others. The survivors began weeping, sorry that they had not entered the ship in time. It was too late; all from the ship who had stayed on the island perished.

This is how life is in this world. One's good deeds are like the ship. Were one to go wholehearted and keep one's watch to serve one's Creator and if one's inclination would not move one to go after the lusts of this world and its follies, one would be among those who enter in peace and who leave in peace.

And so it is with the first group of human beings. There are those who do not wish to go out on the island at all. These are the completely righteous, who have never even tasted sin and who have conquered their inclinations and have never gone after the lusts of this world. They have maintained their charge and watched their place and have never gone on the island, which can be compared to those transgressions that tempt humans by their delights. The one who gives in to such temptations will be lost. The one who keeps from them will be saved.

The second group, those who came ashore on the island and left it immediately, are like those people who, having sinned, immediately repented while they were still young. This is, as we have said, a superior form of repentance.

The third group, those who only left the island when they heard the ship's trumpets, are like those people who repent when they are old. They saw that their time was coming to an end and so they repented before they would die in the state of wickedness. Even though they are penitents, their place is not as grand as the previous group.

The fourth group, those who left only when they saw the ship leaving and who waited until the last moment to leave so that they barely made the ship, are like those who repent only when death is upon them. When they can see that their powers and their lives are declining and they have no more life in this world, they repent out of fear of death. Even though such repentance is acceptable, their position is less than the previous group.

The fifth group, those who remained on the island after the ship departed, going back and forth, weeping and wailing, even though it did not help, are like those people who are so set in their desires of this world that they go about after the stubbornness of their evil hearts and give themselves no chance to repent. So they die in their wickedness. They will go to utter destruction. The joy of this world will be transformed into worms and maggots that will eat their bodies and burn their souls. They shall become a reproach and an eternal detestation, even as the delights of the island became harsh judgments, burning by day, freezing by night, and being attacked by all kinds of evil beasts and snakes and scorpions.

As the *Midrash* noted: "Who cries: Woe? Who [cries:] Alas?" (Proverbs 23:29). The one who leaves much money and brings many transgressions to the grave. Who should this be? The one who amasses money illicitly, about whom Scripture says, ". . . one who gets rich and not by right. In the midst of one's days that person shall leave them" (Jeremiah 17:11). Indeed, when one leaves this world, one is accompanied neither by silver nor gold but only by repentance and good deeds.

This case may be compared to a person who had three friends. The first really loved her. The second merely liked her. The third didn't care for her at all. Once the king sent for her and sent along servants to speed her on the way to the royal court that she might do the king's commands. The person was frightened and terrified of the power of the king. She began to worry. Perhaps someone has lied about me to the king and he will kill me when I get to the court. I will ask a friend, someone I can trust with my life, to come with me to the court so that she can intercede on my behalf. She went to her first friend, who loved her more than the other two, and told her the story. That friend refused to come and would not change her mind. Disappointed, she left her. She said to herself, I will go to my second friend and ask her to come with me. She went to her and the friend said, "I won't go before the king but I will come with you on the way to the court to guard you. As soon as you get to the court, I will leave you and go on my way." The person then went to her third friend, whom she had previously held in low esteem. Asking her friend to go with her, she told her what had happened with the other two friends. The third said, "Don't be afraid, I will go with you! I will appear before the King. I'll defend you. I'll do whatever it takes to save you." As soon as she said it, she accompanied her to the king, spoke up on her behalf, and thereby saved her.

The first friend, the one she loved the most, was her wealth, the dearest thing to her in the world. On the day that she died, she left it. It could do nothing for her, as it says, "One's wealth will not descend after you" (Psalm 49:18). The second friend was her relatives and her friends, who may accompany a person to the grave, but when they are finished with the burial, they depart. Her third friend, the one who recommended her to the king and defended her, was repentance and good deeds. They go with a person at the time of one's death to intercede for the individual, as it is written, "Your righteousness will go before you" (Isaiah 58:8).

The king [in the story] who summoned the person is the Soverign of Soverigns, the Blessed One. God is impartial and cannot be bribed. Only repentance and good deeds can deliver the individual from God's judgment.

CHAPTER FOUR

If anyone is remorseful and wants to repent of his or her misdeeds, let that person confess. One does not have to bring any other offering or seek any other intercession. Remorse alone and oral confession [is sufficient], as we learn in the eighth chapter of *Yoma* (Babylonian Talmud, *Yoma* 86b). Rabbi Isaac said, It is said in the west, in the name of Rabbi Maari: Come and see, the Holy One is not like a human being. Were one human being to offend another, the offended one may or may not be assuaged. Even were you to say that the offended person could be assuaged, it would take words or money to do so. The Holy One is different. God can be assuaged with words, as it is written, "Take with you words, and return to Adonai" (Hosea 14:3). Moreover, God assumes that the person is good, as the verse has the penitent say [in God's presence] "And accept what is good." Indeed, it is as if the penitent has built an altar by pleading and has offered a sacrifice, for the verse continues, "So we will render for bullocks the offering of our lips." You might wonder, "Are the bullocks an obligatory sacrifice?" Therefore, Scripture says, "I will love them freely" (Hosea 14:5).

We learn too in *Pirke deRabbi Eliezer* that the verse "Take with you words" (Hosea 14:3) notes that silver and gold are not mentioned. Rather, the text says, "Take with you *words*."

We also learn in the *Pesikta* that according to Rabbi Judah and Rabbi Nehemiah, the phrase "Take with you words, and return to Adonai" is to be related to [the plea of Cain], "You who can bear all the world, can You not bear [forgive] my sins?"

In the first chapter of *Sotah* (Babylonian Talmud, *Sotah* 7b) we learn: One proclaims [before the errant wife] words of *aggadah* and stories written in ancient texts, such as, "Which of the wise have told from their ancestors, and have not hidden it?" (Job 15:18). Judah confessed and was not ashamed. He merited life in the World to Come. Reuben confessed and was not ashamed. What was his end? He took his portion in the Life to Come! Indeed, what was their reward? We must say, what was their reward in this world? "To whom alone the land was given" (Job 15:19). We are in agreement that Judah confessed, as it is written, "She is more righteous than I" (Genesis 38:26). How do we know that Reuben confessed? Rabbi Samuel bar Nachmani, quoting Rabbi Jonathan, asked, "Why is it written, 'Let Reuben live, and not die' (Deuteronomy 33:6) and 'This is for Judah, and he said' (Deuteronomy 33:7)? It is to teach that for all the years that Israel was in the wilderness, the bones of Judah were rattling around in his coffin until Moses came and asked for mercy on [Judah's] behalf. Moses said, 'Master of the Universe, what caused Reuben to repent? Judah did!" [And thus the verse ". . . for Judah, and he (Reuben) said (confessed)."] Adonai immediately responded to the voice of Judah and the bones returned to their sockets. But the angels would not permit him to enter the College on High. [So, Moses prayed] "Bring him to his people" (Deuteronomy 33:7). He was unable to follow the mode of argument there! He was still unable to secure a decision in accordance with traditional practice [so Moses prayed], "You will be a help to him [in his struggle] against his adversaries." We agree that Judah confessed so that Tamar would not be burnt. Why did Reuben confess? Is it not as Rabbi Sheshet taught, that anyone who specifies one's sin is impudent? Reuben confessed so that his brotherly feeling should not be suspected.

What has already been said, that the one who enumerates one's sins is impudent, refers to one listing sins in the presence of other people. However, one must enumerate one's sins before God. We learn this in the eighth chapter of *Yoma* (Babylonian Talmud, *Yoma* 86b). It was taught, Rabbi Judah ben Baba said, "One must enumerate one's sins, as it is written, 'Oh, this people has sinned a great sin, and has made a god of gold' (Exodus 32:31)." Rabbi Akiba said, "Such elaboration is not necessary, as it is written, 'Happy is the one whose transgression is forgiven, whose sin is pardoned' (Psalm 32:1)." If that is so, then what was the purpose of stating, ". . . and made them a god of gold"? It follows in what Rabbi Yannai stated, "Moses said before the Holy One, 'Master of the Universe, it was the silver and gold that You gave them so abundantly that caused them to make gods of gold!'"

Israel had two good leaders, Moses and David. Moses said, "Let my disgrace be written down as it says, 'Because you did not believe in Me' (Numbers 20:12)." David said, "Let my disgrace not be written down" as it says, 'Happy is the one whose transgression is forgiven, whose sin is *kisui* [here, *hidden*]." How are the differing cases of Moses and David to be understood? It may be compared to two women who were condemned to be whipped by the court. One had gone astray (and had a sexual relationship outside of her marriage). The other had eaten figs produced during the Sabbatical year. The one who ate the figs said, "Please inform everybody why I am being whipped so that people should not say it is for the same reason that the other woman is being whipped." Sabbatical-year figs were immediately brought to her and hung around her neck. An announcement was also made as to why she was being whipped.

If a sin [being repented of] were notorious, then one should confess it publicly, so that all may know that the sinner turned from it. If the sin were one between persons, the offender should publicly seek forgiveness from the one offended. We learn this from the statement of Rabbi Judah. He taught that Rav contrasts two verses, "The one who covers one's transgressions will not prosper" (Proverbs 28:13) and "Happy is the one whose transgression is forgiven and whose sin is hidden" (Psalm 32:1). The first verse relates to the one whose sin is widely known. The second verse relates to the one whose sin is not widely known. Rabbi Zutra bar Tovi said in the name of Rav, "The difference between the two verses is that the first relates to sins between persons and the second relates to sins between an individual and God."

The best thing of all is to enumerate all sins while hiding from other people that sin that is not notorious. For that reason, the Sages created a confessional including every manner of sin, which is to be recited by every person.

Section Two: Dealing with the forsaking of sin. It contains five chapters.

CHAPTER ONE

Even though one may regret one's transgressions and confess them orally, were one not to forsake them, that person would be like the person who immersed oneself [in a ritual bath] while holding on to a contaminating lizard. The immersion will have no [cleaning] effect until the individual gets rid of the lizard. We learn this in the first chapter of *Taanit* (Babylonian Talmud, *Taanit* 16a). The Rabbis taught, "One should confess the sin that one has done. However, if that person does the sin again, to what may that person be compared? To the one who holds on to a lizard. Even were one to immerse oneself in every kind of water in the world, that immersion would not work. As soon as the person casts away the lizard, the immersion works, as it is written, 'But whoever confesses and forsakes them will obtain mercy' (Proverbs 28:13) and as it is also written, 'Let the wicked forsake the [evil] way, and the iniquitious person one's [evil]. Let that person return to Adonai' (Isaiah 55:7)."

Therefore let one who would be penitent forsake any sin that he or she might be still grasping. If such a person still has evil thoughts in one's heart, let them be dispelled. [One who would be penitent] should make every effort never to sin again. Therefore, one should accept the following conditions [of penitence]. First, let him or her intensify the remorse within the heart for the sin that he or she sinned, even were it merely a thought, so that it should not be easy to return to that sin. One's repentance and its duration may be evaluated by the bitterness of one's remorse and the depth of one's suffering, for they indicate the purity of one's soul and the pangs of one's heart. In this regard Scripture says, "A broken and a contrite heart, O God, You will not despise" (Psalm 51:19).

Were one to have sinned with the seeing of the eyes, let those eyes brim now with tears, as it says, "My eyes run down with rivers of water, because they do not observe your law" (Psalm 119:136). Because the heart and the eyes are the agents of sin, the Torah warns us ". . . and that you do not go about after your own heart and your own eyes, after which you used to go astray" (Numbers 15:39). The eye sees, the heart desires, and the person acts!

Were one to have sinned in matters of food and drink, whether of things forbidden or excesses of pleasures, let that person start fasting. Were one to have sinned in matters of sexual desire, let that person greatly lament [the sin] in order to smash desire and the uncircumcised quality of the heart.

From these four principles come all the elements of transgression. The prophet summarized the healing for them in one verse, as it is written, "Yet even now says Adonai, 'Turn to Me with all your heart, with fasting and with weeping, and with lamentation'" (Joel 2:12). What did the prophet mean by "with all your heart"? One should intensify the sorrow [for sin] within one's heart. The pouring forth of tears from their eyes, called "weeping," and the fasting and the lamentation were to subjugate their [the sinners'] bodies and to smash their [wicked] spirits and the power of their [evil] inclinations.

Let no penitent take weeping lightly, for the Sages said that though the gates of prayer might be locked, the gates of tears were never locked, as we learn in the fifth chapter of *Berachot* (Babylonian Talmud, *Berachot* 32b): Rabbi Eliezer said, "Although the gates of prayer may be locked, the gates of tears were never locked."

Were one physically ill, that person would take a kind of medication specific to the illness. The level of unbalance in the individual that the illness caused would be offset by the medication. Similarly, one heals the illnesses of the soul. The soul that was profligate in its love of money must now become accustomed to the giving of *tzedakah*. To avoid constant greed, one must (learn to) rejoice in one's portion. Remembering when death comes suddenly, all is lost. [As a matter of fact,] all may be lost even while one is alive. Such a person should accustom oneself to the company of sick people, reflect on the dead, then go to the cemetery and think, "Here today and tomorrow in the grave."

The soul that is consumed by the love of women can only be healed by distancing oneself from them. The greater the desire [for women], the greater the rejection must be. Such a person should also remember that injury and damage are incurred by lust and what ethical deficiencies follow from it. Indeed, [immoral] women are a net to capture then destroy a person: body and soul.

The soul that is given over to excessive pride can only be healed by walking humbly and modestly.

To heal the soul from its ethical defects, such medications must be applied for many days until they [the defects] are fixed in the [essential] nature of the person [being healed]. Just as the medicine used to treat physical illness does not immediately work, so the healing of the soul may require many days of treatment. One must diligently devote oneself to the *mitzvot* until they become part of one's customary behavior. A Sage once said, "I was an arrogant person from my youth. I never felt any shame in doing anything wrong until I became jealous of my friends.

Thus, my soul grew accustomed to being humble. It did not come easily. It came by necessity and by oath, but when I devoted myself to it for many days, seeing how pleasant it was, I desired it even more. My soul followed after it."

The person who yearns continually to go out drinking and to walk in [self-indulging] gardens can be healed by lessening one's desire for [hedonistic] pleasures. One should increase those things that weaken desire and decrease contact with wicked people. One should get used to being with poor and vulnerable people, thereby weakening one's desire [for pleasure]. One should stick to the right and straight path. This is how all kinds of soul sickness should be treated. On one hand, the soul should train itself. On the other hand, the soul should return to God so that God may heal it.

CHAPTER TWO

The penitent should be ashamed of one's sins, whether one keeps them to oneself or whether one confesses them. Two things will aid the penitent. First, one must curb the pride that once was in the [penitent's] soul. Second, one should forsake even thinking about the desire to transgress. Scripture teaches, "Surely after that I was turned. I repented. And after that I was instructed. I struck my thigh. I was ashamed, yes, even confounded, because I bore the reproach of my youth" (Jeremiah 31:19). The prophet meant to say, "After You chastised me, so that You forced me to turn from my way, I repented, and regretted what I had done. Since I remembered my earlier deeds and acknowledged them in my heart, thinking about them and confessing them, I hit my thigh, to hurt my entire body for the anguish in my heart. With the breaking of my bones, I add more shame and disgrace to my heart for the reproach of the sins of my youth." If one is embarrassed because of the sin of one's friend, which one could ignore, what should one do about one's own sin in the presence of the One who will not ignore the individual? Woe to that shame! Woe to that disgrace! If one sees a person who forgives a friend because of the love of one for the other, one might be embarrassed because of one's irrational love. Indeed, one might add shame to one's heart. The sinner, in seeing that God has overlooked a transgression and the sinner will escape punishment, may become even more ashamed. That's what the prophet meant when he said, "Because I bore the reproach of my youth" (Jeremiah 33:19). Jeremiah meant, "You have forgiven the reproach of my youth" in the same sense as the verse "Happy is the one whose transgression is forgiven" (Psalm 32:1) or what is suggested by the verse "So that you may remember and be confounded and never open your mouth anymore because of your shame. When I have forgiven you all that you have done, says Adonai, God" (Ezekiel 16:63).

We learn in the first chapter of *Berachot* (Babylonian Talmud, *Berachot* 12b) Rabbi Huna the Elder said in the name of Rav: Whoever does something [wrong] and feels ashamed will have all one's sins forgiven, as it says, "that you may remember, and be confounded, and never open your mouth anymore because of your shame. When I have forgiven you all that you have done, says Adonai." One might wonder whether it is different with a congregation, [that their sins would be forgiven]. An answer is provided from this verse: "And Samuel said to Saul: 'Why have you disquieted me, to bring me up?' And Saul answered: 'I am very distressed, for the Philistines are making war against me, and God has left me, answering me no longer, neither by Prophets nor by dreams. Therefore I have called you so you can reveal to me what I should do'" (1 Samuel 28:15). Since Saul had slain those in Nob, the city of priests, and the *Urim* and *Tummim* are not mentioned here, how would we know that Saul was forgiven? It is written, "Moreover, Adonai will deliver Israel with you into the hand of the Philistines. Tomorrow you and your children will be with me. Adonai will deliver the army of Israel into the hand of the Philistines'" (1 Samuel 28:19). Rabbi Yochanan said "with me" means in my division [in heaven]. But the rabbis said [the fact that Saul was forgiven is indicated by] this verse: ". . . and we will hang them up to Adonai in Gibeah of Saul, the chosen of Adonai" (2 Samuel 21:6). "Chosen of Adonai" (*bachur hashem*) is not used here. Instead, "chosen by Adonai" (*bachir hashem*) is used [by the prophetic writer]. A divine voice went out and proclaimed, "Saul is chosen by God." [The Masoretic text has *bachir hashem*, making the *midrash* problematic.]

We also learn why it was written, "And Moses said to Aaron: 'Draw near to the altar'" (Leviticus 9:7) to teach that Aaron was frightened when he saw the altar in the shape of an ox. The sin of the [golden] calf came to mind. Ashamed of that sin, he delayed approaching the altar. [The translation of the last line combines two versions of the text *mitboshesh* and *mitbayish*.] At that moment, Moses our Teacher said to him, "Draw near the altar, for your sin is already forgiven, [simply] because you were ashamed of it."

For that reason [of shame], when the pious of old were guilty of any sin, they would always keep it in mind so that they always would be ashamed of it. Thus, they would fulfill what David said: "For I know my transgressions and my sin is ever before me" (Psalm 51:5). David meant his sin would always be present in his mind so that he might fully reflect on it, to be so ashamed of it that he would never do it again. Ezra said something similar: "O my God, I am ashamed and blush to lift my face to You, my God" (Ezra 9:6). We learn thereby that when one is ashamed of one's sin, one will never do it again. Thus, one achieves atonement for it.

CHAPTER THREE

Submission and humility befit the penitent person because sin comes about through pride in the heart, as the verse has it, "then your heart will be lifted up, and you will forget Adonai your God" (Deuteronomy 8:14). Another verse teaches, "A haughty look, and a proud heart: The tillage of the wicked is sin" (Proverbs 21:4). The medicine for such pride is humility, as the prophet said, "Rend your hearts, not your garments" (Joel 2:13). David said in confessing his sin, "The sacrifices of God are a broken spirit" (Psalm 51:19), by which he meant that God does not want a sacrifice for [the remission of] an intentional transgression, but rather a broken spirit. It is also spoken of Ahab, "And it came to pass, when Ahab heard those words, that he rent his clothes, put sackcloth on his flesh, fasted, lay in sackcloth, and went softly" (1 Kings 21:27). For that reason, God said, "See how Ahab humbles himself before Me" (1 Kings 21:29).

We learn in the *Pesikta* that Zavdi ben Levi, Rabbi Yose ben Pinchas, and the Rabbis commented on the verse "The sacrifices of God are a broken spirit." Said the first, David prayed, "If you will accept my repentance, then I will know that Solomon my son will arise and build the Temple and the altar and will offer every kind of sacrifice on it, as it says, 'The sacrifices of God,'" which is followed by "Do good in Your favor to Zion. Build the walls of Jerusalem. Then you will delight in the sacrifices of righteousness, in burnt-offering and whole offering. Then they will offer bullocks on your altar" (Psalm 51:20, 21). Said the second, "How do we know that the one who repents is considered by God as if he had gone up to Jerusalem, had built the Temple and the altar, and had offered every kind of sacrifice? From the verse "The sacrifices of God are a broken spirit." [The comment of the Rabbis is not given in the text.]

We also learn in the first chapter of *Rosh Hashanah* (Babylonian Talmud, *Rosh Hashanah* 17a) Rabba said, "Whoever foregoes the acts of retribution that are one's own, they [those in heaven] will forgo the individual's sins" as it is written, "Who is a God like You who pardons iniquity, and passes by the transgression of the remnant of Your heritage?" (Micah 7:18). [This verse should be interpreted thus:] "God . . . pardons iniquity" to the one who "passes by the transgression" done to him. It follows that the one who forgoes [and does not retaliate against the injuries and] the sins [done] her will have her sins forgiven by God since such an act of forbearance indicates great humility.

One should improve one's acts in the manner that one had sinned. In the very kind of sin that one had committed, one should now try to fulfill *mitzvot*. It is as the Sages said, "The righteous are those who seek favor in the very sin that they had once committed." The Sages also said, "If you have committed a bunch of transgressions, go now and fulfill a bunch of *mitzvot*."

With all of this, one should pray seeking forgiveness, even as Moses our Teacher said, ". . . Pardon our iniquity and our sin, and take us as Your inheritance" (Exodus 34:9). Daniel said, "And I turn my face to Adonai, God, to seek by prayer and supplication" (Daniel 9:3). And King David said, "We have sinned with our ancestors. We have done iniquitously. We have dealt wickedly" (Psalm 106:6).

We learn too in the first chapter of *Rosh Hashanah* (Babylonian Talmud, *Rosh Hashanah* 18a) it is taught, Rabbi Meir used to say, "If two people go to bed equally sick or if two people approach the bench for judgment equally charged, and if one of the patients leaves the sick bed [and lives] and the other does not [but dies] and if one [who was condemned] is saved [from execution] and one is not, the explanation for both kinds of cases is that one prayed and was answered and the other prayed and was not answered. The one who prayed a complete prayer was answered. The one who did not pray a complete prayer was not answered."

One should also pray not to be gathered [by God at the hour of death] without repentance, as we learn in *Midrash Tehillim*: "Do not gather my soul with sinners" (Psalm 26:9) means that David used to pray before God that God not gather him [at the hour of death] while still a sinner, but [rather] that he be allowed to repent before being taken. Rabbi Yochanan said, "We have found that there are two places [in Scripture] where the righteous prayed that God should not take them with sinners. Daniel said, ". . . that they might ask mercy of God in heaven concerning this secret, that Daniel and his companions should not perish with the rest of the wise men of Babylon" (Daniel 2:18). And David said, "Do not gather my soul with sinners." By this David meant that he should not die suddenly before he had completed his repentance. Rabbi Chalafta in the name of Rabbi Aibo commented on the verse, "And it came to pass after about ten days that Adonai smote (*vayegof*) Nabal, so that he died" (1 Samuel 25:38). He said, "Behold a plague (*magefah*) takes three days. [The interpretation depends on the relation of *vayegof*, "and God smote" to *magefah*, "plague."] It has been taught, 'To die after one day is a death of vehemence. To die after two days of illness is a shocking death. To die after three days of illness is a death by plague. To die after four days' illness is death by excision. To die after five days' illness is an abrupt death. To die after six days' illness is that death spoken of in the Torah. To die after an illness of any longer duration is a death of suffering.'"

God had suspended the seven days of mourning for the righteous Samuel in order not to have it interfere with the mourning of Nabal, who lingered for three days and then died of a plague. Rabbi Berachia in the name of Rabbi Samuel said, "It is not written here 'In ten days.' Rather it is written, 'About ten days,'" like the Ten Days [of repentance] between Rosh Hashanah and Yom Kippur, perhaps one might repent. There is a similar usage in the verse "It came to pass after seven days that the waters flooded the earth" (Genesis 7:10). Rabbi Oshayah commented that this verse taught that God had delayed the days of mourning for the righteous Methusaleh. This suggests the same for "Do not gather my soul with sinners" (Psalm 26:9).

CHAPTER FOUR

What we have discussed concerns sins between persons and God. However, concerning sins between persons, the offender must correct the offense done to the one offended, as it says, "God saw their works, that they had turned from their evil way . . . and from the violence that is in their hands" (Jonah 3:10, 8). Samuel taught (Babylonian Talmud, *Taanit* 16a): "Were one to steal a beam and build with it, [to repent] one should pull down the building and return the beam to its owner."

If one's sin included material things, even though the sinner may have paid one's obligation, the sinner still must ask forgiveness from the injured party, as we learn in the eighth chapter of *Bava Kamma* (Babylonian Talmud, *Bava Kamma* 92a): "It is written, 'Now therefore restore the man's wife, for he is a prophet. He will pray for you and you will live' (Genesis

20:7). From where do we derive the principle that that injured party should not be cruel [and should forgive]? From the verse that follows: 'And Abraham prayed to God and God healed Abimelech . . .' (Genesis 20:7)." In the *Gemara* [of the previous passage] it is said: The Sages taught that in all cases where one must pay damages for the shame inflicted [on another] even were one to offer all the rams of Neviot, one would not be forgiven until one asked forgiveness [from the injured party] as it says, "And now restore the man's wife. . . ."

We learn too in the eighth chapter of *Yoma* (Babylonian Talmud, *Yoma* 87a): Rabbi Isaac said, "Whoever provokes one's fellow, even merely with words, must appease that person, as it says, 'My child, if you are surety for your neighbor, if you have struck your hands for a stranger—you are caught by the words of your mouth—do this now, my child, and deliver yourself . . . God, humble yourself, and urge your neighbor' (Proverbs 6:1-3). If you have money, give her [the one injured] as much as your hand can hold. If you can't, get together a number of friends [to plead your cause and ask for forgiveness]." Rabbi Hisda said, "One must appease [the injured party] with three groups of people [asking her to forgive you] to fulfill the verse 'He comes before people and says: I have sinned, and perverted what was not right, and I did not profit from it" (Job 33:27). If the injured party has died, then one must bring a *minyan* to the grave and say there, 'I have sinned against Adonai and have injured this person.'" When Rabbi Zeira had a dispute with another, he would approach the person again and again, placing himself before that person in order to make reconciliation easier. Let that person say, whatever I thought has gone out of my mind. Thus we learn that in sins between persons, the one who offends must placate the one offended.

In order to effect complete repentance, the penitent should

have as a goal the moving of others from transgression and the leading of them to the proper path. The penitent can do this by warning and rebuking them, making them aware of reward and punishment, telling them how God accepts penitents so that transgressors may turn from their evil ways. This is what David did when he pleaded that God should accept his penitence and forgive him, for he said, "Then I will teach transgressors Your ways and sinners will return to you" (Psalm 51:15).

CHAPTER FIVE

How great is the power of repentance. The Holy Blessed One with great mercy can offer people the opportunity for repentance. We learn in *Bereishit Rabbah* (21:6) that Rabbi Abba bar Kahana, commenting on the verse ". . . and now, in case he puts forth his hand" (Genesis 3:22) said, "The verse teaches that God had presented Adam with an opportunity to repent as indicated by the word[s] 'and now' as in the verse 'And now, Israel, what does Adonai your God require of you, but to fear Adonai your God, to walk in God's ways, and to love God' (Deuteronomy 10:12)."

We also learn there (*Bereishit Rabbah* 22:13) on the verse "and Cain left God's presence" (Genesis 4:16) [that a question was asked], "Where did he go?" Rav Huna said in the name of Rav Nachman bar Isaac that Cain went out to rejoice as [we might learn from] the phrase "and also, behold, he comes forth to meet you and when he sees you, he will be glad in his heart" (Exodus 4:14). Adam met Cain. He asked him, "What happened in your case?" Cain answered, "I repented and my punishment was diminished." At that point, Adam began to hit himself in the face and say, "So great is the power of repentance and I did not know it!" Adam immediately began reciting the Psalm, A Song for the Sabbath day: "It is good to give thanks (*l'hodot*) to

Adonai" (Psalm 92:1). [*L'hodot* can also be translated as "to confess."]

We also learn in *Pesikta deRav Kahana* (*Piska* 3) from Rabbi Levi, commenting on the verse "It is good to give thanks to Adonai," that this psalm was first recited by Adam. It teaches that God receives those who repent and says, "Return to Me" (Malachi 3:7). If I received the *teshuvah* of Ahab, against whom a severe decree was enacted, would I not accept your repentance? About Ahab it is written, "And the word of Adonai came to Elijah the Tishbite, saying: 'Rise up, go down to meet Ahab, king of Israel, who dwells in Samaria. Behold, he is in the vineyard of Navot, where he has gone down to take possession of it. And you must speak to him, saying, "Thus said Adonai: 'Have you killed, and also taken possession?'" And you must speak to him saying, "Thus said Adonai: 'In the place where dogs licked the blood of Navot shall dogs lick your blood, even yours.' . . . And it came to pass, when Ahab heard these words, that he rent his clothes, put sackcloth upon his flesh, fasted, and lay in sackcloth, and went softly" (1 Kings 21:17–19, 27). How long did he fast? Only for three hours! If he were used to eating at nine, he would eat at twelve. If he were used to eating at six, he would eat at nine! Rabbi Joshua ben Levi explained [the phrase] "and went softly" to mean that Ahab went barefoot. What is the meaning of the verses, "And the word of Adonai came to Elijah the Tishbite, saying: 'Do you see how Ahab humbles himself before Me?'" (1 Kings 21:28, 29). [It means that] God said [to Elijah] "Have you seen that Ahab has repented? [Therefore] because he humbles himself before Me, I will not bring the evil during his time" (1 Kings 21:29).

If I could accept the *teshuvah* of the people of Anatot, against whom a severe decree was enacted, would I not accept your repentance? About them it is written, ". . . therefore thus said Adonai Tzevaot: 'Behold, I will punish them. The young people will die by the sword. Their sons and daughters will die by famine. There will be no remnant of them'" (Jeremiah 11:22, 23). Yet when they repented, they were worthy of having 128 descendants, as is specified in the Book of Ezra (2:23).

If I could accept the *teshuvah* of the people of Nineveh, against whom a severe decree was enacted, would I not accept your repentance? About them it is written, "And Jonah began to enter into the city a day's journey, and he proclaimed, and said: 'Yet forty days, and Nineveh will be overthrown.' And the people of Nineveh believed God. They proclaimed a fast . . . and the news reached the king of Nineveh . . . who caused to be proclaimed and published . . . 'Let neither human nor animal . . . taste anything. . . . Who knows whether God will not turn and repent, and turn away from God's fierce anger, so that we might not perish?'" (Jonah 3:4–9). It is then written, "And God saw their works, that they turned from their evil way, and God repented of the evil, which God said God would do to them, and God did not do it" (Jonah 3:10).

It is also written, ". . . rend your heart, and not your garments. Turn to Adonai your God" (Joel 2:13). Rabbi Joshua ben Levi, commenting on the verse, said, "If you rend your hearts in penitence, you will not have to rend your garments [mourning] for your sons and your daughters." Why? [Because the verse continues] "for God is gracious and compassionate, long-suffering, and abundant in mercy."

If I could accept the *teshuvah* of Yochaniah, against whom a severe decree was enacted, would I not accept yours? About him it is written, "Is this man Coniah a despised, broken image?" (Jeremiah 22:28).

Rabbi Aha bar Abin bar Benjamin in the name of Rabbi Abba, the son of Rabbi Pappai, said: God is the power of repentance because it can nullify an oath and nullify a decree. How do we know that it can nullify an oath? Though it is written, "As I live, said Adonai, though Coniah, the son of Yehoiakim, king of Judah, were the signet upon My right hand, yet would I pluck you out" (Jeremiah 22:24), it is also written, "On that day," said Adonai Tzevaot, "will I take you, O Zerubbabel, My servant, the son of Shaltiel," said Adonai, "and will make you like a signet" (Haggai 3:23). How do we know that it can nullify a decree? Though it is written, "Thus said Adonai: 'Write this person childless, a person who shall not prosper in his days. No person from his seed shall prosper, sitting upon the throne of David'" (Jeremiah 23:30), it is also written, "And the sons of Yeconiah—the same is Asir—Shealtiel his son" (1 Chronicles 3:17).

"Your word, Adonai, stands forever fast in heaven" (Psalm 119:89). This verse was spoken in relation to Adam when he first sinned. Were it not that the Holy One had been sitting on the throne of mercy, Adam would not have lasted a moment. God promised Adam's progeny that God would deal with them with the attribute of mercy, as it says, "Your faithfulness is for all generations" (Psalm 119:90).

We also learn in *Pirkei deRabbi Eliezer* (chapter 41): "You should know the power of repentance. Look at the example of Ahab, king of Israel, who robbed, coveted, and murdered, as it says, 'Have you killed, and also taken possession?'" (1 Kings 21:17). Ahab [as a would-be penitent] summoned Yehosaphat, king of Judah, and asked to be beaten with forty stripes, three times a day, each day [in the period of penitence]. From early in the morning to late at night, Ahab would fast and pray before the Holy One. He never again returned to his evil ways. His repentance was accepted, as it says, "Do you see how Ahab humbles himself before Me?" (1 Kings 21:29).

Rabbi Abahu said, "You could learn about the power of

teshuvah from David, king of Israel. The Holy One had promised the Patriarchs that God would increase their seed as the stars
in the heavens, which because of their multitude could not be
counted. Then David came along [and began] to count their
numbers. God said to David, 'David, I have sworn to their ancestors to increase their seed, and you would come to nullify
My word? Because of you, the flock [the Jewish People] will be
devoured!' In only three hours, seventy thousand Israelites died,
as it is written, '. . . and seventy thousand Israelites fell dead'
(1 Chronicles 21:14)." Rabbi Simon said, "The only one of Israel
to die was Avishai ben Zeruyah, whose acts of goodness were
the equivalent of [that done by] seventy thousand people. We
deduce that from the [Hebrew] text saying *ish* (person) rather
than *anashim* (people) in the phrase [translated as] "seventy
thousand people."

When David heard what happened, he rent his clothes, put
on sackcloth and ashes, then fell on his face to the earth before
the Ark of the Covenant of Adonai. He asked God if he were
able to repent and said, "Master of the Universe, I am the one
who sinned. Forgive my sin." His repentance was accepted. God
then said to the Angel of Destruction, "Restrain yourself" as it
is written, "It is enough, restrain yourself" (1 Chronicles 21:15).
What is the meaning of "It is enough"? "Enough Israelites have
fallen." What did the angel then do? The angel took his sword
and wiped it on David's garment. The sight of the angel's sword
caused David's body to tremble until the day he died, as it says,
"But David could not go before . . . to inquire of God. He was
afraid because of the sword of the angel of Adonai" (1 Chronicles
21:30).

Rabbi Joshua said, "You should know the power of
teshuvah from the case of Menasseh, king of Judah, who had
committed all kinds of evil abominations and had sacrificed to

other gods, as it said, 'And he caused his children to pass through the fire in the valley of the son of Hinnom. He also observed time, used enchantments and witchcraft, dealt with familiar spirits and wizards. He brought much evil in the sight of Adonai to provoke God's anger' (2 Chronicles 33:6). Manasseh offered sacrifices to the entire host of heaven. [As a result] the troops of the king of Assyria seized him by his royal necklace, placed him in prison, and set him upon a fiery griddle [to torture him]. Manasseh called upon every god that he had worshiped, but none answered to save him. He said, 'If I can call upon the God of my ancestors with all my heart, maybe God will do for me the same kind of miracle that God did for my ancestors.' With all of his heart he called to the God of his ancestors. His prayer was heard and answered, as it says, 'And he prayed to Adonai . . . and God heard his supplication, and God brought him again to Jerusalem . . . and Manasseh knew that Adonai was God' (1 Chronicles 33:13). At that moment, Manasseh said, 'There is justice and there is a Judge.'"

Ben Azzai said, "You can understand the power of *teshuvah* from the story of Rabbi Simon ben Lakish. He and two of his companions would rob anyone with whom they would come into contact. What did he do? Leaving his companions to remain as robbers in the hills, he sincerely returned to God. Early and late, with fasting and with prayer, he would beseech the Holy One. He occupied himself with the study of Torah and the performance of *mitzvot* and never again returned to his evil deeds. His *teshuvah* was accepted. When he died, his two former companions, the robbers, died. Rabbi Simon was placed in the Treasury of Life and his companions were sent straight to hell. His two companions pleaded with God, saying, 'Do You play favorites?' God answered them, 'He [Rabbi Simon] repented when he was still alive and you did not!' They said, 'All right, we will repent!' God said, 'Repentance works only when you are alive! This [repentance] can be compared to a person going out to the desert. If the person does not take along bread and water, that person won't find them in the desert. Thus, the individual will have nothing to eat and drink. So, if a person does not repent when alive, it is too late to do so when the person is dead, but [as the verse has it] "to give to everyone according to his ways according to the fruit of her doings" (Jeremiah 17:10).'"

Rabbi Nehuniah ben Hakaneh said, "You may know the power of *teshuvah* from the story of Pharaoh, king of Egypt. He rebelled against the Master of the Universe and said, 'Who is Adonai, that I should hearken to Adonai's voice?' (Exodus 5:2). Yet he used the same expression when he repented, saying, 'Who is like You Adonai, among the mighty' (Exodus 15:11). The Holy One had delivered him from among the dead, as it says, 'Surely now I had put forth My hand, and smitten you' (Exodus 15:11). God had him stand among the dead so that he might declare God's power as it says, 'But I have spared you for this purpose, in order to show you My power and so that My reputation may be declared throughout all the earth' (Exodus 9:16). [This interpretation assumes that Pharaoh survived the events at the Re(e)d Sea.] Pharaoh went and became the king in Nineveh. The people of Nineveh were writing out documents of acquisition and robbing one another and were engaged in homosexual intercourse. When the Pharaoh saw that the Holy One sent Jonah to prophesy against Nineveh, he arose from his throne, rent his garments, and put on sackcloth and ashes. He proclaimed throughout his people, 'Whoever will do such things shall be burned in fire.' When the entire people fasted for three days, what did he then do? He had men stand on one side and women on the other; then he placed [ritually] pure animals on one side and [ritually] impure animals on the other. He then placed infants wanting to suckle on one side and their mothers on the other. He would not allow the infants, who wanted to be nursed, [to do so], nor their mothers, who wanted to nurse their children, to do so. As a result, the infants howled and their mothers wept. There were 123,000 people there, more than twelve myriads! [This is the force of the verse] 'And should I not have pity on Nineveh, that great city, where there are more than sixscore thousand persons that cannot discern between their right hand and their left hand, and also many cattle?' (Jonah 4:11). It is also said, 'And repented of the evil' (Jonah 3:10). For forty years God had been patient with them, corresponding to the forty days that God mentioned to Jonah. After forty years, they [the people of Nineveh] returned to their evil ways and their deeds were even worse than before. They were swallowed like the dead and went straight to hell, as it says, 'From out of the populous city people groan' and 'They make oil in the rows of these people' (Job 24:12, 11). It also says, 'But the wind passes and cleanses them' (Job 37:21)."

Therefore [for *teshuvah*] the Holy One has sent divine servants, the Prophets, to prophesy against Israel and to say to them, "Return, O Israel, to Adonai your God" (Hosea 14:2).

Section Three: Dealing with Fasts. It contains three chapters.

CHAPTER ONE

Fasting assists *teshuvah* in two ways. First, it weakens the body and breaks the proud heart by which one sinned. Second, it diminishes one's desires and it purifies one's fat and blood to the level of one's guilt. [Such fasting] is considered more important than the fat and blood of one's sacrifice [brought as an atonement]. When those who are physically ill realize that their illness is due to overeating, they restrict what they eat. Likewise is it with those who are spiritually ill [that they should restrict their desires]. However, were a person not ill or were the person ill due to some physical weakness, the restriction of food would cause illness [in the first case] and further weakness [in the second case]. So it is with one who would unnecessarily afflict the body.

When our Sages of blessed memory reflected on the behavior of human beings, they noted that there were those who would fast for a reason and those who would fast without a reason. They called the former a holy person and the latter a sinner. Even though it would seem that the Sages differed [as to the matter of fasting], with one having one opinion and another having another opinion, in truth there was no disagreement. We learn in the first chapter of *Taanit* (Babylonian Talmud, *Taanit* 11a): Rabbi Samuel said, "Whoever sits and fasts is called a sinner, as it is said, . . . 'and make atonement for him, for that he sinned against the soul' (Numbers 6:11). [This interpretation of *nefesh* is required for the *Midrash*.] Which soul had he sinned against? Against his own! He [the Nazirite] had caused himself trouble by not drinking wine! One can reason from this that if a person who only caused himself trouble by not drinking wine was called a sinner, then how much more should one who afflicts oneself by fasting (be called a sinner)." Rabbi Eliezer [on the other hand] argued that the one who fasts is called holy. He reasons that if the Nazirite is called "holy," as it says about him "he shall be holy" (Numbers 6:5) because he refrains from drinking wine, then one who afflicts oneself by refraining from everything should all the more so be called "holy"! Resh Lakish said that one who fasts is called pious [*chasid*], as it says, "The merciful person [*ish chesed*] does good to one's own soul" (Proverbs 11:17). The Sages explained the matter: "The disciple of the wise does not require affliction. It is forbidden for him to fast, for in so doing he would diminish the work of heaven." Rav Sheshet said, "Were a student [of Torah] to fast, then a dog should eat his meal."

At times, some pious people may afflict their bodies by fasting, by giving up eating meat or drinking wine, by refraining from sexual intercourse, or by putting on garments made of [rough] wool or hair. They did this because they saw in themselves some temporary tendency toward a particular extreme [and therefore moved to the other extreme]. Their acts of abstinence were like the actions of a physician called in to treat persons who had become ill due to some organic imbalance and whose treatment was the restoration of that balance. It may be that some of these pious people accepted suffering as a means of scouring away any evil thought they had or any mistake they had made. Fools, seeing the acts of the pious and not knowing their intentions, thought that those acts were good things to do. If they afflicted their bodies in every possible way, they reasoned, they would acquire such virtue for themselves that they could approach God as if God hates the [human] body and wishes to destroy it! They [the fools] did not know that such acts are harmful to those who do not need [to do] them. This might be compared to a person who knows nothing about the practice of medicine. When he sees a competent physician giving a patient medication, he thinks that he could give a similar medication to a healthy person, reasoning that if the medication healed a sick person it should preserve the health of a healthy person. Of course, that would not be the case. The medication would make the healthy person sick. The same is true with sicknesses of the soul. The same thing would happen to those fools who applied their [proposed] remedy to [the condition of] health. It would be something not in accordance with the Torah, which is perfect, which restores the soul and makes wise the simple. Rather, one should act in a natural manner, that is, within the [golden] mean. One should eat in moderation. One should drink in moderation. Only when there is a tendency toward an extreme should one fast in order to be restored to moderation.

Concerning such a fast, the Sages said in the fifth chapter of tractate *Berachot* (Babylonian Talmud, *Berachot* 32b): Rabbi Eliezer said, "Fasting is greater than giving *tzedakah*, for the former affects one's body and the latter only affects one's money." During such a fast, one should pray to the Creator that the scouring [by fasting] of one's fat and blood should be as acceptable as offering of a sacrifice. We learn too in the second chapter of *Berachot* (Babylonian Talmud, *Berachot* 17a) that while sitting and fasting, Rabbi Sheshet said [in prayer]: "Master of the Universe, it is known to You that while the Temple stood, one might sin and bring a sacrifice, offering only the fat and the blood of that sacrifice and yet gain atonement. Now that my fat and blood have become diminished [by fasting], may they be as sweet savor on the altar and may You grant me favor.'"

Concerning such a fast, we learn in the first chapter of *Shabbat* (Babylonian Talmud, *Shabbat* 11a) that Rabbi Rabba bar Machsia said in the name of Rabbi Chamma bar Gurya in the name of Rav: "A fast will bring on a dream just as fire will ignite flax." Rabbi Joseph said, "It will happen that very day, even if it is the Sabbath." The Sages also say in the fifth chapter of *Berachot* (Babylonian Talmud, *Berachot* 31b), Rabbi Yochanan in the name of Rabbi Yose bar Zimra: "Anyone engaging in a fast on the Sabbath will have any [evil] decree against the individual vacated."

Even so, it was not the intention of our Rabbis to deal with the subject of fasting alone so that one should afflict one's body with fasting. Rather, one should be alerted to search out one's

ways and to return in *teshuvah* in order to nullify an [evil] decree, if such a decree is directed against the individual, and that
one be accorded compassion from on high.

CHAPTER TWO

The matters dealing with fasts and with their associated pleas
are set down in the Written Torah. They were ordered against
the Patriarchs at certain times. Therefore, they ordained that
they should at those times fast and worry and groan, as we learn
in the first chapter of *Rosh Hashanah* (Babylonian Talmud,
Rosh Hashanah 18b). It is taught: Rabbi Simon ben Yochai said,
"There were four matters which Rabbi Akiba expounded with
which I disagree. [They were] the fourth fast on the Seventeenth
of *Tammuz* when a breach was made in the city [wall], as it is
said, 'In the fourth month, in the ninth day of the month, the
famine was in the city' (Jeremiah 52:6). The next verse says,
'Then a breach was made in the city' (Jeremiah 52:7). Why was
it called the fourth [fast]? Because it marked what had occurred
in the fourth month! The fifth fast was the fast of the Ninth of
Av when the House of our God was burnt. Why was it called
the fifth [fast]? Because it marked what had occurred in the fifth
[month]. The seventh fast was on the third of *Tishri* when
Gedaliah ben Ahikum was killed, to teach you that the death of
the righteous is equivalent to the burning of the Temple. Why
was it called the seventh fast? Because it marked what had occurred in the seventh [month]! The tenth fast was on the tenth
of *Tevet*, when the king of Babylon had invested Jerusalem, as
it is written, 'And the word of Adonai came to me in the ninth
year, in the tenth month, on the tenth day of the month, saying: "*Ben Adam*, record the name of this day, this particular day.
On this particular day, the king of Babylon has invested Jerusa-

lem" (Ezekiel 24:1, 2). [This is what Rabbi Akiba held.] I would
not say the same, for I hold that the tenth fast is on the fifth of
Tevet, the time when the report reached the Exile that the city
was smitten, as it says, 'And it came to pass in the twelfth year of
our captivity, in the tenth month, on the fifth day of the month,
that one that had escaped out of Jerusalem came to me, saying:
"The city is smitten"' (Ezekiel 33:21). My view is preferable to
the view of Akiba, for I have dealt with the fasts in order, and he
has inverted their order. [Moreover] I have followed the order
of punishments, and he has followed the order of the months."

We also learn in the tractate *Taanit* (Babylonian Talmud,
Taanit 26a): Five things occurred to our ancestors on the Seventeenth of *Tammuz*, and five things occurred on the Ninth of *Av*.
On the Seventeenth of *Tammuz*, the Tablets [of the Decalogue]
were smashed [by Moses], the offering of the continual sacrifice ceased, the city [wall] was breached, the Torah was burnt
by Vespacian, and an idol was placed in the Sanctuary by him.
On the Ninth of *Av*, it was decreed that our ancestors could not
enter the Land [of Israel], the First and the Second Temple were
destroyed, Betar was captured, and [the destroyed area of] the
city was plowed.

The most important fast of all is the one on the Ninth of
Av because of all the terrible things that had happened on that
day. . . . Because of the evils and suffering that befell our ancestors in scourging their transgressions, Israel is not able to nullify
that day at this time. They [the Sages] added more [restrictions]
in order to diminish that joy which might have occurred when
the month of *Av* began. Thus it is customary not to eat meat
[from the beginning of the month] even at the Cessation Meal
before the fast, unless the Ninth of *Av* occurred on the Sabbath
[at which point it would be postponed until the next day]. One
engages in the restrictions of mourning. One does not study

those passages in the Torah that deal with joy. One engages in the five ways of afflictions related to the Day of Atonement.

It is also customary not to work [on the Ninth of Av] as we learn in the fourth chapter of *Pesachim* (Babylonian Talmud, *Pesachim* 54b): "Where the custom is do work on the Ninth of Av, they may do so. Where the custom is not do work, they may not work. But the disciples of the wise everywhere cease from work. Rabban Simon ben Gamliel says: 'A person should always behave like a disciple of the wise.'" We also learn at the end of the tractate *Taanit* (Babylonian Talmud, *Taanit* 30b): Rabbi Akiba said: "Whoever works on the Ninth of Av will never see a blessing. Whoever eats on the Ninth of Av will never see the [ultimate] joy of Jerusalem as it says, 'Rejoice with Jerusalem, and be glad with her, all you who love her. Rejoice in joy with her, all you who mourn for her' (Isaiah 66:10). Whoever mourns over Jerusalem will merit seeing her joy, as it says, 'Rejoice in joy with her, all you who mourn for her.' The words '. . . whose iniquities are upon their bones' (Ezekiel 32:27) apply to the one who would eat meat and drink wine on the Ninth of Av."

There remains for Israel the possibility of returning to its prior state, as we learn at the end of *Eichah Rabbati*: "Turn us to you, Adonai, and we shall be turned" (Lamentations 5:21) refers to Israel saying before the Holy One: "Master of the Universe, turn us to You," and God saying to Israel, "It [repentance] is up to you," as it says, "Return to Me, and I will return to you" (Malachi 3:7). Israel responds, "Master of the Universe, it is up to You, as it says, 'Restore us, O God of our salvation' (Psalm 85:5)." Therefore it is written, "Turn us to you, Adonai, and we shall be turned. Renew our days as of old" (Lamentations 5:21). What is the meaning of "as of old"? Like the Patriarchs of old, as in the phrase ". . . the ancient mountains" (Deuteronomy 33:15). [*Hararei kedem* can also be translated as "the mountains of old" and "mountains" are midrashically understood to refer to the Patriarchs.] Another interpretation of "Renew our days as of old": the verse may be related to the verse "Then shall the offering of Judah and Jerusalem be pleasant to Adonai, as in the days of old, and as in ancient years" (Malachi 3:7). "The days of old" may refer to the period of Moses, as in the verse "Then God's people remembered the days of old, the days of Moses" (Isaiah 63:11). "And as in ancient years" may refer to the period of Solomon. There is another interpretation that takes "the days of old" to refer to the period of Noah, as in the verse "For this is as the waters of Noah to Me" (Isaiah 54:9). "And as in ancient days" would refer to the period of Abel when there was as yet no idolatry anywhere on earth.

The Holy One has promised us through Jeremiah the prophet that God will transform our mourning into joy, as it is written, "And I will turn their mourning into joy, and will comfort them, and make them rejoice from their sorrow" (Jeremiah 31:13).

CHAPTER THREE

In the same manner that the Sages ordained fasts for those matters considered above, they also ordained that whenever a land, nation, city, or even individuals suffered pain and sorrow or whenever it was the season for rain but no rain fell, people should fast, pray, and blow the *shofar* in order to be moved to examine their deeds and turn toward *teshuvah*. The Holy One might then have pity upon them and save them from any impending sorrow.

The severity of the fasts would depend on the needs and the pressures of time. An order of severity is given in the tractate *Taanit*. [As an example,] it might become necessary to move the Ark [containing the Torah] to the open place of the town in order to shock the hearts of the [local] residents into turning toward repentance. We learn this in the second chapter of *Taanit* (Babylonian Talmud, *Taanit* 15a): "They used to bring out the Ark into the open space of the town and put wood-ashes on the Ark and on the head of the President and the Head of the Court. Everyone [present] then took the ashes and placed them on their [own] head. The oldest person among them admonished all those present saying, 'My brothers [and sisters], it is not said of the people in Nineveh, "And God saw their sackcloth and their fast." Rather, it is written, "And God saw their deeds that they turned from their evil way" (Jonah 3:10).' Tradition further states, 'Rend your heart, not your garments' (Joel 2:13)."

Moreover, it is stated in the *Gemara* (Babylonian Talmud, *Taanit* 15b): "Why should they place ashes on the head of the President and the Head of the Court? Why did they not put ashes on their own heads? Rabbi Abba of Mar Casrei said, 'Being shamed by oneself does not compare to being shamed by another.' Where do they place the ashes? Rabbi Akiba said, 'In the place where one places *tefillin* [on the head], as it says, "To appoint to them who mourn for Zion, to give to them a garland of ashes" (Isaiah 61:3).' Why do they go out to the open space of the town? Rabbi Hiyya bar Abba said, 'It is [as if] to say, "May our exile atone for us! What is the difference between the two views? It is as if they were exiled from synagogue to synagogue."'"

So why do they bring the Ark to the open place? Rabbi Joshua ben Levi answered, "It is [as if] to say, 'We had something that we kept hidden but through our transgressions it was degraded.'" Why did they cover themselves with sackcloth? Rabbi Hiyya bar Abba answered, "It is [as if to say], 'We are considered before You like cattle.'" Why do they put wooden-ashes on the Scroll of the Torah? Rabbi Judah ben Pazzai answered, "It is [as if] to say, 'I am with him in trouble' (Psalm

91:15)." Resh Lakish applied a different verse: "In all their affliction God was afflicted" (Isaiah 63:9). Rabbi Zeira said, "Had
we foreseen that they would place wood-ash upon a Scroll of
the Torah, our entire body would tremble!" And why did they
place wood-ashes on the head of each person present? Rabbi
Levi bar Lachma differed with Rabbi Chama bar Chanina. One
said, "Behold, we are considered before You like ashes." The
other said, "May the ashes of Isaac [at the Akedah] be remembered by You so that You might forgive us!" What is the difference between the two views? The meaning of the ashes!

Why do they go out to the cemeteries? Rabbi Levi bar
Chama differed with Rabbi Chama bar Chanina regarding the
explanation. One said, "[It is as if we say that] O God, we are
considered as if we are already dead." The other said, "May the
dead ask for mercy on our behalf." What is the difference between the two views? The difference is the meaning and the
effect of the graves of non-Jews.

They did all this in order to force their hearts to repent,
that they might direct their prayers so that the Holy One might
hear those prayers. We learn this in the third chapter of *Taanit*
(Babylonian Talmud, *Taanit* 24a): Rabbi Judah the Prince ordered a fast. Although he prayed for mercy, no rain fell from
the time of Samuel to the time of Judah ben Gamliel. He said,
"Woe to the generation that is placed in such a position. Woe
to the one to whom such a thing has happened in one's [own]
days." He was discouraged. Then rain came.

It is also said there that Rabbi Nachman ordered a fast.
Although he prayed for rain, none came. He said, "Take
Nachman up. Then throw him down from a high place to the
earth." He was discouraged. Then rain came.

It is also taught there (Babylonian Talmud, *Taanit* 24b)
that Rabba happened to go to Hagronia. He ordered a fast. Although he prayed for mercy, no rain fell. He said, "Let every-

one go to bed fasting." The next day he said to the people, "Did anyone see anything in a dream?" Rabbi Eliezer of Hagronia answered, "In my dream, they called to me, saying, 'Good health to the good teacher from the good God who does good to the world.'" Rabbi said: "From this you learn that it is a favorable time." He prayed for mercy and the rains came.

This happened to people in olden times. Some, like Honi the Circle Maker, received a response immediately. Others [received a response] only after much complaining, like Rabbi Chama bar Chanina and Levi, who became lame—and also some others.

We learn in the same passage (Babylonian Talmud, *Taanit* 25b): Our Rabbis taught, "It once happened that Rabbi Eliezer ordered thirteen fasts upon the community, but his prayers were not answered. Rain did not fall. The people finally began to leave. He said to them, 'Have you arranged for graves for yourselves?' They began to weep and wail and rain began to fall."

There is another story told about Rabbi Eliezer. He once went before the Ark [to lead services] and said, "There are twenty-four blessings and even so we were not answered." He was followed by Rabbi Akiba [before the Ark], who said, "*Avinu Malkeinu*, we have no Ruler other than You. *Avinu Malkeinu*, have mercy upon us!" He was answered! The people thought that [the reason Akiba was answered was because] Rabbi Akiba was greater than Rabbi Eliezer. Therefore, a divine voice proclaimed, "It is not because one was greater than the other but because one would forbear to recover his slights and the other did not."

Were any individual [to desire] to separate oneself from the community, at a time when the community is enveloped in suffering, then two ministering angels would place their hands on the individual's head and say to that person, "The one who separates oneself from the community will not see its consolation." As we learn in the first chapter of *Taanit* (Babylonian Talmud, *Taanit* 11a): Our Rabbis taught, "Whenever Israel is enveloped in sorrow and an individual wishes to separate from the people, then two angels come [and say that such a person will not see its consolation]." Here is a supporting passage: At a time when the community is enveloped in suffering, let no one say, "I will go home and eat and drink and my soul will be at ease." Let anyone who would wish to do this think of the words of Scripture, "And behold joy and gladness, slaying oxen and killing sheep, eating flesh and drinking wine. Let us eat and drink, for tomorrow we will die" (Isaiah 22:13). Let that person note well what follows: "And Adonai Tzevaot (Lord of Hosts) revealed Godself in my ears: Surely you will not expiate iniquity until you die" (Isaiah 22:14). This applies to someone of average moral qualities. What would Scripture say of one of [really] wicked qualities? "Come, I will fetch wine, and we will fill ourselves with strong drink. Tomorrow will be like today, yet much more abundant" (Isaiah 56:12). What follows that statement? "The righteous perish and no one takes it to heart" (Isaiah 57:1). [The above applies to persons who do not join the community in its sorrow.] However, the one who suffers with the community will be worthy to experience its consolation. We find this to be true in the case of Moses, our master, who suffered along with the community, as it is written, "But Moses' hands were heavy. So they took a stone, put it under him, and he sat on it" (Exodus 17:2). One might wonder, did Moses have no seat or cushion on which to sit? Rather, [we are to understand that] Moses said, "Since Israel is suffering pain, so shall I." Suppose someone said, "[if I don't join in the suffering of the community] who will testify against me?" Rabbi Zeira responded that the two ministering angels who accompany every person will testify against that individual, as the verse has it, "For God will give the angels charge over you, to keep you in all your ways" (Psalm 91:11). Rabbi Hidkah said that a person's soul would testify against the self, as the verse has it, "Keep the doors of your mouth from the one who sleeps in your bosom" (Micah 7:5). The Sages say, "The limbs of a person would testify against him, as it says, '. . . You [all the parts of the body] are My witnesses, says Adonai, I am God' (Isaiah 43:12)."

In addition to this [predicament], those who were pious, who did good deeds, would pray and fast on behalf of the congregation of Israel. Their fast, however, would not interfere with their studies. This is what the people of the assemblies [*maamadot*] would do when the Temple still stood. We learn this in the fourth chapter of the tractate *Taanit* (Babylonian Talmud, *Taanit* 27b): Our Rabbis taught, the [night] guards would pray that the sacrifice of their brothers [and sisters] might be favorably accepted. The members of the Great Assembly entered the synagogue and decreed four fasts for the week: On the second day, for those who go down to the seas; on the third day, for those who go out to the deserts; on the fourth day, to prevent babies from croup; and on the fifth [day] so that pregnant women should not miscarry and nursing mothers should be able to raise their children. Due to the honor of the Sabbath, they did not fast on Sabbath Eve (the sixth day, Friday) and needless to say, not on the Sabbath itself. Why did they not fast on the first day? Because of the Christians! Rabbi Samuel bar Nachmani said, "Because it [the first day] was the third day of creation." Resh Lakish said, "Because of the extra soul [which is given to the individual on the Sabbath]." Rabbi Simon ben Lakish said (Babylonian Talmud, *Beitzah* 16a) "An extra soul is given to a person on *Erev Shabbat* and at *Havdalah* it is taken away, as it says, 'And on the seventh day God ceased from work and rested [*vayinafash*]' (Exodus 31:17)." [*Vayinafash* is understood midrashically as if it were *va-nefesh*: "Woe O soul, when the Sabbath ends, the [extra] soul is lost."]

Those fasts that the Holy One desires are those that are associated with humility, repentance, and charity to the poor. [Be careful,] merely refraining from afflicting the body, bowing the head, and putting on sackcloth may have prideful sin associated with them. This is what the prophet said: "Is this the fast that I have chosen, the day for a person to afflict one's soul? Is it to bow down one's head as a bulrush, and to spread sackcloth and ashes under oneself?" (Isaiah 58:5). Fasts that involve the public should be accompanied by scrutiny of the acts of the public and with prayer in order to motivate the public to make *teshuvah*. We learn this in the first chapter of *Taanit* (Babylonian Talmud, *Taanit* 12b): Rabbi Abuya said, "From morning until midday [of a fast] let them investigate hometown matters. From midday on, one quarter of the day, we read [from the Torah] and complete the reading [from the Prophets], and the last quarter we pray and ask mercy [from God], as the verse states, 'And they stood up in their place, and read in the book of the Law of Adonai their God a fourth part of the day; and another fourth part they confessed and prostrated themselves before Adonai their God' (Nehemiah 9:3). Israel should fast and repent properly so that they can be assured that their prayers will be heard."

Section Four: The Reward of Repentance. There are two chapters.

CHAPTER ONE

One should always think of oneself in a balanced state, so happy is the person who performs one *mitzvah*, for that person leans toward virtue. Woe to the person who commits one transgression, for that person leans toward vice. When a person thinks of this [balance], that person will be eager to perform one *mitzvah* and careful not to commit a transgression. One should also think of all humanity as equally balanced, with the entire world dependent on each individual. By one's virtue or vice one can cause the entire world to fall over. We learn that at the end of the first chapter of the tractate *Kiddushin* (Babylonian Talmud, *Kiddushin* 40b): The Rabbis taught, "One should always see oneself as if one were half innocent and half guilty." We have dealt with this at the end of [my] *lamp of commandment*.

Since there is no greater *mitzvah* than *teshuvah*, the rabbis said that it can permit a person shelter beneath the wings of *Shechinah*. Indeed, repentance can nullify an evil desire directed at any person, as we learn in the first chapter of *Rosh Hashanah* (Babylonian Talmud, *Rosh Hashanah* 16b): "There are four things that nullify an evil decree against a person." . . . It is also taught (Babylonian Talmud, *Rosh Hashanah* 17b): Rabbi Yochanan said, "Great is repentance, for it nullifies an evil decree, as it is said, 'Make the heart of this people fat, and make their ears heavy. Shut their eyes, lest they . . . return and be healed' (Isaiah 6:10)." Rabbi Papa said to Rabbi Abuya, "Could this apply before the fixing of the decree?" He said to him,"[Look at the words] 'Return and be healed!' What has to be healed? You would have to have issued the decree!"

This [*teshuvah*] is one of the things that reflects God's compassion for those things that God has created. For the sake of *teshuvah*, God is willing to retract the evil that God decreed. What God has decreed for good, God does not change, even though people may have [in the interim] become guilty, as the Sages taught, "Whatever comes forth from the mouth of the Holy One will be for good, even what is conditional, for God will not change the divine mind. If Father Jacob was afraid of sin, after the Blessed God had said to him, 'Behold, I will be with you and I will guard you' (Genesis 28:15) and yet even so, 'And Jacob was very afraid' (Genesis 32:8)." The Sages said, "Jacob was afraid that sin might be a factor, perhaps because of the multitude of his sins, for Jacob was very afraid of sin." However, it is a clear matter that whatever God decrees for the good is never retracted. Jeremiah alluded to this when differing with Haninah ben Azor. Jeremiah was prophesying for evil, for death, that Nebuchadnezzar would conquer the cities of Israel and that he would destroy the Temple. Hananiah [on the other hand] was prophesying the reverse—that everything would be good. Jeremiah said, therefore, that even if what he prophesied did not happen, his prophecy would not have been false. God could have mercy upon the people or they might turn in repentance. However, if the words of Hananiah were not fulfilled, that would indicate that he was a false prophet. Thus it is written, "Nevertheless, hear this word that I speak in your ears, and in the ears of all the people: The ancient Prophets that have been before me and before you prophesied against many countries, great kingdoms, of war, of evil, and pestilence. When the word of the prophet who prophesies of peace will come to pass, then the prophet will be known to have been sent by Adonai" (Jeremiah 28:7–9). By this Jeremiah meant that one could not tell whether those Prophets who had prophesied evil had prophesied truly or not because repentance might have nullified the evil decree that had been decreed. [However,] one could tell the truth of their prophesying good should it occur.

We also find that a good mind can use its wisdom [and move to repentance] to deliver the body from the impending evil that might occur. We learn this at the end of the third chapter of *Nedarim* (Babylonian Talmud, *Nedarim* 32b): Rabbi Rami bar Abba said, "Why is it written, 'There was a little city,

with few people in it. A great king came against it, and besieged
it and built greater bulwarks against it' (Ecclesiastes 9:14)? To
teach that the 'little city' stands for the body, 'with few people
in it' stands for [various limbs], and 'a great king came against it
and seized it' stands for the *Yetzer Hara* (Evil Inclination) 'and
built great bulwarks against it' refers to the [various] sins. In it
was found a poor and wise person who by wisdom delivered the
city. Yet no one remembered that 'poor person' refers to the
Good Inclination, 'who by wisdom delivered the city' refers to
repentance and good deeds. Yet, no one remembered that 'poor
person' refers to the fact that the wickedness of the Evil Inclination is so great that no one remembers the *Yetzer Tov* (Good
Inclination). The statement 'Wisdom is a stronghold to the wise'
(Ecclesiastes 7:19) refers to repentance and good deeds. 'More
than ten rulers that are in a city' (Ecclesiastes 7:19) refers to the
two hands, two feet, two ears, and two eyes and the head and
the mouth."

It is clear then that *teshuvah* is that beneficial wisdom that
delivers the body of the sinner from the [evil] decrees and from
the accidents that might befall [a person]. We learn this in the
second chapter of the tractate *Berachot* (Babylonian Talmud,
Berachot 17a): It was a customary statement of Rabba that the
purpose of wisdom was repentance and good deeds. One should
not read and repeat [words of Torah] and then treat one's father and mother and one more learned than oneself with contempt. This is indicated by the verse "The fear of Adonai is the
beginning of wisdom. A good understanding have they that do
thereafter" (Psalm 111:10). Note that the verse does not say,
"those that study them," but it says, "They that do!" "They that
do" refers to those persons who act for the sake [of the *mitzvah*,
that is, for a religious reason] and does not refer to those who
would act without such a reason. Indeed, it would be better for

those who do not act for the sake [of the *mitzvah*, that is, without a religious reason] never to have been created.

We learn in the *midrash* on Psalms: "For the leader, on the Shoshanim, [a psalm] of the sons of Korach. *Maskil*. A Song of loves" (Psalm 45:1). "Come and see what happened to the sons of Korach! They were not called 'lovers' before they repented, but when they did, they were, as it says, '*Maskil*. A Song of loves.'" [The word *Maskil* is also used in the verse] "[A psalm] of David. *Maskil*. Happy is the one whose transgression is forgiven, whose sin is pardoned" (Psalm 32:1). [The word is also used in this verse:] "The path of life goes upward for the wise [*l'maskil*], so that the individual may depart from the netherworld beneath" (Proverbs 15:24). This verse refers to the sons of Korach, who were seen by their Parent in heaven and were delivered, as it says, ". . . the sons of Korach did not die" (Numbers 26:11). Why were they delivered? Because they did not join in the plans of their [earthly] parent. Of the others, it is written, "So they, and all that pertained to them, went down alive into the pit" (Numbers 16:33). Those who were seen from on high were delivered, as it says, "They looked to God and were radiant" (Psalm 34:6). In the same manner, David was seen from on high and was delivered, as it says, "[A Psalm] of David [*l'david* can be understood as 'For David'] *Maskil*. Happy is the one whose transgression is forgiven, whose sin is pardoned" (Psalm 32:1). [*Maskil* is again related to the use in the verse "The path of life goes upward for the wise [*l'maskil*] so that the individual may depart from the netherworld beneath" (Proverbs 15:24).] Not only that, but those wicked persons who wished to look upwards [toward heaven] were delivered. We learn from the case of Nebuchadnezzar, of whom it is written, ". . . I Nebuchadnezzar lifted up my eyes to heaven, and my understanding returned to me, and I blessed the Most High, and I praised and honored the One who lives forever" (Daniel 4:31). Because of this, a portion of his punishment was remitted. Now if the wicked, who are condemned by God, were to raise their eyes to heaven and are forgiven by God, how much the more so would Israel, the children of the righteous, the progeny of Abraham, Isaac, and Jacob [Sarah, Rebecca, Leah, and Rachel], were to raise their eyes to heaven and repent completely be forgiven by the Holy One? Because David was wise [*maskil*], ceased sinning, confessed, repented, and said, "Against You, You alone have I sinned" (Psalm 51:5), the Holy One forgave him.

We find that David established the burnt-offering of *teshuvah*, as we learn in the third chapter of *Moed Katan* (Babylonian Talmud, *Moed Katan* 16b): Rabbi Yonatan asked, "Why is it written, 'The saying of David, the son of Jesse, and the saying of the man raised on high [*hukam al*]' (2 Samuel 23:1)? To teach that David established the burnt-offering [*olah*] of repentance!"

Indeed, as a reward for his [David's] repentance, the matter was revealed to everyone in the world so that they would know that the Holy One forgave him for his sin. As we learn in the second chapter of *Moed Katan* (Babylonian Talmud, *Moed Katan* 9a) and in the tenth chapter of *Sanhedrin* (Babylonian Talmud, *Sanhedrin* 106b) and the second chapter of *Shabbat* (Babylonian Talmud, *Shabbat* 30a), Rabbi Judah said in the name of Rav: "At the moment that Solomon wanted to bring the Ark into the Holy of Holies the gates cleaved to one another. He then said twenty-four prayers of praise, but he was not answered. He [then] said, "Lift up your heads, O gates, and be lifted up, you everlasting doors so that the Glorious Soverign may come in. Who then is the Glorious Soverign? Adonai Tzevaot. God is the Glorious Soverign" (Psalm 24:7–10). He [still] was not answered. Only when Solomon said, "Adonai, O God, do not turn away the face of Your anointed. Remember the mer-

cies of David Your servant" (2 Chronicles 6:42), was he immediately answered. At that very moment, the faces of the enemies
of Israel turned as black as the bottom of a pot. All Israel knew
that the Holy One had forgiven him for his sin, as it is written,
"On the eighth day he sent the people away, and they blessed
the king, and went to their tents joyful and glad of heart for all
the goodness that Adonai had shown to David, God's servant,
and to Israel, God's people" (1 Kings 8:66). We agree that the
words "to Israel" indicate that God had forgiven them on the
Day of Atonement. Why was "David Your servant" said? According to Rabbi Judah, it was said that all Israel might know that
the Holy One had forgiven David for his sin.

They also said that the reward of *teshuvah* increases the life
expectancy of human beings, as we learn in the eighth chapter
of *Yoma* (Babylonian Talmud, *Yoma* 86b): Rabbi Samuel bar
Nachmani said in the name of Rabbi Yonatan: "Great is repentance, for it extends the days and years of each individual" as it
is written, "He shall surely live" (Ezekiel 18:28). In a similar
manner, every manner of good is multiplied for the penitent.

CHAPTER TWO

In the same manner that the Holy One, in great divine compassion, receives the repentance of the individual and nullifies
any [evil] decree ordered against that individual, so God nullifies any [evil] decree ordered against a community if that community fully repents. The events of the city of Nineveh prove
it. The Sages also said that an individual's repentance would
have the merit of causing forgiveness for the group. This we learn
in the eighth chapter of *Yoma* (Babylonian Talmud, *Yoma* 86b):
Rabbi Zutra bar Tuviah said in the name of Rav: "Great is repentance, for if an individual repents, the individual may bring

forgiveness for oneself and for the entire world, as it says, 'I will heal their backsliding, I will love them freely; for my anger is turned away from him' (Hosea 14:5)." We learn in the same passage (Babylonian Talmud, *Yoma* 86a) that repentance brings healing to the entire world, as it is said, "Return, O backsliding children, says Adonai" (Jeremiah 3:14).

Although the transgression that the entire congregation committed is grievous, they should not think that there is no remedy. They should not despair of [doing] repentance. For that reason, Israel was given the example of the sin of the Golden Calf so that they might learn and know that if God could be patient with such a great sin, then there could be no sin that they could do and [then repent of] and not have their repentance accepted. We learn this in the first chapter of *Avodah Zarah* (Babylonian Talmud, *Avodah Zarah* 4b): Rabbi Joshua ben Levi said, "The only reason that Israel sinned with the Golden Calf was in order to give an excuse for those who would be penitent, as it is said, "Oh, that they had such a heart as this always, to fear Me, and keep all My *mitzvot*, that it would be well with them, and with their children forever!" (Deuteronomy 5:26). This relates to what Rabbi Yochanan said: "That generation was not fit for such an act [the Golden Calf] and Israel was not fit for such an act!" That the generation was not fit is indicated by the verse "For I am poor and needy, and my heart is wounded in me" (Psalm 109:5). That Israel was not fit is indicated by the verse "Oh that they had such a heart as this always, to fear Me, and keep all My *mitzvot*" (Deuteronomy 5:26). If so, then why did they sin [by making the Golden Calf]? To teach that if an individual were to sin, then they say to that person, go to an individual [and learn to repent]. If a community sins, they say to them, go to a community [and learn to repent]. Both [the advice to individual and community] are needed, for if the

Compassionate One had only written [in the Torah] about an individual, since that individual's sin was not specified, one might think that repentance might be possible for an individual but not for a community whose sin was specified. On the other hand, had the All Compassionate written [in the Torah] about the repentance and the community, one might think that God's mercy is greater for a community and therefore repentance would be possible for them, but not for an individual. Therefore, both statements about individual and community were necessary. This relates to what Rabbi Samuel bar Nachmani said in the name of Rabbi Yonatan: "Why is it written, 'The saying of David, the son of Jesse, and the saying of the one raised on high [al]' to indicate that he had established the offering [olah] of repentance."

And although it is written, ". . . nevertheless, on the day that I visit, I will visit their sin upon them" (Exodus 32:34), [we are to understand] that refers to another sin that was joined to them. However, the Holy One will forgive them for that sin. We learn this in the fifth chapter of Berachot (Babylonian Talmud, Berachot 32b): "Can a woman forget her suckling child so that she should not have compassion on the child of her womb?" (Isaiah 49:15). "Shall I forget the sucklings of the rams, the first-born of the wombs, which Israel offered in the wilderness for forty years?" Israel [then] said to God, "Since there is no forgetfulness before Your glorious throne, perhaps you won't forget [our making] the Golden Calf?" God replied, "Yea, these I may forget, but I will not forget you" (Isaiah 49:16). Israel responded, "Master of the Universe, were there to be forgetfulness before Your glorious throne, would You forget [the events of] Mount Sinai?" God then said, "These I may forget," which refers to the Golden Calf; "yet I will not forget You" refers to the events of Mount Sinai.

As a reward for *teshuvah*, God will hasten the time of the redemption. We learn this in the eighth chapter of *Yoma* (Babylonian Talmud, *Yoma* 86b): Rabbi Yochanan said, "Great is repentance because it hastens the time of the redemption, as it is said, 'And a redeemer will come to Zion to those who turn from transgression' (Isaiah 59:20)."

The Second Principle: The Days of Repentance

This is divided into two sections. The first section refers to the coming of the day of judgment. The second section is about the coming of the day of atonement.

Section One: The coming of the day of judgment. This has five chapters.

CHAPTER ONE

Any sensible person knowing that he [or she] would be coming for judgment before a human king in matters dealing with money would be filled with anxiety. How much the more so would the individual be filled with anxiety day and night, that person would examine all actions and seek advice from any available counselor, asking for guidance to avoid the judgment. How much more should one be concerned about coming for judgment in matters dealing with one's life, children, and wealth before the Holy One, who is the Sovereign of Sovereigns? God knows all that is hidden. God requires neither witnesses nor evidence. Everything is revealed to God! The only effective defense is repentance and good deeds. Let every person repent of his [or her] sins and seek good counsel from those who know before the individual comes before judgment so that he or she may succeed in his or her case.

Therefore, one should anticipate [the period of attempt-

ing repentance] for at least thirty days. One should start from
the first day of the month of *Elul* to awaken out of the stupor,
[out of the] doldrums in which the individual has been involved
all year. Indeed, that period is the one in which the Holy One
has been inclined to forgive all Israel. In that period, God directed Moses to ascend Mount Sinai for the second time to receive the Tablets of the Covenant again. We find this in *Pirkei
deRabbi Eliezer*: It is taught, on the first day of the month of *Elul*
the Holy One said to Moses, ". . . Come up to Me on the mount"
(Deuteronomy 10:1). At that time, Moses received the second
set of tablets. They passed a *shofar* throughout the camp. Then
Moses went up to the mountain, so that they [the Children of
Israel] would not again err with idolatry. The Holy One, Godself,
was raised by that *shofar* sound, as it is written, "God has gone
up amidst the shouting, Adonai amidst the sound of the horn"
(Psalm 47:6). For that reason, the Sages ordained that the *shofar*
should be sounded every year throughout the month of *Elul* so
that Israel might be moved to repentance, as it is written, "Shall
the horn be blown in the city, and the people not tremble?"
(Amos 3:6), and that Satan be disturbed.

We also found this response of Rabbenu Hai: It is our custom to recite supplicatory prayers only during the Ten Days [of
Repentance]. We have heard that in some places, like Persia, it
is the custom to recite such prayers from the first day of the
month of *Elul*. The reason given is that Moses ascended Mount
Sinai for the third time with the second set of tablets, remaining there until the Day of Atonement. Whoever prays all the
more for mercy is meritorious. According to Rabbi Ibn Giat of
blessed memory: It is our custom to do as those who ask for mercy
from the first day of *Elul*.

According to Rabbenu Nissim: Many Sages and many
homeowners would sound the *shofar* beginning with the first

day of *Elul*. I have a basis for this practice in the *Midrash*: It is taught that on the first day of *Elul* the Holy One said to Moses. . . . (This *midrash* has been cited above.)

We have also found that it is customary to fast on the eve of the New Year. A basis for this [practice] is found in [the midrashic exposition of] the verse "And you shall take you on the first day" (Leviticus 23:40). [The verse is interpreted as "You will take yourselves as an offering on the first day of the year, that is, Rosh Hashanah, the New Year.] After all, was it "the first day"? No, it [the festival of Sukkot] falls on the fifteenth day! Rather "the first day" refers to the first day of the accounting of transgressions [*Tanchuma Emor*]. It may be compared to a city that owed a tax to the king that it had not paid. The king approached the city with his army to collect. As he came closer — still ten miles away — a delegation of the notables of the city came to him and said, "We have nothing to give you." The king remitted one-third of the tax. When he came still closer, the guards (*biryonei*) [and some texts read (*baynonei*) "average people"] came out and the king remitted what remained. The king is the Holy Blessed One. The people of the city are Israel, who all year long heap up transgressions. On the eve of the New Year, the notable persons among them fast, and one-third of the transgressions of Israel are forgiven. Then during the Ten Days of Repentance, the average people fast, causing another third of their transgressions to be forgiven. On the Day of Atonement, everyone fasts, and God forgives them all. At the end of the Day of Atonement, the people of Israel busy themselves with the *mitzvot* of *sukkah* and *lulav* and do not engage in transgressions. For that reason, the Torah calls it (Sukkot) "first holiday," that is, "the first for the accounting of transgressions."

Even though they may fast on the eve of the New Year, they wash and cut their hair and dress in white garments, for as we have found in the statement in the *Midrash* (Jerusalem Talmud, *Rosh Hashanah* 1:3) that Rabbi Simon stated, "It is written, 'For what great nation is there, that has God so close to them, as Adonai our God is [close] whenever we call to God' (Deuteronomy 4:7)." Rabbi Hanina and Rabbi Joshua commented on the verse ". . . What great nation is there? A nation that knows the characteristics of its God!" By "characteristics" we mean God's way of acting and God's judgments. It is customary that when a person faces judgment, one puts on dark clothes, wraps oneself in a dark mantle, lets one's beard grow, and does not trim one's nails, for the individual does not know what will be the disposition of one's case. It is different for the people of Israel. They put on white clothes, wrap themselves in white mantles, trim their beards, cut their fingernails, eat, drink, and rejoice on the New Year. They know that the Holy One will work a miracle on their behalf.

We also find a Geonic response that states, "Regarding fasting on the first two days of the New Year, we find it better not to fast. This follows what those ancient leaders said concerning the New Year: 'Go your way. Eat the fat and drink the sweet. Send portions to the one for whom nothing is prepared, for this day is holy to our God" (Nehemiah 8:10)." Similarly, it is unseemly to fast on the Sabbath of Repentance [Shabbat Shuva]. Although the fast of the Ninth of *Av* [*Tisha B'av*] is an important fast, the Sages did not allow it to occur on the Sabbath but postponed it to the next day. Even the completing of fasts on the eve of the Sabbath troubled many generations. Finally, the law was established: "Fasting on the eve of the Sabbath must complete the fast" (Babylonian Talmud, *Eruvin* 41a).

This follows what we learn in the *Yerushalmi* (Jerusalem Talmud, *Nedarim* 8:2): Rabbi Jacob would charge the teachers, "Should someone come to you and ask, you should answer them, 'One may fast at any time with the exceptions of Sabbaths, holidays, New Moons, and Purim.'" In the *Bavli* (Babylonian Talmud, *Yoma* 81a), we learn, "Is it not logical to say that if fasting that is not done on Sabbaths and holidays would incur punishment [if not done on the day of Atonement] then should not work that could be done on Sabbaths and holidays incur punishment [if done on the Day of Atonement]? We learn thereby that one does not fast on the Sabbath or the holidays."

We have a response to the question of fasting on the New Year and on the Sabbath of Repentance. Those who would fast do not know that one can have repentance without fasting. Fasting is only one of the ways to repent, but the others are more important.

CHAPTER TWO

There is a day of judgment set for every person, whether as an individual or as a member of a community. That day in this life occurs on the New Year. We learn this in the first chapter of *Rosh Hashanah* (Babylonian Talmud, *Rosh Hashanah* 8a): The Rabbis taught, "From the verse 'For it is a statute for Israel, an ordinance of the God of Jacob' (Psalm 81:5) we learn that the Court on High cannot proceed to judgment until the court below has proclaimed the beginning of the new month. There is a supporting passage. From the verse 'For it is a statute for Israel,' I would understand that the New Year [as a day of judgment] applies only to Israel. From where would I derive that it applies to the nations as well? From the scriptural passage 'An ordinance of the God of Jacob.' If that is so, what is the force of 'For it is a statute of Israel'? It teaches that Israel enters into judg-

ment first, as Rabbi Hisda said, 'When a king and his community come to be judged, the king is judged first, to fulfill the verse
". . . that God maintain the cause of God's servant, and the cause
of God's people Israel" (1 Kings 8:59).' Why is this so? One may
say that it is not proper etiquette to have the king sit outside
[while the community is judged] or one may say that the king
enters first to absorb the divine wrath."

We also find it written in the *Mishnah* (Babylonian Talmud, *Rosh Hashanah* 16a), "The world is judged four times a
year: at Passover, through grain; at Shavout, through the fruits
of the tree; on New Year's Day, when all who come into the
world pass before God like legions of soldiers, for it is written,
'The one who fashions the hearts of all who considers all their
works' (Psalm 33:15); and at Sukkot, they are judged through
water."

The first of *Tishri* is the Day of Judgment. According to
Rabbi Eliezer, Adam was created on that day. We learn in the
Gemara (Babylonian Talmud, *Rosh Hashanah* 10b) that Rabbi
Eliezer taught that in *Tishri* was the world created. In that month
were the Patriarchs born and in that month did they die. Isaac
was born on Passover. Sarah, Rachel, and Hannah became pregnant on the New Year. Joseph was freed from prison on the New
Year. Our ancestors were freed from labor in [Pharaoh's] Egypt
on the New Year. They were delivered in the month of *Nisan*.
They [all Israel] will be redeemed during *Tishri*. Another supporting passage: Rabbi Eliezer said, "How do we know that the
world was created in *Tishri*? From what we learn from 'And God
said: "Let the earth put forth grass, herb yielding seed, and fruit-
tree bearing fruit after its kind, in which is its seed, on the earth"
(Genesis 1:11).' In what month does the earth put forth grass
and trees bear fruit? You would have to say: the month of *Nisan*!
In the same season do wild and domestic animals mate, as the

verse has it, "The meadows are clothed with flocks" (Psalm 65:14).

Rabbi Eliezer said, "How do we know that the Patriarchs were born in *Tishri*? From the verse 'And all the men of Israel assembled themselves before King Solomon at the feast, in the month of *Ethanim*, which is the seventh month' (1 Kings 8:2). It was the month in which the ancients (*ethanei*) of the world were born! Why does the word *ethan* suggest power? From its use in the verse 'Though firm (*ethan*) by Your dwelling place' (Numbers 24:21)."

One verse says, "Hear, O you mountain, Adonai's controversy" (Micah 6:2). Another verse says, "Hark! My beloved! Behold, he comes, leaping on the mountains, skipping on the hills" (Song of Songs 2:8). [The mountains are midrashically understood to refer to the Patriarchs.] "Leaping on the mountains" refers to the merit of the Patriarchs. "Skipping on the hills" refers to the merit of the Matriarchs. Rabbi Joshua said, "How do we know that the Patriarchs were born in *Nisan*? [We know it] from the verse 'It occurred in the four hundred and eightieth year after the Israelites had left the land of Egypt, in the month of *Ziv*—which is the second month—that he began to build Adonai's house' (1 Kings 6:1). In that month [*Ziv*] the nobles of the world [*zivtanai*] were born!" How do those who hold such a view deal with the proof text ". . . in the month of *Ethanim*"? They hold that the word *Ethanim* refers to those powers [implicit] in the fulfillment of the commandments rather than to the Patriarchs. How do those who believe that the Patriarchs were born in *Tishri* deal with the verse "in the month of *Ziv*"? They contend that the verse refers to the beauty [*ziv*] of the trees [which is then to be seen]. It is like what Rabbi Judah said: "Whoever goes about in the month of *Nisan* will see the trees blossom." He would also say, "Blessed is the One who has caused the world to lack for nothing, creating things that are good and trees that are beautiful that humans may derive pleasure from them."

There are those who hold that the Patriarchs were born in the month of *Tishri* and in that month they died. There are those who hold that the Patriarchs were born in the month of *Nisan* and in that month they died. How important is it to us? It is written, "And he [Moses] said to them: 'I am a hundred and twenty years old today'" (Deuteronomy 31:2). What is the scriptural force of "today"? [By having Moses say "today"] I fulfill my days and my years, Scripture is teaching that the Holy One counts the years of the righteous from day to day and from month to month, as it says, "I will fulfill the number of your days" (Exodus 23:26).

Isaac was born on Passover, as the verse indicates, "At the set time [*moayd*, also translated as "holiday"] I will return to you, when the season comes around, and Sarah will have a son" (Genesis 18:14). What was that "set time"? Were I to say that the announcement was made at Passover, would one say that Sarah bore a son fifty days later at Shavuot? Were one to say that the announcement was made at Shavuot, would one say that Sarah bore a son five months later at Sukkot? One must say that the announcement was made in *Tishri* and Isaac was born in *Nisan*! Could one say that Isaac was born after [a gestation period of only] six months? It was taught that Isaac was born in an intercalated year [so that there were two months of *Adar* and hence he was born after seven months]. Are not unclean days to be deducted? Mar Zuta said, "Even according to the one who says that a woman giving birth to a nine-month baby will fulfill her allotted days of pregnancy, the one giving birth following a pregnancy of seven months will not. [The months of her pregnancy will be incomplete.] This is indicated by the verse 'And it came to pass, when the time had come about [lit. 'And it was according to the periods of the days'] (1 Samuel 1:20). The minimum for 'periods' is two as is the minimum for 'days' [suggesting that Samuel's birth did not fulfill the allotted days of his gestation]."

Sarah, Rachel, and Hannah were visited on the New Year. How do we know this? Rabbi Elazar said, "The term 'remembered' and the term 'visited' are both found. About Rachel it is written, 'And Adonai remembered Rachel' (Genesis 30:22). It is written about Hannah, 'And Adonai remembered her' (1 Samuel 1:19). There is mention of remembrance with regard to the New Year, as it says, 'In the first month, in the first day of the month, there shall be a solemn rest to you, a memorial [*zechron*] proclaimed with the blast of horns, a holy convocation' (Leviticus 23:24). Visiting is mentioned in connection with Hannah as we read, 'So Adonai remembered [*pakad*, lit. 'visited'] Hannah' (1 Samuel 2:21). Visiting is mentioned in connection with Sarah as we read, 'And Adonai visited Sarah' (Genesis 21:1)."

Joseph was freed from prison on the New Year. How do we know that? From what is written in the psalm: "Blow the horn at the new moon, at the full moon for our feast-day for it is a statute for Israel, an ordinance of the God of Jacob. God has appointed it in Joseph as a testimony" (Psalm 81:5–6).

Our ancestors were freed from their labors in Egypt on the New Year. How do we know this? From the use of the word "burden" in the aforementioned psalm [which is related to the New Year]: "I removed his shoulder from the burden" (Psalm 81:7) and the use of the same word [in the promises of salvation] in the verse "And I will bring you out from the burdens of the Egyptians" (Exodus 6:6).

They (the Israelites) were redeemed in *Nisan* and they will be redeemed in *Tishri*. We know that because the word *shofar* (horn) is used in the context of past deliverance and in the context of future deliverance. Regarding the past, it is written in the psalm, "Blow the horn (*shofar*) at the new moon. . . . For it is a statute for Israel. . . . When God went forth against the land of Egypt" (Psalm 81: 4–6). Of the future, it is written, "And it shall come to pass on that day, that a great horn (*shofar*) shall be blown; and they . . . that were lost . . . and they that were dispersed . . . shall worship Adonai in the holy mountain in Jerusalem" (Isaiah 27:13). Rabbi Joshua said, "They were redeemed in *Nisan* and they will be redeemed in *Nisan*." What reason does he adduce? The statement in the verse "It was a watch night (*shmurim*) for bringing them out from the land of Egypt; this same night is a watch night to Adonai for all the Israelites throughout their generations" (Exodus 12:42). It was set aside (*meshumar*) from the Six Days of Creation. It was protected (*meshumar*) from all manner of demons.

We learn from this that it was the [same] day on which Adam was created. Therefore, it is truly fitting that the New Year should begin for all who come into the world on that day. It is a day fitting for divine visitation and is the day upon which those who needed such visitation were visited.

On the very day that Adam was created, he sinned. On that day, he repented and received atonement. It is fitting that day [the New Year] also be the day of judgment, the day of repentance, and the day of atonement. That very day, the Holy One said to Adam, just as I have forgiven you on this day, so will I forgive your children on this day. We learn in the *Pesikta* (*Pesikta deRav Kahana, Piska* 23) that two verses were contrasted: "Forever, O Adonai, Your word stands fast in heaven" (Psalm 119:89) and "They stand this day according to Your ordinances" (Psalm 119:91). [Note the difference between the divine word standing "forever" and standing "this day."] Rabbi Eliezer said, on

the twenty-fifth of *Elul*, the world was created. For that individual, it was if "this day" [in the aforementioned verse meant]
"This day is the beginning of Your works!" One must say then
that Adam was created on the New Year. It occurred to God to
create Adam in the first hour [of that day]. During the second
hour, God took counsel with the ministering angels. God gathered the [necessary] dust in the third hour. In the fourth hour,
God kneaded it. In the fifth hour, God shaped it. In the sixth
hour, God formed Adam's body. In the seventh hour, God
breathed a soul into it. In the eighth hour, God brought Adam
into the Garden of Eden. In the ninth hour, Adam received
mitzvot. In the tenth hour, Adam sinned. In the eleventh hour,
Adam was judged. In the twelfth hour, Adam was pardoned. The
Holy One said to Adam, "This will be a sign for your descendants. Just as you stood before Me on this day [the New Year]
and were pardoned, so will your descendants stand before Me
in the future on this day and be pardoned."

Nevertheless, there are things that have depended on
[other] specific times, from [the period of] Adam on, like when
the Temple still stood and people were offering sacrifices to
obtain divine favor. As we learned in the first chapter of *Rosh
Hashanah* (Babylonian Talmud, *Rosh Hashanah* 16a): It is
taught that all are judged on the New Year, but the verdicts of
individuals are deferred to different times. Some receive [reward
or punishment with regard to] produce on the Festival of Passover, some receive [differing amounts of] the fruits of the tree
during Shavuot, and some receive their judgment with regard
to rain during Sukkot. One may be judged on Rosh Hashanah,
but the verdict is sealed on Yom Kippur. Rabbi Yose said, "One
may be judged every day, as it is said, '. . . You should remember him every morning' (Job 7:18)." Arguing from the continuation of the verse, "And try him every moment," Rabbi Nathan

said that one is tried every moment. We learn further that Rabbi Judah said in the name of Rabbi Akiba: "Why does the Torah say bring a sheaf on Passover" [Leviticus 23:10]? Because Passover is the time of produce! The Holy One says, "Offer before Me a sheaf so that the produce that is in the field may be blessed." Why does the Torah say, "Bring before Me the shewbread during Shavuot" [Leviticus 23:17]? That festival is the time of the fruits of the tree. It is as if the Holy One were saying, "Bring before Me the shewbread during Shavuot so that the fruits of the tree might be blessed on your account." Why then does the Torah say, "Offer a water libation during Sukkot" [*Sukkah* 4:1, 9]? The seasonal rains may [thus] be blessed on your account! Why should verses relating to God's sovereignty [*malchuyot*], God's memory [*zichronot*], and to the ram's horn [*shofrot*] be recited on Rosh Hashanah? The sovereignty verses are recited so that you might accept My sovereignty over you. Memory verses should be recited so that I will have a good recollection of you. How should this be accomplished? With the ram's horn, the *shofar*. Rabbi Abahu asked, "Why is a ram's horn sounded on Rosh Hashanah? [Because] the Holy One said, "So that I may remember for your benefit the Binding of Isaac, son of Abraham, and so that I may account the sounding of the *shofar* as you had bound yourselves [as a sacrifice] before Me."

The Binding of Isaac is of great importance to the seed of Abraham. Their Creator will always love them because of what Abraham our Patriarch was willing to do to fulfill the Divine Will. That love will always be available to them no matter how perilous their situation, simply because Abraham passed that great test. We learn about this in the eleventh chapter of *Sanhedrin* (Babylonian Talmud, *Sanhedrin* 89b). It is written, "And it came to pass after these *words*" (Genesis 22:1). [The word *devarim* can be translated either as "words" or "things."] After whose words? Rabbi Yose ben Zimra answered, "After the words of Satan as it is written, 'And the boy grew and was (*vayegamel*) weaned' (Genesis 21:8). [This assumes the *midrash* (*Bereishit Rabbah*) that Isaac was delivered (also *vayegamel*) from the power of the Evil Inclination.]

For this reason, God has instructed us to sound the ram's horn to keep in mind the ram that was substituted for Isaac and was slaughtered in his place. The quoted verses and the sounding of the ram's horn have our movement toward repentance and our accepting God as our Ruler as their purpose. We ask God to remember those righteous women who were visited with child at this season and the Binding [and near sacrifice] of Isaac, although we may not have repented properly. [We also ask] God to remember us for good, that God have mercy upon us. [Thus,] we read on the first day on the New Year the visiting of Sarah (Genesis 21) as the Torah portion and the visiting of Hannah (1 Samuel 1) as the *Haftarah*. On the second day we read the Binding of Isaac (Genesis 22) as the Torah portion and we read "After I was turned" (Jeremiah 31:18ff) as the *Haftarah*.

CHAPTER THREE

Every element of the Torah, every aspect of Jewish faith, depends on the belief in Divine Providence. One must believe that the Creator provides for the individual and the group in the most perfect manner that corresponds to their deeds, as it is written, "Great in counsel, and mighty in work, whose eyes are open upon all the ways of the sons of humankind, to give every one according to one's ways, and according to the fruit of one's doings" (Jeremiah 32:19). Another verse attests, ". . . the eyes of Adonai run to and fro throughout the whole earth" (Zechariah 4:10). The verses of the Torah that teach this are beyond number. The Rabbis in the third chapter of *Pirkei Avot* (*Pirkei Avot* 3:16) taught, "All is foreseen, but freedom of choice is given."

Even though providence and reward [and punishment] operate at all times and in all places, on the Day of Judgment all things come into account; all things are weighed. It is the month for the use of scales. It is the time for all the deeds of people to be examined to see which side weighs heavier. There is no forgetfulness before the Throne of Glory. All is recalled by God as if all were inscribed and set forth. In order for us humans to understand, the matter is compared to something written down in books, as the Rabbis said in the first chapter of *Rosh Hashanah* (Babylonian Talmud, *Rosh Hashanah* 16b). Rabbi Crospodai said in the name of Rabbi Yochanan, "Three books are open on Rosh Hashanah. One [open book contains] completely righteous people. One [book contains] completely wicked people. One [book contains] those [people] in the middle. Those who are completely righteous are immediately inscribed for life. Those who are completely wicked are immediately sentenced to death. The fate of those who are in the middle is held in abeyance from the New Year until Yom Kippur. If they merit it, they will be inscribed for life. If not, they are sentenced to death." Rabbi Abin said this verse applies: "Let them be blotted out of the book of the living and not be written with the righteous" (Psalm 69:29). "Let them be blotted out of the book" refers to the completely wicked. "Of the living" refers to the book of the absolutely righteous. "And not be written with the righteous" refers to the book of those in between. Rabbi Nachman bar Isaac said, "This relates to what is written: '. . . blot me, I pray, out of Your book which You have written' (Exodus 32:32). 'Blot me' refers to the book of the wicked. 'Your book' refers to the book of the wicked. 'Which You have written' refers to the book of those in the middle."

There has been great confusion about this matter. Many have said that a righteous person may perish even though that person is righteous, while a wicked person may live long even though that person is wicked. Even the Psalmist said, "But as for me, my feet were almost gone. My steps had nearly slipped. I was envious of the arrogant. When I saw the prosperity of the wicked" (Psalm 73:2). The Psalmist was not satisfied until reaching the following conclusion: "Until I entered the sanctuary of God and considered their end" (Psalm 73:17). By "their end" the Psalmist meant the end of the matter, whether that meant the end of the days of humankind or the other world, that is, the World to Come. Jeremiah spoke about this when he said, "Why does the way of the wicked prosper? Why are those who deal very treacherously secure?" (Jeremiah 12:2). It would seem from their words [those of the Psalmist and Jeremiah] that they were more troubled by the ease of the wicked than the suffering of the righteous. Since ". . . there is not a righteous person on earth that does good and does not sin" (Ecclesiastes 7:20), anyone who appears to be righteous may have committed a secret sin. However, when we see a person commit many sins publicly and yet live a life of ease, we would be greatly perplexed were it not for that statement of our Rabbis (Babylonian Talmud, *Taanit* 11a) expounding the verse "A God of faithfulness without iniquity" (Deuteronomy 32:4). God has no partiality. The wicked person who constantly sins may have some merit for which that person will be rewarded in this world. Yet that person may get what he [or she] deserves when entering the World to Come laden with guilt. On the other hand, the righteous person who may have sinned in the least way will be punished in this world but will get his [or her] full reward in the World to Come. Therefore, should we see those who seem to us to be righteous die young while the wicked live long, we should know that the judgment on Rosh Hashanah deals only with bodies. That's what Rabbi

Yochanan meant when he spoke [in Babylonian Talmud, *Rosh Hashanah* 16b] of "completely righteous persons." He referred to those judged righteous in this world. That's also what he meant when he spoke of "completely wicked persons." He referred to those so judged in this world, for the ultimate judgment of souls is in the World to Come on the Day of Judgment, as was indicated in the similar statement [Babylonian Talmud, *Rosh Hashanah* 16b] that it was taught according to Bet Shammai. There were three groups who would be judged on the Day of Judgment: those who were completely righteous, those who were completely wicked, and those who were in the middle (Babylonian Talmud, *Rosh Hashanah* 16b).

There are those who say that even the righteous cannot merit two tables [in other words, have a reward in both worlds]. Were the Creator to give wealth, ease, and long life to the righteous in this world and keep these good things from the wicked and moreover, were God to constantly punish the wicked, people would be moved to righteousness, not for the sake of heaven but for the sake of their own self-interest. They would want to get those good things that were tangible and flee from their opposites. They would not be interested in those higher spiritual purposes promised us by the Torah. Immediate gratification or the immediate avoidance of pain would be their motivations. Like all humans, they would seek what is pleasant and flee from what is unpleasant in a manner no different from all other animals. A cow just seeing grass when it is hungry or seeing water when it is thirsty immediately goes after what it needs to live. Just as that cow seeks to avoid pits and the goad, so it would be with human beings doing what is natural [and thus choosing virtue and not vice in order to gain pleasure and avoid pain]. After all, even a little child would choose a pearl rather than a coal were the two placed before him [or her]. When that ultimate good is not perceptible even to the righteous person, the Rabbis said, "Don't serve God on the condition of receiving a reward but rather for the sake of heaven to understand the truth and the glory yet to come" [a paraphrase of *Pirkei Avot* 1:3]. How much more would there be the wrong intention [in serving God] if that ultimate good is immediately perceptible?

Furthermore, were all the righteous to experience good with no exceptions and all the wicked to experience evil with no exceptions, then the nature of varying accidents related to corruptible matter would be nullified. Then it would be possible for even this pious person to continually eat bad food and never suffer, never get sick. Even were such a person to hurl oneself from a high tower, that person would never get hurt! On the other hand, were a wicked person to cast seed on fertile soil, it would not grow. Were the pious person and the wicked person to have adjoining fields, rain would not fall on the one, lest it fall on the other. Were a wicked person to have sexual intercourse with a woman, then he should not [be able] to have children with her [but he will]. All of this is impossible. It is contrary to the nature of the existing things in their origin in the Divine Will. It is enough for us that all the good of this world is nothing compared to the ease in the world to come. Although the righteous person will fall, that person will arise. The wicked person will fall in his [or her] evil. There may be immeasurable goods in this life. However, they pale by comparison to the pleasure to be inherited in the life to come, about which Scripture says, "Neither has the eye seen . . ." (Isaiah 64:3).

It follows that repentance and good deeds are acceptable at all times. However, in connection to that day of judgment [the New Year] pertaining to one's body, children, and sustenance, it is [even more fitting] for one to repent from one's sins, that one be judged innocent in order to be inscribed at that

moment for life. If he [or she] is a person in the middle and yet
be meritorious, then the scale of justice will be inclined on his
[or her] behalf toward life. That's what the Sages said (Babylonian Talmud, *Rosh Hashanah* 16b): "Were the individual not
meritorious, and therefore inscribed for death" refers to that person who has transgressed against the *mitzvah* of *teshuvah* and
therefore has postured oneself toward death. *Teshuvah* is a
mitzvah incumbent on everyone, just as the Torah instructs,
"And you shall return to Adonai your God and you shall respond
to God's voice" (Deuteronomy 4:31). Our Rabbis said in the first
chapter of Rosh Hashanah (Babylonian Talmud, *Rosh Hashanah*
18a), "But what about the individual? On the ten days between
the New Year and the Day of Atonement God is available to
accept repentance, just as they [the Rabbis] interpreted the verse
'Seek Adonai where God may be found' (Isaiah 55:6). It is also
stated, 'But from that time, you shall seek Adonai your God'
(Deuteronomy 4:29).

CHAPTER FOUR

As God has mercy for all of God's creatures, so has God given
them the opportunity to return in repentance. Thus, they might
not be destroyed in their wickedness, since the inclination of
the heart of the human is evil from youth. By nature, humans
pursue material things and abandon ideas. For that reason,
humans need to examine our ways at all times and turn toward
repentance, as it is written, "Let us search and try our ways, and
return to Adonai" (Lamentations 3:40).

Since we humans are sunk into lust and do not move ourselves to repentance throughout the year, the Torah instructs
[us] to sound the *shofar* on the New Year in order to awaken
us—and make us remember—as if to say, "Wake up, you who

sleep from your slumbers, for the time of your visitation approaches." God, may You be blessed, does not desire the wicked to be destroyed but rather that they repent and live. Therefore the *shofar* is sounded on the New Year so that the people of Israel should repent. If the *shofar* is sounded in the city and the people do not tremble, [they are culpable] their blood is on their own head [an allusion to Amos 3:6].

We learn in the *Pesikta*: "And God speaks before God's army, for God's camp is very great" refers to Israel. "For God does what God says" refers to the righteous, whom God strengthens when they do God's will. "Terrifying and great is the day of Adonai" refers to the Day of Atonement. Regarding "who can abide it," according to Rabbi Crospodai in the name of Rabbi Yochanan, there are three ledgers: one for those who are completely righteous, one for those who are completely wicked, and one for those in the middle. Those who are completely righteous "shall awake . . . to everlasting life" (Daniel 12:2). Those who are completely wicked "shall awake . . . to reproaches and everlasting abhorrence" (Daniel 12:2). Another verse, "Let them be blotted out of the book of the living and not be written with the righteous" (Psalm 69:29), [is interpreted in this manner]: "Let them be blotted out" refers to the wicked. "The living" refers to the righteous. "And not be written with the righteous" refers to those in the middle. The Holy One has given the ten days from the New Year to the Day of Atonement to repent. If they do repent, they will be inscribed with the righteous. If they do not repent, they will be inscribed along with the wicked.

The Torah, by requiring that a horn be sounded in a three-fold manner (*tekiah*, then *teruah*, then *tekiah* again) alludes to the three principles of *teshuvah*. The first *tekiah* alludes to the first requirement of repentance: the would-be penitent must earnestly investigate past actions and if he [or she] finds any sin —

whether it is an act, intention or thought—the individual must rid oneself completely of it, as it is written, "Let the wicked forsake the way, and the iniquitous one, one's thoughts. Let that person return to Adonai" (Isaiah 55:7). The sounding of *teruah*, sounded between the two *tekiot*, suggests the groaning and wailing one expresses when one's evil deeds and sins, as it is written, "Surely after that I was turned, I repented. And after that I was instructed . . . I was ashamed, yes even confounded" (Jeremiah 31:18). The final *tekiah* is to set it firmly in mind: to commit oneself never again to return to one's former [evil] thoughts and acts, as it is written, "Neither shall we call the work of our hands our gods anymore" (Hosea 14:4).

Further, the Torah alludes to this when it says, "But the word is very close to you, in your mouth, and in your heart, that you may do it" (Deuteronomy 30:14). First, the Torah says that the repentance it commands is close to us, easier than anything that the [non-Jewish] nations have to do. When they sin, they have to go to their priests to ask advice regarding the ways of *teshuvah*. Their priests tell them to fast for many days, to go overseas and to walk around barefoot, weary, and fatigued. Also, they [are told to] beat themselves with iron sticks and undergo other kinds of great suffering. However, our holy Torah has mercy for Israel and does not wish to multiply fasts or increase suffering. It does not ask that one [the would-be penitent] should go on long journeys, nor does it direct us to climb to some high spot that one cannot reach or to take a long trip overseas. That is why it says, "It is not in heaven . . . neither is it beyond the sea . . . but the word is very close to you, in your mouth, and in your heart, that you may do it" (Deuteronomy 30:12–14). The Torah suggests three things: mouth, heart, and hand. The first deals with the confession made with the mouth, when the penitent says that he [or she] has given up sin. The second reflects the groaning and heartbreak felt by the penitent, reflecting on what has been done. The third [represents] the determination that the penitent will not return to the sinful act. Were one to interpret the verse in relationship to the Torah and not to *teshuvah*, then one would understand that all the *mitzvot* of the Torah, positive and negative, deal with speech, thought, and deed.

The rabbis determined that the *shofar* should sound *tekiah* and *teruah* a second time when they [the congregation] stands to recite the *Musaf* service. We learn this in the first chapter of *Rosh Hashanah* (Babylonian Talmud, *Rosh Hashanah* 16a). Rabbi Isaac said, "Why do they sound *tekiah* and *teruah* when they are sitting down? Why do they do the same thing when they are standing? They do so in order to disturb Satan."

The *Midrash* states that Satan gets frightened when they begin and are sitting. When they are about to conclude and are standing, Satan gets even more frightened for [he wonders] perhaps if it is his time to be swallowed up, as it is written, "He will swallow up death forever" (Isaiah 25:8). Further, it would seem that Satan remembers that when he hears the sound of the Great *Shofar* at the end of days, his time will come to be swallowed up forever. Just as a person becomes confused and unable to argue when told the day of one's own death, so it is with Satan.

It is also written in the responsa of Rabbi Isaac Ibn Giat (Numbers 175 and 176), "Rav Amram, Saadia Gaon, and Rabbenu Hai said that it was already the custom in their time to sound *teruah* after the completion of the [*Amidah*] Prayer without sounding *tekiah* and three *shevarim* in order to disturb Satan."

This day is called *Yom Teruah* [the day of blowing of the *shofar*] and not *Yom Tekiah* [the day of sounding of the *shofar*] because the one who repents of one's sins, weeps, wails, and groans because of them. The individual determines in one's mind that having forsaken such sins, he [or she] will never again do them. It would seem that the second element of repentance alluded to by *teruah* is the most important of all. For that reason the Torah says, ". . . it is a day of blowing of the horn to you" (Numbers 29:1). The term *teruah* is also related to the breaking of one's heart, as the verse has it, "You will break them [*teroaym*] with a rod of iron" (Psalm 2:9). Changing the letters [of *teruah*] suggests the word for "awakening" [*haarah*].

The Psalmist, while speaking of the understanding of the notion suggested by the Torah, said, "Happy is the people who know the joyous shout [*teruah*]" (Psalm 89:16). The reason the verse continues "They walk, Adonai, in the light of Your countenance" is because God will enlighten the face of every penitent and will in love bring that person close.

CHAPTER FIVE

The *mitzvot* have many particular qualities beneficial to body and soul. Since it is the Holy One's intention to grant merit to Israel chosen from among all peoples, God gave them much Torah and many *mitzvot* for their own benefit. The *mitzvah* of sounding the *shofar* on the New Year has many purposes that can be summed up in the verse "The path of life ascends for the wise, so that he [or she] may depart from the netherworld beneath" (Proverbs 15:24). These purposes are also subsumed in the Decalogue.

First, this day [the New Year] is the very day of the original creation of the human person. It was for that creation that this lower world was created. The Holy One became sovereign over this terrestrial world, which had proceeded from potency to act that very day. It is common that on the day when a mortal king ascends to the throne, his servants assemble before him, sound trumpets, proclaim his sovereignty, and declare, "Long live the king!" How much the more should it be for the Sovereign of Sovereigns, the Holy One, whose sovereignty preceded the people, and who will be Ruler over all the earth! How much more should God's people mark the day each year that began God's dominion over the world and proclaim that God's sovereignty is ongoing, without end. This is as the Psalmist said: "With trumpets and sound of the horn, you should shout before the Sovereign, Adonai" (Psalm 98:6).

Second, these days [between the New Year and the Day of Atonement] are fitting to receive penitents. Thus, the Torah instructs us to sound the *shofar* in order to announce that whoever wants to repent, may repent. The one who will not repent will be responsible for not doing so. There can be no greater warning than this! Any ruler makes a public announcement to warn people not to transgress a new decree before enacting it. Anyone who then does [what is forbidden] is culpable. When a ruler wants to forgive sinners, the ruler makes a public announcement: "Anyone who will come to such and such a place and who will return to the royal service will be forgiven for any action. Anyone who won't [return] will suffer the consequences." *Teshuvah* is the same kind of thing.

Third, when we remember that it was the *shofar* that was sounded when the Torah was given at Sinai, as it is written, "And . . . the voice of the horn [*shofar*] gets louder and louder . . ." (Exodus 19:19), then when we hear the sound of the *shofar* [on the New Year] we will remember the day of the giving of the Torah. Fear of God will enter our hearts, and we will try to do God's *mitzvot*. Then we will return in *teshuvah*.

Fourth, when we remember the words of the Prophets— whose words were compared to the sounding of the *shofar*, as it says, "Then whoever hears the sound of the horn [*shofar*] and takes no warning, [and then] if the sword comes and takes him away, the individual will be responsible" (Ezekiel 33:4)—we are warned. We may deliver our household and all that we have.

Fifth, when we remember the destruction of the Temple, which was accompanied by the sounds and the *shofar* blasts of war conducted by our enemies, as it is written, "Because you have heard, O my soul, the sound of the horn, the alarm of war" (Jeremiah 4:19), then hear the sound of the *shofar*, we pray to God, we implore God to deliver us from the hands of our enemies, that God may speedily rebuild the Temple, which, because of our sins, our enemies had destroyed. God had promised us this [the rebuilding of the Temple] through God's servants, the Prophets.

Sixth, we remember the Binding of Isaac our patriarch, who for the Glory of God and the fulfillment of the divine will had given himself over to death. When we remember Abraham his father, who loved Isaac like his own soul and yet wished to fulfill the divine word [and would have] had the Holy One not had pity upon the father and the son and had shown Abraham the ram prepared from Creation, so that Abraham offered up the ram in Isaac's place. That offering was considered to be the equivalent of Abraham's sacrificing his son as a perfect offering. If only we were to walk in God's ways, then our Creator would have compassion for us and would remember to be merciful, as the Rabbis taught that [God says,] "Sound the horn of the ram before Me so that I may remember for your sake the Binding of Isaac, son of Abraham [and Sarah], and that I may accept your *teshuvah* and deliver you from your enemies, from those who hate you" (Babylonian Talmud, *Rosh Hashanah* 16a).

Seventh, the nature of the sound of the *shofar* causes us to fear when we hear it. That fear causes us to submit to our Creator, even as it is said, "Shall the horn [*shofar*] be blown in a city and the people not tremble?" (Amos 3:7). Therefore, on hearing the *shofar*, let one say to the other, "Why should the *shofar* be sounded this particular day?" And let the other say, "Because of this and that which was done." This is what Maimonides meant when he wrote (in the *Mishneh Torah*, *Hilchot Teshuvah* 3:4) "Even though the sounding of the *shofar* on the New Year is a scriptural ordinance, it has its message, as if to say, 'You who are asleep, awake from your slumber. Search your deeds! Remember your Creator and repent! Don't be like those who forget the truth because of the vanities of the time, who waste their days in things that have no meaning, no purpose, and no benefit. Look to your souls. Start doing good.' Let everyone turn away from one's evil way and one's wicked thoughts, as it says, 'And let him return to Adonai. Let him return to Adonai' (Isaiah 55:7)."

Eighth, when we remember the great Day of Judgment and we become afraid, as it is said, "The great day of Adonai is near. It is near and is coming quickly. Even the voice of the day of Adonai in which the mighty one cries bitterly. That is the day of the trouble and distress, a day of waste and desolation, a day of darkness and gloominess, a day of clouds and thick darkness, a day of the horn and alarm" (Zephaniah 1:15, 16). It is also said about this, "Gather yourselves together, indeed, gather together, O shameless nation" (Zephaniah 2:11).

Ninth, we sound the *shofar* with the hope that the Holy One will gather the dispersed of Israel as God has promised us through Isaiah the prophet, as it says, "And it shall come to pass on that day that a great horn shall be blown" (Isaiah 27:12).

Tenth, when we remember the day of the resurrection of the dead, which the prophet said that they would arise to life, that the *shofar* would be sounded, and that they would be gath-

ered together when they hear the *shofar*, as it says, "All you inhabitants of the world, and you dwellers on the earth, when an
ensign is lifted up on the mountains, look! And when the horn
is blown, listen!" (Isaiah 18:3). "Inhabitants of the world" refers
to those of the people of Israel who are in the Diaspora. "Dwellers on the earth" refer to those who are dead. That the last refers to the dead is proven by "Awake and sing, you who dwell in
the dust" (Isaiah 26:19).

Therefore, we are obligated to keep these things in mind
and to concentrate on the *mitzvah* of the *shofar*, to be careful of
it as the Torah has commanded. Our reward is to be increased,
as it is written, "And Adonai instructed us to do all these statutes, to fear Adonai our God, for our good always . . ." (Deuteronomy 6:24).

We discussed the matter of the prayer and the [biblical]
verses in the Lamp of Commandment, the last chapter of the
section on prayer. The particulars were explained in the Table
of the Shewbread [sections in *Menorat Hamaor*].

From every place we have learned that the only purpose
of the sounding of the *shofar* was to encourage repentance. We
learned in the *Mechilta* [actually found in *Leviticus Rabbah*
29:6] "And in the seventh month (*bachodesh*)," (Numbers 29:1)
is to be [midrashically] understood thus: "Renew (*chadeshu*)
yourselves." Similarly, "Blow the horn (*shofar*) at the New
Moon" (Psalm 81:4) means, "Improve (*shapru*) yourselves." The
Holy One said to Israel, "If you will improve (*shipartem*) your
deeds before Me, then I will be, as it were, your *shofar*. Just as a
shofar is blown from one end and the sound comes out from
the other, so will I get up from the Throne of Justice and I will
sit down on the Throne of Mercy. I will have compassion on
you. All things are suspended by our acts of repentance and may
they from heaven have compassion for us."

Section Two: On the Onset of the Day of Atonement

Every God-fearing, intelligent person should tremble knowing that every deed is recorded and that God judges for good or ill every hidden act. Judgment begins on the New Year. The verdict is sealed on the Day of Atonement. A person, being judged by a flesh-and-blood king, fearfully tries to avoid that judgment. How does one avoid being judged by the Judge of the Universe? A way out is in one's grasp. One need only begin to repent before the verdict, as it says, "What shall we do for our sister when she shall be spoken for" (Song of Songs 8:8). ["Our sister" is midrashically understood as the soul. "When she shall be spoken for" is understood as the time of judgment.]

Therefore, it is fitting that everyone who fears God should bestir oneself during the [Ten] Days of Penitence before the day of the sealing of the verdict [the Day of Atonement]. One should engage in business less and devote oneself to examine one's ways and engage in the ways of repentance. This period is one of divine favor, as it is written, "In an acceptable time, I have answered you" (Isaiah 49:8) and as another verse has it, "Seek Adonai while God may be found" (Isaiah 55:6). The Rabbis said (Babylonian Talmud, *Rosh Hashanah* 18a) these verses refer to the ten days between the New Year and the Day of Atonement. We learn further (*Midrash Tehillim* 26:7) that Rabbi Berachia in the name of Rabbi Samuel said [the phrase] "And it came to pass about ten days" [*k'aseret yamin,* lit. "like the ten days"] and not "in ten days" [*b'aseret yamin*] relates to the ten days between the New Year and the Day of Atonement and suggested that Nabal had the opportunity for repentance. [This passage is found in the third chapter of *Midrash Tehillim.*]

Even though the Holy One is compassionate and grants atonement for those sins between the individual and God, were a person to sin against another person, that person must appease the other person and win favor with word and deed. We learn in the eighth chapter of *Yoma* (Babylonian Talmud, *Yoma* 85b) Rabbi Eliezer ben Azariah interpreted the verse "For on this day shall atonement be made for you, to cleanse you. From all your sins shall you be clean before Adonai" (Leviticus 16:30) thus, for sins between the individual and God the Day of Atonement brings atonement. However, for sins between persons the Day of Atonement brings atonement only when the one who has offended has appeased the one offended.

The following was said in the *Gemara* (Babylonian Talmud, *Yoma* 87a): Rabbi Isaac said that whoever provokes another [must appease that person] and the same was stated above in *Midrash Tehillim* in the passage cited.

Even though one ought to quickly appease a person offended any day of the year, one should do so even quicker, paying back [whatever is owed] and asking forgiveness when the Day of Atonement approaches. The one offended should not delay [forgiving the offender], for in so doing one's own sins will be forgiven. This we learn in the fifth chapter of the tractate *Eruvin* (Babylonian Talmud, *Eruvin* 54a) and in the seventh chapter of the tractate *Nedarim* (Babylonian Talmud, *Nedarim* 55a): Rabba had once offended Rabbi Joseph bar Hamma. [This has been discussed above in the third chapter of the third section of "The Behavior of Those Who Study Torah."] When the Day of Atonement was approaching, Rabba said [to himself] I should go and appease him [Joseph bar Hamma]. He went and found that his [Rabbi Joseph's] attendant was mixing a cup of wine. Rabba said to him, "Give me the cup and let me mix the wine for him." He then mixed the wine. When Rabbi Joseph tasted the wine, he said, "It seems to me that Rabba did the mixing." Rabba said, "Yes, it was me." Rabbi Joseph responded,

"Before you take your seat, explain why Scripture says, 'And from Mattanah to Nahaliel and from Nahaliel to Bamot' (Numbers 21:9)." Rabba said to him, "Were a person to consider oneself as if he [or she] were this wilderness that everyone may trample, then it [the knowledge of Torah] would be given to him [or her] as a gift, as the Torah states, 'And from the wilderness to Mattanah [which means *gift* in Hebrew]' (Numbers 21:18). Since it was given as a gift, it is as if God had caused the individual to inherit it [*nachal El*] as the verse had it, 'From Mattanah to Nahaliel.'" Since God has caused the individual to inherit it, that person has ascended to greatness, as the verse continued, "from Nahaliel to Bamot" [*Bamot* in Hebrew means "high places"]. Were a person to become arrogant, God would bring that person low, as the next verse states, "and from Bamot to the valley" (Numbers 21:20). If, however, that person would now repent, then the Holy One would raise that person, as the verse states, "Every valley shall be lifted up" (Isaiah 40:4).

We also read in the eighth chapter of *Yoma* (Babylonian Talmud, *Yoma* 87a) that Rav once had a quarrel with a butcher. Twelve months went by and the butcher had not come to appease him. Even when the Day of Atonement arrived, he had not come. Rav said, "I will go [and appease him]." On the way, he met Rav Huna. He asked, "Where are you going?" He answered, "I am going to appease Mr. so-and-so [the butcher]." Rav said, "Are you going to kill somebody?" He went [to the butcher's house] and called at the door. He [the butcher] called out, "Go away, I will have nothing to do with you." When the butcher was [at work and was] splitting a head, a bone flew off and struck his throat [severing an artery] and killed him.

They were accustomed to immerse themselves on the eve of the Day of Atonement. Those who did found warrant for this practice in the *midrash* of *Pirkei deRabbi Eliezer* (chapter 46) that one should be as clean as the ministering angels. We have also found in the *Respona of the Geonim* (*Otzar Hageonim, Rosh Hashanah*, p. 27) a statement in the name of Rabbi Isaac Ibn Giat that this act of immersion does not require a blessing because it is an enactment of the early Sages. Therefore, one should immerse oneself in the usual manner without a blessing because a blessing is not required for something done in the usual manner. This is as Rabbi (Judah the Prince) said concerning the willows [used on Sukkot], that one may beat them without a blessing. He held that such a practice followed the custom of the Prophets (Babylonian Talmud, *Sukkot* 44b). Therefore, one may say that one does not recite a blessing for a customary usage.

They [the Sages] ordained that one should eat a festival meal on the eve of the Day of Atonement to show that one rejoices when the time of one's atonement comes near. We learn in the eighth chapter of the tractate *Yoma* (Babylonian Talmud, *Yoma* 81b): It was taught that Rabbi Hiyya bar Rav Midapti asked concerning the verse "And you shall afflict your souls, in the ninth day of the month at evening" (Leviticus 23:32), "Do we fast on the ninth day? We fast on the tenth day!" [He continued, "Then why does the Torah say 'the ninth day'?] It is to tell you that whoever eats and drinks on the ninth day will be accounted [and will receive the reward] as if he had fasted on the ninth and on the tenth!"

It is told in the *Midrash* (*Bereishit Rabbah* 11:4) of a police officer of a city who told his servant to buy a fish. The servant found only one fish [in the market] and was willing to pay two gold coins for it. The servant then bid four golden coins for the fish but the tailor upped his bid to five and got the fish. When the servant came home and told his employer what had happened, the officer sent for the tailor. He asked him, "What do you do?" He answered, "I am a tailor." The officer asked, "Why did you pay five gold coins for a fish? I sent my servant to buy a fish for me and you took it!" The tailor answered, "I would have paid ten gold coins for it so that I could eat on such a day as this which the Holy One has instructed that we eat and drink. We are certain that God will grant us atonement for all of our sins." The officer said, "If that was the reason, you have done well!" From this we learn that whoever acts for the sake of heaven will not be injured in doing so.

On such a day, the Holy One shows that God will be merciful to all of Israel. God asks that we fast only one day a year. God asks that we enjoy eating and drinking before the fast so that we may strengthen our bodies and be able to fast. It may be compared to a king who had an only son and he instructed him to fast one day. However, the king also commanded his son to eat and drink well so that he would be able to fast.

Further, since on Sabbaths and festivals we eat festival meals for our own joy and for the sake of heaven and since we cannot eat such a meal on the Day of Atonement because it is a fast day, we are obligated to have such a meal prior to the [onset of the] eve of the Day of Atonement. There are those who say that if a person were to have one's festival prior to the fast, it makes the discomfort of the fast greater. For that reason, they [the Sages] say that whoever eats and drinks on the ninth, it is as if that person had fasted on the ninth and the tenth! Because the individual got used to the enjoyment of eating and drinking on the day before [the fast], the fast seemed to that person to have endured for two days!

In any case, anyone with sense will be happy when the day comes for the atonement of one's sins. The individual ought to prepare for it with repentance so that he [or she] will be ready for atonement. Doing so, the individual would act like a physician who, anticipating the crisis of a patient's illness, would remove whatever caused the illness, whether an overfilled stomach or a surplus of blood. At the onset of the crisis, the individual would find the physician prepared to deal with it. Had the physician not prepared for it, the crisis would bring death to the patient. So it is with the Day of Atonement: it is the crisis for sickness of the soul. Were the sinner to remain with his transgression, he would be judged guilty and his verdict would come speedily. Were s/he to repent, s/he would be found innocent and his/her sins would be scoured away, so that s/he would be cleansed and granted atonement, as it is written, "Though your sins be as scarlet, they shall be whiter than snow" (Isaiah 1:18).

For this reason, one should search one's ways and turn from one's sins and confess them on the eve [of the Day of Atonement] before one's meal. It is even better for one to immerse oneself and [as it were] one's soul. One should not be like the individual who immerses oneself while holding onto a contaminating reptile, for in such a case, immersion has no effect. One should prepare oneself so that one may enter into the Day [of Atonement] purified and prepared for repentance so that the atoning day may arrive and the Creator, the Holy One, may through the quality of mercy grant the individual atonement, as it is written, "For on this day shall atonement be made for you, to cleanse you. From all your sins you will be clean before Adonai" (Leviticus 16:30).

CHAPTER TWO

When the Day [of Atonement] begins, let every person sanctify their body and their soul so that they can be like an angel of God, who is free of all sin, as we learn in the fortieth chapter of *Pirkei deRabbi Eliezer*: When Samael sees that Israel is free of sin on the Day of Atonement, he says, "Master of the Universe, is there any other people in all the world who are like the ministering angels? Just as the ministering angels go about barefoot, so does Israel on the Day of Atonement. Just as the ministering angels are free of sin, so is Israel on the Day of Atonement. Just as peace reigns among the ministering angels, so does peace reign among Israel on the Day of Atonement." Hearing such testimony from Israel's accuser, the Holy One grants Israel atonement.

It is also written in *Deuteronomy Rabbah* in the section *veetchanan* that when Moses ascended to heaven, he heard the ministering angels praise the Holy One, as they said, "Praised be the Name of God's glorious kingdom forever and ever." Moses brought that praise down to Israel. It may be compared to a person who stole jewelry from the king's palace and gave it to his wife. He cautioned her, "Put it on only when you are alone inside the house." Thus, during the rest of the year, Israel recites, "Praised be the Name of God's glorious kingdom" in a whisper. On the Day of Atonement, they recite it loudly, as if to say, "We Israel are as the ministering angels." Likewise, they stand on their feet throughout the Day of Atonement, as if to say, "We stand because we are compared to the ministering angels and we can stand as erect as they." We could also say that this day is fit for atonement, for on that day Abraham our patriarch circumcised himself. The foreskin that was removed formed a covenant to circumcise [as it were] other foreskins, those of the heart, of the ear, and of the lips. It was also on the Day of Atonement that atonement was granted for making the Golden Calf and the second set of tablets was given.

The Sages also said that the daughters of Israel would honor that day by being dressed in clothes more beautiful than those worn on any other holiday. We learn this at the end of the tractate *Taanit* (Babylonian Talmud, *Taanit* 26b) and in the eighth chapter of *Bava Batra* (Babylonian Talmud, *Bava Batra* 121a): Rabbi Shimon ben Gamliel said, "There were no happier days for Israel than the fifteenth of *Av* and the Day of Atonement, for on them the daughters of Israel would go out to dance in the vineyards in white garments that were borrowed, so that none should be embarrassed who did not own them." [This has been covered above.]

We can also say that the Holy One, for whom schemes are devised, has commanded that this day [of Atonement] should occur when it does because it is a time of contention [lit. "kicking"] and rebelliousness. Why? Because during the summer the warehouses are filled throughout the land of Israel with corn, grain, wine, and every other kind of good thing. That is the reason that one must be stirred from one's lethargy and turn oneself from one's wealth and contention and turn from one's usual ways, which are the pursuit of desire and pleasure. One should turn, too, from every kind of false belief that is heresy. This is what the Torah warned about when it said, ". . . and that you do not go after your own heart and your own eyes, after which you used to go astray" (Numbers 15:39). The rabbis expounded this verse (in Babylonian Talmud, *Berachot* 12b) in this manner: "after your own heart" refers to heresy. "After your own eyes" refers to lewdness. They meant that one should think only of what one should believe. One should fulfill one's desires only to maintain one's body and to maintain the species. In doing this, one will achieve human perfection.

Hence, let everyone watch out for those sins that are brought on by desire. One is enmired in such sins throughout the year. [Sexual] desire should be pursued only for the sake of heaven. Therefore, the sin-offering of a goat was brought every month. It was called a "sin-offering to Adonai" (Numbers 28:15) to alert us to the way one should conduct one's life in acts and in belief to bring atonement for the sin that one committed in enjoying the world for sake of [mere] desire. Let no one despair. One can repent and save one's soul from one's body, which is the enemy. Satan is the one who really is one's enemy. Satan is the Evil Inclination. Satan is the Angel of Death. However, on the Day of Atonement, a day intended for repentance, the two goats come [as offerings] corresponding to the two kinds of sin. The first [goat] corresponds to those sins that derive from those bodily desires that precede from the nature of the corruptible and mortal body. Such desires should not be totally rejected but should be held off with one's left hand and brought near with one's right hand. The [goat], the "one lot for Adonai" (Leviticus 16:8), is offered for such sins. It is slaughtered and offered to Adonai and not the one that is sent out [into the wilderness]. The one that was sent was the one to be retained, though repressed and afflicted, that it might be subjugated to serve divine purposes. Since the five senses seek excessive pleasures, the Holy One has instructed for the Day [of Atonement] five afflictions in order to affect and subjugate them. The goat that was slaughtered fulfills this purpose. The goat that was sent out relates to the sins of the evil thought, which is the false belief that something profane may, in one way or another, be associated with the divine. Such is the belief of the [non-Jewish] nations. Those things in the Torah that are misleading because "the Torah speaks in the language of the children of humankind" (Babylonian Talmud, *Yevamot* 71a) should [as it were] "be sent out alive." Such an error corresponds to that portion of the living thing that sins. That is what Samael said: "You have not given me domination over Israel since you have already warned them, 'You shall have no other gods before Me' (Exodus 20:3)." The Holy One responded, "You shall have power over them on the Day of Atonement, if they have any sin." God meant that the day is designed for sanctification and for repentance. If any sin related to belief remains with them, you have them in your power. Why is the goat [that is sent out] sent to *Azazel*? The word [*Azazel*] is made up of *az* and *azel* ["strong" and "left"] to inform them that the goat has left and gone away from them. As we say, the goat has been sent out to inform them that it has completely sent away so that no memory [or that goat] would remain in the settled land. This is what the prophet Joel referred to when he said, "But I will remove far off from you the northern [*hazaphoni*] one, and will drive him into a land barren and desolate" (Joel 2:20). The Rabbis (in Babylonian Talmud, *Sukkah* 52a) interpreted this to refer to the Evil Inclination, which is hidden [*zaphon*] in every person's heart. The same is Satan, who leads people astray.

When the people of Israel conduct themselves properly, Satan has no power over them on the Day of Atonement. We learn this in the first chapter of *Yoma* (Babylonian Talmud, *Yoma* 19b): Elijah said to Rabbi Judah, the brother of Rabbi Sala the Pious, "You have said, 'Why has the Messiah not come? Today is the Day of Atonement and how many virgins will have intercourse in Nehardea?'" He [Rabbi Judah] asked, "What would the Holy One say?" He [Elijah] answered, "Sin couches at the door" (Genesis 4:7). He [Rabbi Judah then] asked, "What would Satan say?" "On the Day of Atonement, I have no power to lead you astray!" How do we know that? Rabbi Rami bar Hamma said, "The numerical value of [the Hebrew letters making up the word *satan*] Satan is 364. For 364 days of the year, Satan has the power to lead astray [but not on the Day of Atonement]."

Because the goats [described in Leviticus 16] are related to other goats that are dangerous by nature, they allude to those dangers that have been removed from Israel, that is, heresy. That one goat remained [alive] alludes to lewdness, so that there would remain what is necessary for the health of the body and the maintenance of the species. It is necessary that all one's acts should be for the sake of heaven.

CHAPTER THREE

Even though the Day of Atonement is the one promised by the Holy One to atone for Israel's sins, still one must forsake one's sin, regret what one has done, and determine never again to sin. Only this kind of repentance can bring atonement, as we learn in the eighth chapter of *Yoma* (Babylonian Talmud, *Yoma* 85b): If a person said, "I will sin and repent, and sin again, and repent," that person will be given no chance to repent. [If that person said,] "I will sin and the Day of Atonement will effect atonement," then the Day of Atonement effects no atonement. For transgressions that are between God and people the Day of Atonement effects atonement, but for transgressions that are between an individual and one's fellow, the Day of Atonement effects atonement only if that person has appeased one's fellow. All this teaches us that the day brings atonement only to the one who has properly repented.

The purpose of fasting is not that one should afflict one's body while remaining polluted by sin. Such a fast is not desired; indeed, it is despised by God. Rather, one should correct one's ways and one's acts. This is what the prophet meant (in the prophetic reading for the Day of Atonement) when Israel complained, "Why have we fasted, and you did not see it? Why have we afflicted our soul, and you take no knowledge?" (Isaiah 58:3). He answered them, "Behold, in the day of your fast you pursue your business and exact all your labors. Behold, you fast for strife and contention, to smite with the first of wickedness. You do not fast this day in order to make your voice be heard on high" (Isaiah 58:3–5). The prophet was showing them the proper path to repentance, what God would desire by telling them, "Is this not the fast that I have chosen? To loose the fetters of wickedness, to undo the bonds of the yoke, and to let the oppressed go free, and that you break every yoke?" (Isaiah 58:6). The prophet also said that giving charity to the poor was good along with the fasting, as it is written, "Is it not to share your bread with the hungry?" (Isaiah 58:7).

Charity, fasting, and prayer are excellent means to nullify the evil decree, as we read in *Pesikta d'Rav Kahanah* (p. 191a): Rabbi Yudan said in the name of Rabbi Eliezer, "Three things that nullify the evil decree. They are prayer, charity and repentance." [This has been discussed above in the section on prayer.]

Since unlike the Sabbath and the festivals the Day of Atonement is honored by physical pleasure, let each person honor it with nice clothing as he [or she] can afford. We learn this in the sixteenth chapter of the tractate *Shabbat* (Babylonian Talmud, *Shabbat* 119a): The Exilarch said to Rabbi Hamununah, "Why is it written, 'And the holy of Adonai honorable' (Isaiah 58:13)?" He replied, "The verse refers to the Day of Atonement, which has neither eating nor drinking. Therefore, the Torah says, 'Honor it [the Day of Atonement] with clean clothes.'"

Because of our sins, our Sanctuary was destroyed and we are no longer able to offer the sin-offering goats. The rabbis ordained that we read the section "After the death" [Leviticus 16], which describes those goats and the bullock [which were offered as sacrifices], and the prophetic reading and the *Musaf* Service, which tells of the order of sacrifices, as they were properly accomplished so that the reading may be considered by God as if we had been involved in the sacrificial service. We learn this from the fourth chapter of the tractate *Taanit* (Babylonian

Talmud, *Taanit* 27b) and from the third chapter of *Megillah* (Babylonian Talmud, *Megillah* 31b): [God says,] "I have ordained from them [Israel] an order of sacrifices. When they read that order, I will account it to them as if they had performed all the sacrifices before Me. I will forgive them for all their transgressions."

It is also written in *Shemot Rabbah* (38:4): "Now, this is what you shall offer on the altar" (Exodus 29:38), namely, "Take with you words" (Hoseah 14:3). . . .

The section on forbidden sexual relations (Leviticus 18:1–30) is read on the afternoon of the Day of Atonement because it deals with those sexual sins that, in thought or in act, form a net that traps many people. The Book of Jonah is read as the prophetic reading so that one may learn about complete repentance from the people of Nineveh. Even though they were not of the seed of Israel, their repentance was complete. For that reason, what happened to them was recorded in the Book of the Prophets.

The rabbis also ordained that when fasts would call [to God's mercy] in time of difficulty, passages suggesting forgiveness from the story of the repentance of Nineveh would be read. We read of this in the third chapter of *Taanit* (Babylonian Talmud, *Taanit* 16a): Brethren, neither sackcloth nor fasting have an effect. Only repentance and good deeds, as we find in the case of the people of Nineveh, for it is not said, "And God saw their sackcloth and their fasting" but rather it is said, "And God saw their works, that they turned from their evil ways" (Jonah 3:10).

Since on such a holy day, the Divine Presence rests here below with Israel and in the evening, it ascends to the Seven Heavens and then descends again. The rabbis said in the name of Rabbi Judah Gaon, it was ordained that seven times the phrase

"Adonai you are God" should be said to demonstrate to us that God has ascended with shouting and the sound of the *shofar*, as it is written, "God has gone up amidst shouting, Adonai amidst the sound of the horn" (Psalm 47:7). There is also that which may be understood from Mount Sinai, ". . . when the ram's horn sounds long, they shall come up the mount" (Exodus 19:13). The rabbis (*Mechilta, Yitro*) explained the verse to mean that the sound of the *shofar* was a signal that the Divine Presence would ascend. Then the people were permitted to go up the mountain.

We find in the responsa of the *Geonim* (*Otzar HaGeonim Yoma* p. 42) that Rabbenu Hai wrote in a responsum: "It is our custom to sound the *shofar* at the end of the Day of Atonement, though we have found no legal requirement to do so. It may be an allusion to the Jubilee Year or it may be that [the sounding of the *shofar* at the end of the Day of Atonement] is to distract Satan."

We may say that the sounding of that *shofar* is connected to the *shofar* of liberty (Leviticus 25:9, 10), for the day that brings atonement has many souls freed from subjugation to the body and also the bodies deserve eternal freedom. Therefore, the *shofar* is sounded, as it says, "And it shall come to pass on that day, that a great horn shall be blown. And they who were lost in the land of Assyria shall come, and they who were dispersed in the land of Egypt. And they shall worship Adonai on the holy mountain at Jerusalem" (Isaiah 27:13).

❧ 2 ❧

Pesikta deRav Kahana
(Discourses of Rabbi Kahana)

Rav Kahana

This Aramaic work is one of the oldest extant collections of homiletic *midrashim*. It contains homilies or classic rabbinic sermons that focus on the Torah and *Haftarah* readings for festivals and special Sabbaths. The *Pesikta* can probably be dated to fifth-century Palestine and is attributed to Rav Kahana, whose sermon introduces the material on Rosh Hashanah and the Sabbath after 17 *Tammuz*. Since Rosh Hashanah represents the beginning of the Jewish religious year—and perhaps the most intensive period of introspection and self-discovery—this collection is attributed to him. Solomon Buber published an edition in 1868 that he based on four manuscripts. His edition became the one most commonly used in the Jewish community.

The material included from the *Pesikta* for this collection reflects the religious psyche of its author. Since it was prepared for the High Holiday period, you can easily use its message to gain insight from the text. Use the words of our tradition—as taught by master teachers—to gently guide you in the process of change. It only takes one slight turn to begin to face another direction. As a start, go to your neighbor—your friend—and ask her for your forgiveness. Then you can join her in the synagogue with a cleansed heart and a clear conscience.

———◆———

SHABBAT SHUVAH
PISKAH 25

"Return, O Israel, to Adonai your God" (Hosea 14:2). "Shall the
horn be blown in a city and the people not tremble? Shall evil
befall a city without Adonai doing it?" (Amos 3:6). This may be
compared to a city that was invaded by ravaging troops. An old
person there was warning all the people. All who listened to that
person were saved. All who did not were killed by the invaders,
fulfilling the verse "So you, O mortal one, I have set you as a
guardian for the house of Israel. Therefore, when you hear the
word at My mouth, warn them from Me. When I say to the
wicked: 'O wicked one, you will surely die,' and you do not speak
to warn the wicked from [their wicked] way, that wicked person will die as a result of iniquity, but you are responsible for
his [or her] blood. Nevertheless, if you warn the wicked about
his [or her] way to turn from it, and that person does turn, he
[or she] will die in inquity, but you have redeemed your soul"
(Ezekiel 33:7–9). Thus is the meaning of "Shall the horn be
blown in a city" on Rosh Hashanah. "And the people not
tremble?"—these are Israel. "Shall evil befall a city without
Adonai doing it?" The Holy Blessed One does not wish the death
of the wicked, as it is written, "As I live, says Adonai, God, I have
no pleasure in the death of the wicked" (Ezekiel 33:11). My
people, what is it that I want of you? "Turn, turn from your evil
ways, for why will you die, O house of Israel" (Ezekiel 33:11).
If you wish, you may find further scriptural support in "Seek Me
and live" (Amos 5:4). "My people [says God], what do I ask of
you? Seek Me and live." Therefore, Hosea warns the people and
says to them, "Return, O Israel, to Adonai your God" (Hosea
14:2).

"With wondrous works do You answer us in righteousness, O saving God" (Psalm 65:6). Rabbi Judah, in the name of Rabbi Isaac, explains, "With wondrous works that You have done with us in this world and because of the suffering that You have brought upon us in this world." Rabbi Haggai said, in the name of Rabbi Isaac, "The . . . 'wondrous works' are those that You will bring in the World to Come because of the suffering that You have brought upon us in this world. 'You are the confidence of all the ends of the earth' (Psalm 65:6)—You are the One who will requite those who are violent, and all who are on a journey trust in Your reputation, indeed, those who venture out in caravans or are far away at sea trust in You."

He said to them, "Repentance is like the sea, for just as the sea is always open, so the gates of *teshuvah* are always open. Prayer may be compared to *mikveh*, a ritual bath. Just as a ritual bath is open at times and closed at times, so the gates of prayer are sometimes open and sometimes closed. A person entering a *mikveh* might find his father or his teacher there and become embarrassed and leave before he immersed himself. However, at the seashore, he only has to move away a short distance and enter the waters and immerse himself. Rabbi Berachia, in the name of Rabbi Anan, son of Rabbi Yose, said, "The gates of prayer *are* always open." Yose, son of Tachalifa, said, "There are times for prayer, just as David specified, 'But as for me, let my prayer be to You, Adonai, an acceptable time' (Psalm 69:14). David said before the Holy One, Sovereign of the Universe, When I pray before You, may it be a favorable time. 'O God, in the abundance of Your mercy, answer me with your true salvation' (Psalm 69:14)."

It was taught in the name of Rabbi Eliezer, "You are hope, *mikveh*, of Israel" (Jeremiah 17:13). Just as a *mikveh* purifies those unclean, so the Holy Blessed One purifies Israel. Therefore Hosea warns Israel and says to them, "Return, O Israel."

"And God speaks the divine voice, before God's army" (Joel 2:11). This refers to Rosh Hashanah. "For God's camp is great" (Joel 2:11). This refers to Israel. "For the one who executes God's word is mighty." God strengthens the power of the righteous who perform God's word. "For great and awesome is the day of Adonai" refers to the Day of Atonement. "And who can abide it?" This refers to what Rabbi Crisfa taught in the name of Rabbi Jochanan: "There are three ledgers. One is for those who are completely righteous. One is for those who are completely wicked. And one is for those who are neither one nor the other." "And many of them who sleep in the dust will awake, some to everlasting life" (Daniel 12:2). [This verse refers to the completely righteous.] "Some to reproaches and everlasting abhorrence" (Daniel 12:2). This refers to the completely wicked. [There is also another verse that applies:] "Let them be blotted out of the book of the living and not be written with the righteous" (Psalm 69:29). Those who will "be blotted out from the book" are the completely wicked. Those who will be among "the living" are the completely righteous. And those who "will not be written with the righteous" are those who are neither completely righteous nor completely wicked. To such persons, God has given the ten days between Rosh Hashanah and Yom Kippur. If they repent, they will be inscribed with the completely righteous. If they do not, they will be inscribed with the completely wicked. Therefore, Hosea has adjured all Israel, saying, "Return, O Israel."

"Tremble and do not sin. Meditate in your own heart on your bed and be still. Selah" (Psalm 4:5). Rabbi Jacob bar Avinah and the Rabbis discussed the verse. Rabbi Jacob bar Avinah interpreted it as if God said, "I will bind up your [Evil] Inclination and you will not come within sin's power." This verse was taught in the name of Rabbi Eliezer. "You are hope, *mikveh*, of Israel, Adonai" (Jeremiah 17:13) means that God says to Israel, "I say to you, you should pray in the synagogue in your city, as well as in the midst of your field. And if you are not able to do so, pray in your house. Pray on your bed. And if you are not able to pray on your bed, meditate in your heart and be still. Selah" (Psalm 4:5).

Rabbi Yehudah said that the last means "Quit your transgressions." Thus, Hosea cautioned Israel, saying, "Return, O Israel."

Zavdi ben Levi, Rabbi Yose bar Petrus, and the Rabbis discussed the verse "The sacrifices of God are a broken spirit" (Psalm 51:19). One imagined David saying before God, "If you will receive me in *teshuvah*, then I will know that my son Solomon will arise, build the Temple and the altar, and offer the [various] sacrifices on it." This might be deduced from the continuation of the verse "A broken and contrite heart, Adonai, You will not despise" and from the verses that follow: "Do good in Your favor to Zion" (Psalm 51:20) and "Then You will delight in the sacrifices of righteousness" (Psalm 51:21). The other asked about the scriptural basis for the notion that if one repents, the Holy One accounts it as if the individual had gone up to Jerusalem, built the altar, and offered up the [various] sacrifices. We learned it from the verse "You will not despise a broken and contrite heart" (Psalm 51:19) and from the verses "Do good in Your favor to Zion (Psalm 51:20) and from "Then you will delight in the sacrifices of righteousness" (Psalm 51:21). The Rabbis deduced the principle from the same verse, and the two that follow it, that the one who leads services must mention the building of the Temple and the sacrifices—and then bow. For them, these verses were the basis of the blessing "May you dwell in Zion, Your city, and may Your children worship You in Jerusalem."

Rabbi Abba bar Yudan said that what makes an animal unfit to be a sacrifice has been made by God acceptable for a person to approach God. Thus, if an animal were ". . . blind, broken, or maimed, or having a wen . . . you should not offer these to Adonai" (Leviticus 22:22). God has declared acceptable ". . . a broken and contrite heart"! Rabbi Alexandri said, "It would be a disgrace if an ordinary person used a broken vessel. However, the Holy One is different. All whom God would use are broken vessels, as it is said, "Adonai is close to those who are broken of heart" (Psalm 34:19) and "Who heals the broken of heart" (Psalm 147:3) and "A broken and contrite heart, O God, You will not despise" (Psalm 51:19). Therefore, Hosea urges Israel, "Return, O Israel."

"Behold, God does loftily in divine power. Who is a teacher like God?" (Job 36:22). Rabbi Berachia understood the first word of the verse, *hen* ("Behold"), as the Greek word for "one." Thus, the verse means that the One and unique God acts loftily in divine power by strengthening the righteous in their power to do God's will. "Who is a teacher like God to teach the wicked how to repent?" Thus, Hosea charges Israel, saying, "Return, O Israel."

"Good and upright is Adonai. Therefore does God instruct sinners in the way" (Psalm 25:8). They asked of wisdom, "What is the punishment of the sinner?" Wisdom responded, ". . . the soul that sins shall die" (Ezekiel 18:4). They asked the Torah, "What is the punishment of the sinner?" The Torah responded, "Let one bring a guilt offering and it will atone," as it is written, "And it shall be accepted for the person to make an atonement" (Leviticus 1:43). They asked the Holy Blessed One, "What is the punishment of the sinner?" God answered, "Let one repent and that repentance will atone, as it is written, 'Good and upright is Adonai. Therefore does God instruct sinners in the way' (Psalm 25:8)."

My children, what do I ask of you? Only that you seek Me and live. Rabbi Pinchas asked, "Why is God described in the above psalm as 'good'? Because God is 'upright'! Why is God described as 'upright'? Because God is 'good'!" Therefore does God instruct sinners in the way. God teaches them the way that they can repent. Thus Hosea admonishes Israel, "Return, O Israel."

Following the tradition of Rabbi Simon ben Chalafta, Rabbi Sima and Rabbi Joshua ben Levi discussed the verse "The one who covers one's transgression will not prosper. But whoever confesses and forsakes them will receive mercy" (Proverbs 28:13). They said that when you cover the roots of the nut plants, they do not flourish. This is like the case of a brigand who is being questioned before a magistrate. As long as he is recalcitrant, he is beaten. However, when he does confess, he is doomed. Not so with the Holy One. As long as the sinner is recalcitrant he is doomed. As soon as he confesses, he is pardoned. This is as the verse has it: ". . . whoever confesses and forsakes them [one's transgressions] will receive mercy." Rabbi Isaac said, "Let the sinner confess in order to forsake one's sins and receive mercy." To this end, Hosea pleads, "Return, O Israel."

"A person's belly shall be filled with the fruit of one's mouth" (Proverb 18:21). "And Reuben returned to the pit" (Genesis 37:29). Rabbi Eliezer, Rabbi Joshua, and the Rabbis discussed these verses. Rabbi Eliezer said, "Reuben returned from sitting in sackcloth and fasting, repenting his sin" [with Bilhah his father's concubine (Genesis 35:22). Thus Reuben's belly suffered because of what he had said and done]. When Reuben concluded his penance, he returned to the pit that had held Joseph. Seeing that Joseph was not there, "He rent his clothes" (Genesis 35:22). Rabbi Joshua said, "Reuben returned from the household responsibilities that had been placed upon

him. When he was finished with them, he returned to the pit.
Looking in it, he saw that Joseph was not there, so "he rent his
clothes." [It was Reuben's concerns with the necessities of eating that would give him pain in the belly when he found that
Joseph had disappeared.] The Rabbis said that the Holy One
said to Reuben, "You wished to restore a beloved son to his father. By your life, your grandson will restore all Israel to their
parent in heaven. Who was that? It was Hosea, as it says, 'The
word of Adonai that came to Hosea, the son of Berri' (Hosea
1:1)." Another verse says, "Beerah his son [in the line of Reuben,
cf. 1 Chronicles. 51 ff.] whom Tillegat-Pilneser, king of Assyria,
had carried away captive" (1 Chronicles 5:6) [Berri and Berrah
are read as the same person.] Why was he called Beerah? Because he was a well (*be'eir*) of Torah. Why did he die in the exile?
So that the ten tribes might turn in *teshuvah*. Why did Moses
die in the wilderness? So that the generation of the wilderness
might be moved to repent on account of his merit. Rabbi
Berachia said: The Holy One said to Reuben, "You were the
first to come in *teshuvah*. By your life, your grandson will begin
with *teshuvah*, as he has said, 'Return, O Israel.'"

   "For My thoughts are not your thoughts" (Isaiah 55:8). This
text can be compared to the acts of a magistrate questioning a
criminal. First he reads the charge. Then the magistrate has the
criminal beaten. Finally, the criminal is taken out to be executed. The Holy Blessed One is different. First God reads the
charge: though ". . . they sin more and more and have molten
images of silver" (Hosea 13:2). Only then does God beat them:
"Ephraim is smitten. Their root is dried up" (Hosea 9:16). Then
God puts them in a dungeon: "The iniquity of Ephraim is
bound up. Ephraim's sin is stored up" (Hosea 13:12). Then God
gives them over to execution: "Samaria shall bear her guilt, for
she has rebelled against her God. They shall fall by their sword"

(Hosea 14:1). Yet even here God will accept their *teshuvah*: "Return, O Israel, to Adonai your God" (Hosea 14:2).

It is written, "Samaria shall bear her guilt, for she has rebelled against her God" (Hosea 14:1). Following that statement, it is written, "Return, O Israel, to Adonai your God" (Hosea 14:2). Rabbi Eliezer, in the name of Rabbi Samuel bar Nachmani, compared the two verses to a city that had rebelled against its king, so the king sent a general to destroy it. Being thoughtful, the general said to the people of the city, "Take the time to think of what you have done [and give up the rebellion]. Otherwise, the king will do to you what he has already done to such and such [a rebellious] city and its surrounding towns." This is what Hosea did. He said to Israel, "My children, repent, lest the Holy One do to you what was done to Samaria and its surrounding towns."

Israel said before the Holy Blessed One, "Master of the Universe, if we make *teshuvah*, will You receive our repentance?" God said to them, "If I accepted Cain's *teshuvah*, will I not receive yours? Upon Cain was a severe decree enacted: "When you till the ground, it will no longer yield to you its strength. [Thus,] you will become a fugitive and a wanderer on the earth" (Genesis 4:12). When Cain repented, half of the decree was rescinded. How do we know that Cain repented? From the verse that follows: "And Cain said to Adonai: 'My punishment is greater than I can bear'" [interpreted as 'My guilt is greater than I can bear']. How do we know that half of the decree was rescinded? From the verse "And Cain went out from Adonai's presence and dwelled in the land of Nod [interpreted as 'wandering'], east of Eden" (Genesis 4:16). [He no longer had to be "a fugitive"!]

What is the meaning of "And Cain went out"? Rabbi Yudan said in the name of Aibo, "Cain went off casting the words [that

he had heard] behind him, like one thinking to fool God." Rabbi
Berachia said in the name of Rabbi Eliezer Bar Simon, "Cain
went out to deceitfully assuage his Creator." Rabbi Huna said
in the name of Rabbi Hanina bar Pappa, "He went out joyously,
[for going out has that sense] as in ". . . he comes forth to meet
you, when he sees you, he will be glad in his heart" (Exodus
4:14).

When Cain went out, he met Adam. Adam asked him,
"What happened to the judgment against you?" Cain answered,
"I repented and half my sentence was remitted." When Adam
heard this, he began hitting himself in the face, saying, "Such
is the power of repentance and I did not know it!" At that moment, Adam began reciting, "It is a good thing to give thanks to
Adonai and to sing praises to Your name, O Most High" (Psalm
92:2). Rabbi Levi [agreeing] said that the psalm Adam recited
was A Psalm: A Song for the Sabbath Day (Psalm 92).

[The Holy One said:] "I accepted Ahab's *teshuvah* upon
whom was a most severe decree directed. Will I not accept your
repentance? As it says, '. . . Have you killed and also taken possession? You will speak thus to him.' Thus said Adonai. 'In the
place where dogs licked the blood of Naboth will dogs lick your
blood, [yes] even yours' (1 Kings 21:19)." "And it came to pass,
when Ahab heard those words, that he rent his clothes, and put
sackcloth on his flesh, and fasted, and lay in sackcloth, and went
softly" (1 Kings 21:27). How did Ahab fast? Were he accustomed
to breakfast at nine in the morning, he delayed eating until noon.
What he was used to eating at noon, he now delayed until three
in the afternoon. What is meant by "and went softly"? Rabbi
Joshua ben Levi said, "He went barefoot—as may be deduced
from the verses 'And the word of Adonai came to Elijah the
Tishbite, saying: "Do you see how Ahab humbles himself before Me? Since he humbles himself before Me, I will not bring

the evil in his days. . . ." (1 Kings 21:27, 28). [Elijah could see that Ahab was barefoot.] The Holy One said to Elijah, "You see how Ahab humbles himself before Me." [God says to Israel: If I could accept the repentance of Ahab, should I not accept your repentance?]'"

[The Holy One says,] "If I received the *teshuvah* of the people of Anatot, would I not accept your *teshuvah*? They received a severe decree, as it says, 'Therefore, thus says Adonai concerning the people of Anatot . . . therefore, thus says Adonai Tzevaot: "Behold, I will punish them. The young men will die by the sword. Their sons and their daughters will die by famine" (Jeremiah 11:21, 22) and by war, "and there will be no remnant of them" (Jeremiah 11:23).' However, 128 persons were associated with them when they repented, as it says, "The people of Anatot 128" (Ezra 2:28). [If I accepted their repentance,] would I not accept yours?

"I accepted the repentance of the people of Nineveh. Would I not accept your repentance? Against the people of Nineveh was a severe decree enacted, as it says, 'And Jonah began to enter into the city a day's journey, and he proclaimed, and said: "Yet forty days, and Nineveh shall be overthrown"' (Jonah 3:4). 'And the tidings reached the king of Nineveh. . . . And he caused it to be proclaimed and published through Nineveh by the decree of the king and the nobles, saying: "Let neither human nor beast, herd nor flock, taste anything. Let them not feed, nor drink water. Instead, let them be covered in sackcloth . . . let them turn every one from his evil way, and from the violence that is in their hands"' (Jonah 3:6, 7, 8)." Resh Lakish said that their repentance was false. According to Rabbi Huna, who said in the name of Rabbi Simon ben Chalafta, the people of Nineveh took a bunch of calves and put them inside an enclosure with their mothers on the outside, so that the calves

were bellowing and the cows were bellowing. The people of
Nineveh then said to Adonai, "Master of the Universe, if You
won't have compassion on us, we won't have compassion on
them." Rabbi Acha said, "This is done in Arabia even now in
the time of a fast," as it says, "How the beasts groan! The herds
of cattle are preplexed, because they have no pasture. The flocks
of sheep are made desolate" (Joel 1:18).

"But let them be covered with sackcloth, both human and
beast, and let them cry mightily to God" (Jonah 3:8). What is
the meaning of "mightily"? Rabbi Simon ben Chalafta said,
"Fervent prayer will vanquish the Evil One. How much more
will it win over the Good One of the world! 'Let every one turn
from his evil way, and from the violence that is in their hands'
(Jonah 3:8)." Rabbi Yochanan said, "What they had in their
hands they returned. What they had in the safe, chest, or closet,
they did not return."

"And rend your heart, and not your garments, and turn to
Adonai your God" (Joel 2:13). Rabbi Joshua ben Levi commented, "If you have rent your hearts in penitence, you will not
need to rend your clothes [in mourning] for your sons and
daughters. Why? 'For God is gracious and compassionate, long-
suffering, and abundant in mercy' (Joel 2:13)."

Rabbi Acha and Rabbi Tanchum said in the name of Rabbi
Hiyya, in the name of Rabbi Jochanan: "*Erech af* is not the
Hebrew text for 'compassionate' but rather *erech apayim* [sug-
gesting twice the compassion]. God extends the divine spirit to
the innocent. God punishes them for the few evil deeds that they
have done in this world in order to give them their reward in
the future yet to come. God grants well-being to the wicked in
this world in order to reward them for their few goods in this
world, to punish them in the future yet to come as it is written,
'. . . and repays them that hate God to their face, to destroy them'
(Deuteronomy 7:10)."

Rabbi Samuel said in the name of Rabbi Yochanan: "*Erach af* is not written here but rather *erach apayim*, which means that God extends the divine spirit so as not to requite[the wicked]. Yet when God comes to requite, God will delay and then requite."

Rabbi Hanina said, "Anyone who says that God is indulgent, let his bowels become loose. Rather one should say that God is patient and then collects from the wicked."

Rabbi Levi asked, "What is the meaning of *erech apayim* [compassionate]? God moves away from anger. This may be compared to a king who had two fierce legions. The king said that should the legions be headquartered in a city where the inhabitants might provoke him, the legions would immediately destroy them. He had better station those legions in a far-off place so that should the people of the city provoke him, they would have the chance to appease him before the legions came."

[God says,] "I would accept their appeals, as it is written, 'They come from a far country, from the end of the heaven, even Adonai and the weapons of God's indignation, to destroy the whole earth' (Isaiah 13:5)."

Rabbi Isaac said, "Not only that, God had locked the door before them [i.e., God had prevented their *teshuvah*], as it says, "Adonai has opened the armory and has brought forth the divine weapons of indignation" (Jeremiah 50:25). Thus when God is involved, God's associates [the weapons of divine indignation] come forward.

It was taught in the name of Rabbi Meir that the verse "For behold, God comes forth from God's place" (Isaiah 26:21) means that Adonai will move from one quality to another, from the quality of justice [*midat hadin*] to the quality of mercy [*midat rachamin*] for the sake of Israel.

[The Holy One says,] "I received the repentance of Manasseh, should I not accept your *teshuvah*? Against him a severe decree was enacted, as it says, 'And Adonai thus spoke to

Manasseh, and to his people, but they gave no heed. . . . Wherefore Adonai brought upon them the captains of the host of the king of Assyria, who took Manasseh with hooks, and bound him with fetters . . .' (1 Chronicles 3:10, 11)." What is the meaning of "hooks"? Rabbi Abba bar Kahana said "handcuffs." What is the meaning of "fetters"? Rabbi Levi bar Hiyyata said, "They made a brass mule with holes in it, placed him inside of it, and began to apply heat beneath it. As he began to suffer, he began to cry out to each and every idol in the world, saying, 'O Idol, come and save me!' When nothing availed him, Manasseh said, 'I remember when my father would have me read this verse: "In your distress, when all these things are come upon you, at the end of days, you will return to Adonai, your God, and hearken to God's voice, for Adonai your God is a merciful God. God will not fail you or destroy you" (Deuteronomy 4:30, 31). Now I will read it. If God will answer me, fine. If not, then all religions are the same!' At that moment, the angels began closing all the windows of heaven in order to prevent the prayer of Manasseh from rising up to God. The angels asked God, 'Shall a person who placed an idol in the Temple be able to repent?' The Holy One answered, 'If I do not accept Manasseh's repentance, I will be locking the door of *teshuvah* to all other penitents.' What did God then do? God dug out a small hole beneath the Throne of Glory, in order to hear Manasseh's plea, as it says, 'And he prayed to God and God was entreated of him, and heard his supplication' (2 Chronicles 33:13)." What is the meaning of *vayeatar*, "God was entreated"? Rabbi Eleazar bar Simon said, "They pronounce the word *chatitrata* (digging out) *atitrta* (entreaty) in Arabia."

The biblical text continued, ". . . and brought him [Manasseh] back to Jerusalem into his kingdom." What was the meaning of *vayishivayhu*, "and brought him back" [from the root *shuv*, "return"]? Rabbi Samuel bar Nachmani interpreted the words in the name of Rabbi Adah that Manasseh was blown back to Jerusalem by the wind, [taking *vayishivayhu* as if it came from the root *nashav*], as in the liturgical usage *mashiv haruach*, "causing the wind to blow." "Then Manasseh knew that Adonai was God" (2 Chronicles 33:13). At that moment, Manasseh said, "There is a Law and there is a Judge."

[The Holy One says,] "I accepted the *teshuvah* of Coniah; shall I not accept your repentance?" A severe decree was enacted against him, as it says, "Is this man Coniah a despised broken image?" (Jeremiah 22:28). Rabbi Abba bar Kahana compared him to a marrow bone, which when smashed can be used for nothing. Rabbi Helbo compared him to a mat used for wrapping dates, which when emptied can be used for nothing else. "Is he a vessel in which there is no pleasure?" (Jeremiah 22:28). Rabbi Hiyya ban Hanina compared Coniah to a vessel used to collect urine. Rabbi Samuel compared him to a vessel used in bloodletting. Rabbi said that the Holy One has vowed not to raise up a king from Coniah, the son of Jehoiakim king of Judah, as it says, "As I live, says Adonai, were Coniah, the son of Jehoiakim, king of Judah a signet upon My right hand, would I yet pluck you [instead]" (Jeremiah 23:24). Rabbi Hanina bar Isaac interpreted the last word *etkeneka*, "I would pluck you," to mean that God says, "I will pluck (*notek*) the kingdom of David from you." There is another interpretation possible: *etkeneka* could be understood as deriving from the root *taken* (correct, improve) rather than from the root *natak* (pluck up). Then God would be saying, "I will improve you through *teshuvah*." [There is yet another interpretation that seeks to incorporate both meanings:] "From the place that you will be plucked, there you will be corrected."

Rabbi Zeira said that he once heard Rabbi Samuel bar Isaac

expounding the meaning of one word and did not know what that meaning was. Rabbi Abba Aricha said, "Perhaps it was this: 'Thus says Adonai, "Write this person childless, a person who will not prosper in his days (*b'yamav*) for no person of his seed shall prosper, sitting upon the throne of David, ruling any more in Judah" (Jeremiah 22:30).'"

Rabbi Zeira responded, "That is it! In his days *b'yamav*, he shall not prosper, but in his son's days, he will!"

Rabbi Aha bar Abin bar Benjamin, in the name of Rabbi Abba, the son of Rabbi Pappai, said, "Great is the power of *teshuvah* because it can nullify an oath [even a divine oath!]. It can nullify a [severe] decree. What is the scriptural proof that it can nullify an oath? The oath is given in the verse "As I live, says Adonai, were Coniah, the son of Jehoiakim, king of Judah the signet upon My right hand, I would yet pluck you [instead]" (Jeremiah 22:24). Its nullification is given in the verse "On that day, says Adonai Tzevaot, I will take you, O Zerubbabel, My servant, the son of Shalteil, and will make you as a signet. I have chosen you, says Adonai Tzevaot" (Haggai 2:23). The decree is given in the words "Thus says Adonai: Write this person childless" (Jeremiah 22:30). Its nullification is given in the words "And the sons of Jeconiah—the same as Asir—Shealteil his son and Malchiram, and Pedaiah, and Shenazzar, Jekamiah, Hoshama, and Nedabiah" (1 Chronicles 3:17).

Rabbi Tanhum bar Jeremiah explained the name "Assir" in the aforementioned verse as indicating that Jeconiah was imprisoned (*asar*). He explained the name Shealtiel, indicating that from him was established (*husthatlah*), the kingdom of the House of David. Rabbi Tanhuma explained the name Assir, indicating that God had bound (*asar*) God by oath, and said Shealteil suggests that God had made application to the Court on High and been freed of the divine oath. Rabbi Judah the

Prince said in the name of Rabbi Judah bar Simon, "One may shoot an arrow and reach the end of a large field or even twice as far, but the power of *teshuvah* is far greater, for it can reach the Throne of Glory! Even as it says, "Return, O Israel.""

Rabbi Yose interpreted the verse "Open to me, my sister, my love, my dove, my undefiled" (Song of Songs 5:2) to mean that the Holy One says [to Israel]: "Make an opening [for repentance] as small as the eye of a needle and I will make an opening for you through tents that siege engines could pass." Rabbi Tanhum said in the name of Rabbi Hanina, as did Rabbi Aibo in the name of Resh Lakish, "You can repent in the blink of an eye (*k'heref ayin*), as it says, 'Let be (*harpu*) and know that I am God' (Psalm 46:11)." *Harpu* [can also be translated as] "Let go" of your evil ways and know that I am Adonai, interpreting "Today, if you would only hearken to God's voice" (Psalm 95:7). Rabbi Levi said if Israel would repent just one day, they would be redeemed! Rabbi Judah bar Simon said that the verse "Return, O Israel, to Adonai your God" (Hosea 14:2) means that *teshuvah* is possible even if one in the past had denied God. Rabbi Elazar said, "It is customary that if one insulted another publicly and then wished to make amends privately, the one insulted would say, 'What, would you insult me publicly and apologize privately? Go bring here those persons in whose presence I was insulted and then [and only then] will I forgive you.' God is different. One may blaspheme publicly and the Holy One says to that person, 'Repent just between the two of us, and I will accept your *teshuvah*.'"

Rabbi Issachar of Kefar Mando interpreted the verse "For God knows base people. When God sees iniquity, will God not consider it?" (Job 11:11) in this manner: Though in this life, one may pile up sins, when one repents, then "when God sees iniquity, God will not consider it!"

It was taught in the name of Rabbi Meir: "Return, O Israel (ad), to Adonai your God" (Hosea 14:2) may have this meaning: Since ad (to) may also mean "while," the verse can mean "Return, O Israel, while God is Adonai [the Tetragrammaton and its substitutions were understood to reflect God's attribute of mercy while Elohim was understood to reflect God's attribute of justice] and before God takes on the attribute of justice—and before the plea of the defense becomes the case for the prosecution."

Rabbi Samuel Patrigirta, in the name of Rabbi Meir, spoke about the verse "Rejoice, O young man, in your youth" [as problematic]. [The Sages wanted to suppress the Book of Kohelet because it contained what many considered to be heresy.] Kohelet said, "Rejoice, O young person, in your youth . . . and walk in the ways of your heart, and in the sight of your eyes" (Kohelet 11:9). Had not Moses said, ". . . do not go about after your own heart and your own eyes" (Numbers 15:39)? If this Kohelet can get away saying what he did, then "the reins are loosed" [anything is possible] and there is neither Judge nor judgment! When, however, Kohelet [whom the Rabbis took to be Solomon] added, "but know that for all these things, God will bring you into judgment" (Kohelet 11:9), the Rabbis said that Kohelet had spoken well. Rabbi Hiyya Rabba compared the last clause to a fleeing felon being pursued by a magistrate who said, "Don't run so far that you won't be tired out coming back." The same clause, "But know that for all these things, God will bring you into judgment" was compared by Rabbi Simon ben Chalafta to a swimmer who was warned not to go out too far from shore lest she be exhausted while swimming back. Rabbi Yoshaiya compared the last few words, "God will bring you into judgment" to one who had stolen some tolls. When he was arrested, his captors said to him, "Hand back the tolls." He said to them, "You figure out how much was collected." They answered, "Do you think we are going to figure out the time and place of the particular toll collection? We want you to give back all the tolls from the time you stole the particular toll." That is the meaning of the verse "for all these things God will bring you into judgment."

Rabbi Levi made another application of the verse. He related it to a bird put into a coop. Another bird stood next to it and said, "You should be happy. Your food is provided." The first bird replied, "You are looking at the food. Look rather at the netting!" That is the meaning of "But know that for all these things, God will bring you into judgment."

Rabbi Tanhuma compared the meaning of the verse to the case of a ruffian who entered a tavern and said to the shopkeeper, "Give me some good wine, some nice bread, and a piece of fat meat." The shopkeeper did, so the ruffian ate and drank. The shopkeeper then said, "Pay your bill." The ruffian said, "Go take it out of my belly!" The shopkeeper replied, "Do you think that you are going to get rid of me this way?" Being a clever man, the shopkeeper grabbed the hooligan, tied him up, wrapped him in a mat, and set the mat at the opening of the tavern. To every passerby, the shopkeeper would say, "[Give some money and] gain the merit of burying this dead man." An even worse ruffian [who did not give anything] came by and said, "How long has he been in this condition?" Said the shopkeeper, "Since he did not pay his bill!" When [the shopkeeper collected enough to pay the bill] he said [to the one who didn't pay the bill], "Get up and go to your ancestor's grave." Someone else said, "It is enough for him that his ultimate end will be bad." This [story] illuminates the meaning of "Know that for all these things God will bring you into judgment."

Rabbi Elazar, son of Rabbi Jose the Galilean, said that Israel had said before the Holy One, "O Master of the Universe, if we repent, who will testify on our behalf?" God answered, "If I am a witness against you for evil, will I not be a witness for you for good? The scriptural proof that I am witness against you for evil is given in the verse 'And I will come near to you to judgment, and I will be a swift witness against the sorcerers and against the adulterers' (Malachi 3:5). Shall I not be a witness on your behalf for good? Was I not a witness for Ahab ben Koliya and for Zedekaiah ben Maaseheh, who were false prophets and who were adulterers with the wives of their neighbors, as it is written, '. . . because they have wrought evil deeds in Israel, and have committed adultery with their neighbors' wives, and have spoken words in My name falsely, which I did not instruct them. But I am the one who knows and am witness, says Adonai' (Jeremiah 29:23)." How would they commit adultery with their neighbors' wives? One would go to the wife [of a neighbor] and say to her, "Prophecy has told me that my friend is coming to you. Make love with him and you will be able to raise up a prophet in Israel!" In this manner, one would pimp for another! However, when the time came for their downfall, they came to the wife of Nebuchadnezzar. They told her the usual story. She, however, said to them, "I don't do anything without clearing it with [my husband] the king." When Nebuchadnezzar came, she told him what they had said. He answered, "That is impossible. The God of that people hates lewdness. However, I will test them in the same way that I tested Hananiah, Meshael, and Azariah [and throw them into a fiery furnace]. If they are saved, fine. If not, they were false prophets!" Here is what he did: he took a brass barrel and put perforations in it. Next, he took them and put them in it. Then he lit a fire beneath the barrel. When they began suffering, they joined their cause to Joshua ben Yehozadak, who had been put in with them, saying, "Maybe his innocence will save us!" What happened? He was saved and they were burned! This the Holy One did to fulfill the verse "All of them shall be taken up as a curse by all the captivity of Judah that are in Babylon, saying: May Adonai make you like Zedekiah and like Ahab, whom the king of Babylon roasted in the fire" (Jeremiah 29:22). [One should note that] the text does not say, "whom the king of Babylon *burned* in the fire," but rather it says, "whom the king of Babylon *roasted* in the fire." They were roasted like roasted grain!

Rabbi Levi and Rabbi Isaac were discussing *teshuvah*. Rabbi Levi said that the Holy One has said to Jeremiah, "Go and tell Israel to repent!" He went and told them. They then said to him, "Rabbi Jeremiah, how can we repent? How can we come with these faces before the Holy One? Have we not provoked God? Have we not vexed God? Don't those mountains and hills upon which we worshiped idols still stand? Was it not taught, 'They sacrifice upon the tops of the mountains, and offer upon the hills' (Hosea 4:13)? 'Let us lie down in our shame and let our confusion cover us. We have sinned against Adonai our God' (Jeremiah 3:25). Jeremiah came before the Holy One and told God. God replied, 'Go and tell them, did I not write in My Torah, ". . . I will . . . set My face against the soul, and will cut him off from among the people" (Leviticus 20:6)? Yet [said God] did I ever do that? I have not set My face against you because ". . . I am merciful, says Adonai, I will not bear a grudge forever" (Jeremiah 3:12).'"

Rabbi Isaac [on the other hand] said, The Holy One said to Jeremiah, "Go and tell Israel to repent." Jeremiah went and the people said to him, "Our master, how can we repent? Can we with these very faces come before God? Have we not provoked God? Have we not vexed God? Do not the mountains and the hills upon which we worshiped idols still stand? Does not the verse teach, 'They sacrifice upon the tops of the mountains, and offer upon the hills' (Hosea 4:13)? Let us lie down in our shame and let our confusion cover us, for we have sinned against Adonai our God" (Jeremiah 3:25). Jeremiah came before the Holy One and told God. God replied, "Go back and tell them: if you came back to Me, you are coming back to your parent in heaven! It is written, 'For I am a parent to Israel and Ephraim is My firstborn' (Jeremiah 31:9)."

It is written, "For you have stumbled in your iniquity" (Hosea 14:2). Rabbi Simai compared this to a great rock standing in an intersection against which people would crash. The king said to the people [of the locality], "Start chipping some pieces off it. One of these days, I will come and take it away altogether." This is what is meant by ". . . I will take away the stony heart out of your flesh, and I will give you a heart of flesh" (Ezekiel 36:26).

Rabbi Isaac said it is customary that if a person stumbled in sin and incurred the punishment of death by the hands of heaven, that person's ox would die, his rooster would be lost, and his flask would be broken. Even were that person to break a finger, [the suffering of] a portion of his soul would count as [the suffering of] his entire soul. This is what is meant by ". . . adding one thing to another, to find out the account" (Ecclesiastes 7:27). What is the meaning of "one thing to another"? These are added up [i.e., these minor calamities atone for the sin of the sinner] and they "find the account" [i.e., they balance out the sin].

"Take with you words and return to Adonai" (Hosea 14:3). Both Rabbi Judah and Rabbi Nehemiah commented on the verse. Rabbi Judah said [God said], "Was it not with words that you beguiled Me at Sinai?" The verse says, "But they beguiled

God with their mouth and lied to God with their tongue" (Psalm 78:36). Rabbi Nehemiah said, "Take with you words" means take with you those who are eloquent, those who are good biblical scholars, and those who are good expositors, like Levi ben Sisi and his associates. As for Levi ben Sisi, once when a rampaging band entered his city he took a Torah scroll, went up on a roof, and said, "Master of the Universe, if You have made null one word contained [in the Torah], then let these brigands enter [the city]. However, if not, let them go their way." Immediately, they [the brigands] attempted to find him, but they could not. One of his students tried to do the same [i.e., to take a Torah and go up to the roof], but his right hand withered. The band departed. At another time, the same thing occurred. A student of one of his students did the same [as had Levi ben Sisi]. His right hand did not wither but the band did not depart. There is a proverb that says a fool does not get hurt and dead flesh doesn't feel a scalpel.

"And return to Adonai." Say to God: "Forgive all iniquity and accept what is good." (Hosea 14:3). The two, Rabbi Judah and Rabbi Nehemia, commented on this verse as well. Rabbi Judah said, "If You can forgive all iniquity, can't You forgive our iniquities?" Rabbi Nehemia said, "Forgive all [of our iniquity] or [if not,] forgive half and remit half."

Rabbi Natan and Rabbi Acha commented in the name of Rabbi Simon on "and accept what is good." They said that the letters of the word *tov* (good), when set against a reversed alphabet, correspond to the letters *nun, pay,* and *shin,* which spell the word *nephesh* (soul). Hence ". . . accept what is good" means "accept the soul [of the penitent]."

"So shall we render *uneshalmah* for bullocks the offering of our lips" (Hosea 14:3). Rabbi Abahu said, "What shall make up (*meshalem*) for the bullocks we used to offer before You? Our

lips! Our lips [which speak] in the prayers we will pray before
You!" Rabbi Isaac said, "How great was the good that You would
bring to our souls when You would effect atonement for them!
What would we do [in response]? We would say, "It is [for] a
good thing [the bringing of atonement] to give thanks to Adonai"
(Psalm 92:2). [This too is the meaning of] "O give thanks to
Adonai, for you are [interpreted as "do"] good" (Psalm 136:1).

❊ 3 ❊

Hegyon Hanefesh Ha'atzuvah (Meditations of the Sad Soul)

Abraham bar Chiyyah

Abraham bar Chiyyah was a Spanish philosopher (also mathematician, astronomer, and translator) who lived in Barcelona most of his life. While little is known about his life, he was called Savasorda, a corruption of the word for "captain of the bodyguard," which, unlike its contemporary counterpart, probably reflected some judicial post with civil responsibility. This position—more like the *nasi*—was an office in the community that included the power to impose punishment and regulate taxation, but its specific role is unclear.

Hegyon Hanefesh Ha'atzuvah deals with creation, repentance, good and evil, and the righteous life. Its emphasis is generally ethical and the author uses a homiletical approach in order to reach his listeners (now readers). For bar Chiyyah, the righteous person must live a good life here in order to be rewarded in the next life. The individual has free will and can choose between good and evil. If the individual chooses a life of sin, then he or she is given the opportunity to repent. Affirming the sense of Jewish tradition, the author communicates to us in this section that the gates of repentance are always open.

PART THREE: HOW THE SINNER
MAY BE DELIVERED FROM WICKEDNESS
THROUGH REMORSE AND REPENTANCE

One verse teaches, "Return, O Israel, to Adonai your God, for you have stumbled in your iniquity" (Hosea 14:2) and another verse teaches, "Return to Me and I will return to you" (Malachi 3:7). Thus you find that "returning" is used with regard to the person who returns to the service of God, seeking forgiveness for sins, however committed, and is used with regard to God, who returns to God's servants who seek God's mercy.

[There are other verses that use the same root, *shuv*, "turn" or "return."] Says one verse, "But if the wicked turn from all one's sins that one has committed and keep all My statutes and do what is lawful and right" (Ezekiel 18:21). Says another, "But when the righteous person turns away from righteousness and commits iniquity, does all the abominations that the wicked person does" (Ezekiel 18:24). Thus "turning" in the two verses can be used with regard to the righteous and the wicked, for one can turn from an evil path and one can turn from a good one. Linguistically, both are acceptable. Thus, we learn that in Hebrew, the verb *shuv*, "turn or return," can be used in different ways with different meanings. In order to truly understand *teshuvah*, "repentance" [derived from the same root], we will have to investigate those meanings. Only then will we understand who is truly penitent.

We will find that there are seven different meanings for the root *shav*, "return," and those terms derived from it:

1. The most obvious meaning is physically turning from one path to another or mentally turning from one notion to another. Thus, "Your children will return to their own border" (Jeremiah 31:17); "Adonai did not turn from the fierceness of the divine

wrath . . ." (2 Kings 23:26); "I returned and saw under the sun" (Ecclesiastes 9:11); "Who knows whether God will not turn and repent, and turn away from God's fierce anger" (Jonah 3:9); "And the dust returns to the earth as it was" (Ecclesiastes 12:7). The root is not transitive in the *kal* but only in the *hiphil* conjugation as in ". . . he shall return what he took by robbery" (Leviticus 5:23) or in ". . . you shall return it to him" (Deuteronomy 22:2).

2. The second meaning is reversing or restoring, as in ". . . then Adonai your God will turn your captivity" (Deuteronomy 30:3), where the sense is "God will reverse your captivity." There are similar senses in "Restore us, O God of our salvation" (Psalm 85:4); "Behold, I will turn the captivity of Jacob's tents" (Jeremiah 30:4); and "Turn our captivity, O Adonai" (Psalm 126:4).

3. The third meaning is giving or paying or exchanging, as in ". . . the amount repaid [*hamushav*] shall go to Adonai for the priest" (Numbers 5:8) and in ". . . and he rendered to the king of Israel the wool of one hundred thousand lambs" (2 Kings 3:4). The difference between ". . . he shall return what he took by robbery" (Leviticus 5:23) and ". . . the amount repaid shall go to Adonai for the priest" (Numbers 5:8) is that in the first case, one brings back to the rightful owner what was stolen and in the second case, one brings a substitute. "And he rendered to the king of Israel . . ." has the sense of providing a present or a gift. Thus, the *hiphil* conjugation is used differently here than was noted above.

4. The fourth sense is resting or dwelling, as in the phrase "When Adonai rested [*beshuv*] those who dwelled in Zion" (Psalm 126:1), where the meaning is "caused them to stay." *Shivah* in the phrase *shivat Zion*, "who dwelled in Zion," follows the grammatical pattern of *kimah*, so that *shivah* is derived from *shav* as *kimah* is derived from *kam*. There is the use of *shov*,

as in "if you will abide *shov teshvu* in the land" (Jeremiah 42:10); the meaning of that verse is "if indeed you will dwell in the land." There is a similar usage in "I will dwell [*veshavti*] in the House of Adonai forever" (Psalm 23:6).

    5. The fifth sense is that of continual linkage. This uses the *polel* (i.e., the doubling of the third root letter) form of the verb. Thus, "He went linked [*shovav*] to the way of the heart" (Isaiah 57:17). The Hebrew word *shovav* comes from *shav* in the same manner that *komeim* comes from *kam*. Just as *komeim*, "established" or "set," signifies the intensification of meaning of *kam*, "arisen," so *shovav* is an intensification of the meaning of *shav* in the sense of cleaving, that is, an intense and persistent linkage to a particular path from which one does not turn aside. The use of the *kal* form to mean "cleave" is seen in the verse "After I persisted *shuvi* I repented" (Jeremiah 31:19). The verse does not mean "After I turned from my sin, I repented" or "After my repentance, I repented" [for both such interpretations of *shuvi* would make "I repented" redundant]. It means that "after I walked in the stubbornness of my heart and I persisted in my wickedness, then I repented." [Support for such an interpretation is given by the continuation of the verse.] As it is said, "After that I was instructed and I struck my thigh" meaning "after I understood my folly and the stubbornness of my heart, I struck my thigh." The root has a similar meaning in the verse "And the persistence [*meshuvat*] of the thoughtless shall slay them" (Proverbs 1:32), that is, if they do not repent of their folly.

    6. The sixth sense is settle in comfort or dwell in security. Thus the verse "Settle [*shuvah*], O Adonai, the ten thousands of the families of Israel" (Numbers 10:36), whose meaning is "Cause them to dwell in safety." This may be the meaning of *beshuv* in the verse "When Adonai caused those who dwelled in Zion to settle" (Psalm 126:1), that is, "God caused them to

settle in security." There is the verse "You settle [*yeshovev*] my soul" (Psalm 23:3) whose meaning is, God will keep it securely and let it be satisfied by its good deeds and lead it in the ways of righteousness.

7. The seventh sense is the real reason that we have investigated this verb. It is to turn from one's iniquity and to repent of one's sins. It has the same meaning as the first, that of turning away from some matter. This seventh meaning is different in that it deals with matters of the World to Come and the ways of heaven.

On investigating the ways of repentance, one will discover at the outset that there are two kinds: the first reflects the righteous person who repents of sin whether committed inadvertently or intentionally; the second reflects the action of the wicked person who repents of sin. Repentance may also be divided into what is perfect and complete and what is imperfect and deficient. This latter distinction may be a better one since the full definition of repentance suggests that the individual must regret the evil deed and sin committed. Such a definition requires that the transgressor believes in the transgressed *mitzvah*, then regrets the deed, whether done intentionally or inadvertently. Note the difference: an intentional transgression requires confession. However, an inadvertent transgression does not [require confession] since most such transgressions are done unknowingly. They require only regret and a request for forgiveness and atonement. In both kinds of transgressions, the penitent must believe that he [or she] has indeed transgressed divine instruction. Those who do are called genuine penitents.

However, if the sinner did not originally believe that he [or she] had transgressed a *mitzvah* and only later came to realize it and now rues the act, only by a flexible use of language can we call such a person a penitent. We might [however] call such a person a convert or a seeker of the way of faith. We follow here the sense of the verse "And when the wicked person turns from wickedness and does what is lawful and right, that person will, as a result, live" (Ezekiel 33:19). That sinner may not have believed at first. That person's faith is here considered repentance [because he or she *turned*]. It follows that whoever seeks the proper path and previously had not done so is called a penitent. To fully explain this matter, we will approach it a different way.

The sense of the verse above is "to turn from the transgression," that is, after it was done. That can be understood in two different ways: it may mean that the transgression was done inadvertently or it may mean that the transgression was done intentionally. The latter relates to the one who believes in the *mitzvah*. The former may relate to either a believer or a nonbeliever. The punishment or the reward for acts done inadvertently or intentionally is not the same. I would say that the punishment for an inadvertent sin is far less than the punishment for an intentional sin. Similarly, the reward for one who truly repents of an intentional sin is greater than the reward for the one who repents of an inadvertent sin. However, in the mind of most believers, the reverse should be true. Both cases of repentance reflect *teshuvah after* the act [of sinning].

There are two kinds of penitents who repent *before* the act. One repents after thinking and planning to sin. This kind of repentance only occurs because the sinner has considered the punishment for the intended sin. It is as if the Evil Inclination had come to tempt the individual, but God had rebuked Satan and driven him away. Alternately, the other repents even though the person did not plan a specific sin. This kind of repentance occurs because, as a believer, the penitent knows that there is always punishment for sins. That person refrains from any transgression. Such an act of faith is so glorious, and the person is considered a penitent *after* the act.

According to the Sages, those who repent before the act are far more meritorious in God's sight than those who repent after the act. They acquire reward and are in no danger of punishment. Those who repent after the act do so to remove their [otherwise merited] punishment. If God out of divine goodness gives the latter a reward, it is not because they merit it. To have their transgression forgiven would suffice.

From this discussion, we may come to understand that there are three categories of penitents. We have already come to understand that there are five kinds of persons proceeding in the proper path or turning from it.

The first two kinds are persons who are completely righteous. The first kind is called "lowly in spirit." Such a person is one whose soul and quality of goodness rule over one's Evil Inclination from the day of one's birth to the day of one's death. Since such a person is holy, the term "repentance" can never apply [since that person has never sinned].

The second kind is referred to as "contrite of heart." Such a person, though attracted by this world, throughout life has weakened, defeated, and finally conquered the inclination to evil. This individual is in control of the Evil Inclination. Thus, that person has moved the heart away from desire. Because that person had to control the inclination to evil, the term "repentance" can be applied. Indeed, that person is the best and the most praiseworthy kind of penitent.

After these two kinds of absolutely righteous persons, there are three kinds who are neither absolutely righteous nor may they be simply called righteous. However, to the first and second of these, the term "repentance" can be applied. The first is

the one who repents of one's sin. That person is so sorry that he
or she will never again do it.

The second is one who repents of sin but still does it again.
When that person repents, it is not complete repentance.

The third is the absolutely wicked person. Throughout
one's entire life, that person persists in doing evil. The absolutely
righteous person was too holy to have the term "repentance" applied. Repentance is too holy to apply to the absolutely wicked
person. It follows that there are three types of penitents. The first
is one who is entirely righteous. The second is one who is neither entirely righteous nor entirely wicked. The third is the one
who is entirely wicked. We may find these three types in the
Book of Jonah.

The book [of Jonah] begins, "Now the word of Adonai
came to Jonah, the son of Amittai: 'Arise, go to Nineveh, that
great city, and proclaim against it; for their wickedness has come
before Me.' But Jonah rose up to flee unto Tarshish from the
presence of Adonai; and he went down to Yafo. . . . But Adonai
hurled a great wind into the sea . . . so that the ship [he was on]
was threatened with destruction" (Jonah 1:1, 2, 4).

[Reading the story of Jonah,] the first thing we need to determine is why he did not follow Adonai's word and why he did
not perform his mission. As pious believers, we would have to
maintain that his intentions must have been for good and not
for evil. It could never have occurred to him to transgress
Adonai's word; rather, he must have acted out of humility and
wholeheartedness. One might compare his actions to those of
Moses when God said to him, "Come now therefore, and I will
send you to Pharaoh, so that you may bring forth My people,
the Israelites, out of Egypt" (Exodus 3:10). Moses replied, "Who
am I, that I should go to Pharaoh, and that I should bring forth
the children of Israel out of Egypt?" (Exodus 3:11). Jonah must

have reasoned in this manner: "If Moses, who was sent to deliver the innocent out of the iron furnace, delayed until he was assisted by his brother Aaron, should not I, who have been sent [merely] to warn the wicked, delay until I see what more Adonai has to say to me?"

The text [of the Book of Jonah] continues, "And he went down to Yafo" (Jonah 1:3). This means he understood the beauty of what he had been advised to do. [Note the wordplay on the Hebrew *Yafo* and beauty *yofi*.] When Jonah found a ship going to Tarshish, what he had been charged to do was now confirmed, [in his mind]. He immediately paid the fare and boarded the ship to go to Tarshish. His reason for going to Tarshish was to leave the land [of Israel]—where God had revealed the divine self to the Prophets—and to go to a land where [he thought that] God would not reveal Godself. Hence the text says, ". . . to Tarshish, from the presence of the Adonai" (Jonah 1:3). [This suggests that Jonah hoped] that God would accomplish God's mission through another prophet. He did not want to be the messenger for the wicked. Reasoning in this manner, we can consider Jonah's going to Yafo as an act of a righteous person or a prophet.

If this investigation has shown that Jonah's thoughts and intentions were for good, we must then ask why he was punished. We would answer that he was not punished for his good thoughts but because the Holy Blessed One has commanded the Prophets to warn the wicked, as Ezekiel said, "When I say to the wicked: O wicked person, you will surely die, and you do not speak to warn the wicked person from his way; that wicked person will die in his iniquity, but his blood will I require at your hand. Nevertheless, if you warn the wicked of his way to turn from it, and he does not turn from his way; he will die in his iniquity, but you have delivered your soul" (Ezekiel 33:8, 9).

Thus, Jonah did not warn the wicked, although his intentions were good, he was commanded to do so. He did not act. Therefore, he was punished. Were one to argue that this prophecy of Ezekiel [commanding the Prophets to warn the wicked] was directed only to Israel as the preceding verse has it, "So you, mortal one, I have set you as a guardian over the house of Israel; therefore, when you will hear the word at My mouth, warn them for Me" (Ezekiel 33:7), and such warning does not apply to other peoples, I would respond that God specifically said to Jonah, "Arise, go to Nineveh, that great city, and proclaim against it" (Jonah 1:2). Jonah, therefore, was obligated to warn them. Since he failed to do so, their blood might have been required of him, not because of honor due them but because of honor due to the divine word that he had not carried out. Jonah's act is not comparable to the act of Moses, who responded to God's command, saying, "Oh, Adonai, please send whomever you will send" (Exodus 4:13) because God did not send him to warn wicked Pharaoh but rather to save the people Israel. God, because of divine compassion and kindness, was going to ultimately take out the people even if Moses had not gone to them.

God immediately punishes sinners as soon as God is aware of their wickedness. We see that in the case of Sodom, "I will go down now, and see whether they have done altogether according to the cry that has arrived before Me" (Genesis 18:21). On that very day, as it is written, "And the two angels came to Sodom at evening . . ." (Genesis 19:1). Similarly, God said to Jonah, ". . . for their wickedness has come before Me" (Jonah 1:2). Immediately, Jonah was sent to them and when he delayed acting, he was punished, as it says, "But Adonai hurled a great wind into the sea, and there was a mighty tempest in the sea, so that the ship was threatened to be destroyed" (Jonah 1:4). Thus, you see, when God is angry with the Prophets and those who fear God, God punishes them through elements of the natural order such as whirlwinds. When God wants to save the Prophets and those who fear God, God delivers them by way of miracles and wonders. This was the case with Jonah. When God was angry with him, God brought a great wind and storm upon the sea—such occurrences are natural at sea. When God wanted to save Jonah, God delivered him through a great miracle [the great fish].

When the sailors saw the storm, they did what sailors do, as it is written, "And the mariners were afraid, and cried every person to his god; and they cast forth the cargo that was in the ship into the sea, to lighten it for them" (Jonah 1:5). Their actions were the same as any other sailor facing a storm at sea. Those sailors did not have much confidence in their gods, for having cried out to them, they did not wait. Instead, they cast their wares into the sea. The sailors sensed that their gods could not save them. Hence, they did not cry out again to their gods. Not so with Jonah: he accepted the divine judgment and put his faith in the compassion of heaven, as it is written, "But Jonah had gone down to the deepest part of the ship; and he lay and was fast asleep" (Jonah 1:5). It never occurred to Jonah when he saw the great storm that he was its cause, because his thoughts and intentions in his fleeing [to Tarshish] were for the sake of heaven. He was certain that God would deliver him as God had delivered other righteous persons, as it is written, "Many are the ills of the righteous, but Adonai delivers from them all" (Psalm 34:20). Jonah lay down like one who is certain that there is nothing to fear, as the text says, "And he lay, and was fast asleep" (Jonah 1:5).

[The text continues] "So the ship's captain came to him, and said to him: 'How can you sleep? Get up, call upon your God, hopefully God will think about us, and we will not perish"' (Jonah 1:6). The captain was a wise man and what he meant was this: "How is it that you sleep like a person lying down without fear? If you are so certain of your own virtue and so sure that God will save you, then ask for God's mercy so that God will speedily deliver us! Get up and call upon your God; maybe your God will be interested in us and we won't die!"

The captain spoke appropriately, since it is known that if anyone is troubled in this world, he or she may be delivered by prayer, and it is written, "They cried, and Adonai heard, and delivered them out of all their troubles" (Psalm 34:18). God will hear the cry of someone being hurt or oppressed and will graciously save that person, as it is written, "And it shall come to pass, when someone cries out to Me, that I will hear, for I am gracious" (Exodus 22:26). Because of God's gracious compassion, the Holy One hears the voice of every distressed person when that person cries out. Should such a person silently suffer a robbery, then God will give that person the reward for such forbearance in the World to Come and will punish the robber. If the robbed person cries out to God, then God will punish the robber, if the robber has not made amends to the person robbed. However, the person robbed will not receive a reward in the World to Come because of the kind of compassion received in this world. From such an analysis, we may say that the captain spoke appropriately, that Jonah maintained his silence in order to increase his reward in the World to Come.

We now should investigate whether Jonah called out to God when he was asked by the captain, "Arise and call to your God" (Jonah 1:6). When examining the matter, we discover that Jonah did not pray at that time. It became clear to him that he had made a mistake. He realized that he should be silent rather than pray and thus to fulfill the verse "Let him sit alone and keep silent, because God has laid it upon him" (Lamentations 3:28).

When God places divine chastisement upon those who fear God, they remain silent and accept the divine judgment upon themselves. Thus they love the chastisement of Adonai. This is the meaning of the text "He lay, and was fast asleep" (Jonah 1:5), namely, Jonah went down into the depths of the ship and was silent. When the sailors, having each cried out to his god — and yet the storm got worse — came to search out those who remained to urge them to pray, as it is written, "And they said every one to his fellow: 'Come, and let us cast lots, so that we may know who caused this evil to come upon us'" (Jonah 1:7) meaning that they were casting lots to see who did and who did not pray, they discovered that everyone because of the fear of the storm had prayed to his god, all except Jonah, as it says, "And the lot fell upon Jonah" (Jonah 1:7). [The text continued] "Then they said to him: 'Tell us, please, for whose cause the evil is upon us'" (Jonah 1:8). This statement is similar to the previous verse, ". . . for who caused this evil to come upon us" (Jonah 1:7). Both statements mean "who is causing us this great evil?" When they were seeking to learn which person that was, they learned that it was Jonah. They then wanted to find out why he was the cause of this evil, as it says, "Who caused" (Jonah 1:8). Then they asked, "What is your occupation, and where do you come from? What is your [native] country? And of what people are you a part?" (Jonah 1:8). They asked about four things: his work, his journey, his land, and his people, in order to find out what it was that caused the evil to happen. First, they asked about his work, as it says, "What is your occupation?" (Jonah 1:8). They wondered whether he was a magician or a wizard and by some magic means he had brought the storm upon them. Then they asked where he was going, as it says, "And where do you come from?" (Jonah 1:8), thinking that he might be a messenger for some wicked people. After that they asked, "What is your country?"

(Jonah 1:8), fearing that he might be from some evil country or from a city whose inhabitants hated them. Finally they asked about his people, as it says, "And of what people are you a part?" (Jonah 1:8), figuring that he might be from a people accustomed to doing evil.

Jonah, however, did not answer the questions in the order they asked. They had asked about his people last. He responded to that question first, as it says, "And he said to them: 'I am a Hebrew'" (Jonah 1:9). That meant: you need not fear me since I belong to a people to whom all manner of dangerous acts or notions are forbidden. Moreover, "I am a Hebrew and I fear Adonai." One who fears God is not predisposed to involvement with anything evil, as it is written, "I fear Adonai, the God of heaven, who made the sea and the dry land" (Jonah 1:9). When the sailors realized that Jonah could not be suspected of being the cause of their trouble, they become even more frightened, fearing the storm could get even worse and they could die, as it is written, "Then were the men exceedingly afraid" (Jonah 1:10). Seeing that the storm was affecting only them ". . . [they] said to him: 'What is it that you have done?' For the men knew that he fled from the presence of Adonai, because he had told them" (Jonah 1:10). In other words, from what he had told them, they deduced that he was fleeing. It was not that he had explicitly told them that he was fleeing from God, rather they understood that from what he had been saying. His statement "For I fear God" suggests another use of "for" as in the verse "The hunger of the laboring person labors for him, for his mouth compels him" (Proverbs 16:26). "Compels" (in Hebrew *acaf*) suggests in turn the use of the root in "Neither shall my pressure *achpi* be heavy upon you" (Job 33:7). The words "my pressure" are interpreted as "my sin" or "my transgression." Hence the meaning of the verse in Proverbs is that the transgression of the mouth of the one who labors caused his soul to labor. In other words, the transgression of his mouth and his pressure/sin caused his labor. There is a similar usage in "And he returned to be healed in Jezreel *for* they had wounded him" (2 Chronicles 2:6). In sum, one can see that the sailors understood from what Jonah said that he was fleeing.

The sailors were now afraid that it was due to their sin in bringing Jonah aboard and accepting his passage money that God had brought the storm to the sea. Thus the verse says, "Then they said to him: 'What shall we do with you in order to calm the sea?' For the sea grew more and more tempestuous" (Jonah 1:11). "[All this is happening] because we brought you with us!" "Said Jonah, 'It is because of me, not because of you.'"

[The text continues] "And so he [Jonah] said to them: 'Take me and throw me into the sea; and thus will the sea be calm for you; for I know that it is my fault that you are beset by a great storm'" (Jonah 1:12). When the sailors heard that he had given himself over to death, they took pity upon him. They said, "If we can get him back to land where we picked him up, then God can do what God wants and we will be innocent." Thus the text continues, "Nevertheless the men rowed hard to bring it to land; but they could not. The storm prevented them from reaching land. The sea grew more and more tempestuous against them" (Jonah 1:13).

When the sailors realized that they would not be able to reach land, they asked God's mercy regarding two matters: (1) that God deliver them from the storm; and (2) that God keep them from transgression, as the text says, "thus they cried to Adonai and said: 'We beg of you Adonai, we beg of you, let us not perish for this man's life, and do not lay innocent blood upon us'" (Jonah 1:14). In other words, "let us not perish"—if we keep him with us and "do not lay innocent blood upon us"—if we act basely against him and cast him into the sea, even though he has handed himself over to You, "For You, Adonai, have done as You please" (Jonah 1:14).

After they had presented their case before Adonai, they threw Jonah off the ship, as it is written, "So they took Jonah, and cast him into the sea; and the sea ceased its raging" (Jonah 1:15). One should understand "its raging" as God's raging, that is, the raging of the sea caused by God, the suffix referring to God and not to sea. Usually, the Hebrew word for storm is *saar*. The word for "its raging," *zaapho*, is used only with reference to God, as in "I will bear the raging *zaaph* of Adonai, because I have sinned against God" (Micah 7:9). Hence there was a storm at sea because of the raging of Adonai. When the raging ceased, the storm ended.

"Then the men really feared Adonai, so they offered a sacrifice to God, and made vows" (Jonah 1:16). There is an important distinction to be made in understanding the fear mentioned in this verse and the fear mentioned in the previous verse, "Then the men were really afraid and they said to him: 'What is it that you have done?'" (Jonah 1:10). The earlier verse dealt with a fear of things happening in this world; the later verse dealt with fear of heaven, dread of punishment in the World to Come, and repentance that moves [the individual] toward the path of truth. This is proven by the end of the latter verse, ". . . and they offered a sacrifice to Adonai, and made vows" (Jonah 1:16). Believing in God's Torah, the sailors humbled themselves and controlled their Evil Inclination. This was accounted to them as if it had been a sacrifice, as it is written, "The sacrifices of God are a broken spirit; A broken and a contrite heart, O God, You will not despise" (Psalm 51:19). After all, they could hardly have offered real sacrifices in the midst of the sea. Moreover, they did not know the laws of sacrifice, nor were they the appropriate persons to offer sacrifices! We should understand the phrase "and made vows" (Jonah 1:16) as meaning that the sailors agreed among themselves that they would maintain their fear of heaven with unswerving devotion when they returned to land and to home.

So far the story has presented two kinds of repentance that we have already mentioned at the beginning. The first refers to a righteous person of perfect faith: the case of Jonah. The second concerns a wicked person: the case of the sailors. The sailors were saved from punishment by their prayers and repentance. It is quite clear that had Jonah prayed for mercy at that time, his prayer would have been heard. However, he had no desire for prayer until he had received divine chastisement for his inadvertent sin in this world. Jonah knew full well that God would not punish him with death but rather would work miracles on his behalf, even as God punished him. And so, even at the beginning of Jonah's punishment, God was about to save him, as it is written, "And Adonai prepared a great fish to swallow up Jonah; and Jonah was in the belly of the fish three days and three nights" (Jonah 2:1). We should not understand the term "great fish" as a reference to the size of the fish. There were many bigger fish. Rather, ["great fish"] refers to its age and status. As far as its age is concerned, it had been prepared from the Six Days of Creation to accomplish this feat. As far as its status is concerned, it had been prepared to save the life of a righteous person. The phrase "to swallow Jonah up" is to be understood as meaning "to hide" or "to cover" or "to secrete." There is a similar usage in reference to the Sanctuary, ". . . they shall not go in to see the holy things as they are being covered, lest they die" (Numbers 4:20). There the meaning [of the root *bala*] is "covering" or "hiding." Thus, the meaning of "to swallow Jonah up" is "to hide Jonah" or "to cover Jonah." The infinitive "to swallow" is written defectively in the Hebrew to suggest that Jonah was already covered.

The reason that the text says "to swallow Jonah" when it could have said "and it swallowed Jonah up" is to indicate that the fish was part of the divine plan. It was not that God suddenly designated a fish to do God's bidding. This is clear when one compares the language relating to the gourd found later in the book. There it says, "And Adonai prepared a gourd, and made it come up over Jonah, to serve as a shadow over his head, to save him from his evil" (Jonah 4:6). No sooner had God designated it than it grew. The great fish was from the very beginning [of the world].

It may be that "to swallow Jonah" [and not "to kill him"] may indicate that God did not give the fish permission to harm Jonah or in any way control him. Animals should not have power over humans. How then should a fish have power over a righteous person? One must say that God caused Jonah to be swallowed by the fish in order to hide him there.

"And Jonah was in the belly of the fish three days and three nights" (Jonah 2:1). For all three days, Jonah felt rejected by God and was unable to pray. He felt deeply ashamed because of that divine rejection. The three days of Jonah's being in the belly of the fish correspond to the three days of darkness suffered by the Israelites in Egypt. Just as God delivered the Israelites immediately after the three days, so God brought Jonah out of the depths of the sea, out of the darkness of the big fish's belly. Thus, the verse says, "three days and three nights" (Jonah 2:2). Although the order of Creation has the nights come first, the mentioning of days first indicates the parallel of these three days of darkness with the three days of darkness in the land of Egypt. Just as God took the Israelites out of Egypt immediately following the three days of darkness, so God took Jonah immediately out of the belly of the fish after the three days of darkness.

You would have to say that just as the Israelites during those three days of darkness [in the land of Egypt] were dwelling in light both day and night, yet recognized when it was night, as it is written, ". . . but all the Israelites had light in their dwellings" (Exodus 10:23). In other words, they had light even in the period of darkness, so Jonah even in the belly of the fish had light, like the light of day, even while he could recognize the periods of the night. That is why the text has "days" precede "nights." When Jonah realized that the three days corresponding to the three days of darkness of Egypt were complete, he felt certain that God's salvation would come to him. He immediately began to pray, as indicated in the very next verse: "Then Jonah prayed to Adonai his God out of the fish's belly" (Jonah 2:2). There is a difference in the spelling of the word for fish, *dagah*, in this verse and *dag* in the previous verse to indicate that when Jonah first entered the belly of the fish, it was alive, but when he reached its depths, it was dead. The fish's only purpose, which was determined during the Six Days of Creation, was to swallow up Jonah. As soon as that was done, the fish had fulfilled its purpose and died. Dating back to the Six Days of Creation, that fish had only one purpose: to swallow Jonah. Having accomplished that task, the fish fulfilled its purpose and died. Its death is indicated by the use of the term *dagah* for fish, a term seen before in the verse "And the fish (*dagah*) that were in the river died" (Exodus 7:21). In both contexts, *dagah* refers to a dead fish.

Jonah's prayer suggests as much, for he said, "I cried out of my affliction to Adonai and God answered me. Out of the belly of the netherworld I cried, and You heard my voice" (Jonah 2:3).

In other words, "I cried from the belly of a dead fish, which was in the netherworld." When one is in the belly of anything dead, it is as if one is in the belly of the netherworld. There is something marvelous here. Normally, a dead fish floats to the surface. Yet the dead fish in which Jonah lay remained in the depths of the sea, as indicated by the next verse: "For You cast me into the depths, into the heart of the seas" (Jonah 2:4). The fish and Jonah had reached the very bottom of the sea.

The verse continues, "All the flood was round about me" (Jonah 2:4), because streams may enter the sea but they do not descend to its depths. Because Jonah was in the depths of the sea, all the waters of all the streams surrounded him and all the breakers of the sea went past him in every direction, as it says, "All Your waves and billows passed over me. And I said, 'I am cast out from before your sight. Yet, I will look again toward Your Holy Temple. The waters encompassed me, even to my soul. The deep was round about me. The reeds were wrapped around my head'" (Jonah 2:4–6). One may wonder why the Re(e)d Sea is mentioned in connection with the depths more than any other sea. If, however, one rearranges the order of the two verses, all becomes clear: "And I said: 'I am cast from before Your sight,'" then, "The waters encompassed me even to my soul," in other words, "When the waters of the deep encompassed me on every side, I said, 'I am cast out from before Your sight.' However, when I saw 'the reeds around my head,' in other words, they were behind my head like some kind of bandage, then I said, 'Yet, I will look again toward Your Holy Temple.'" The Re(e)d Sea is west of the Land of Israel and its waters were coming at Jonah and wrapping his head from behind so that his face was turned toward the Land of Israel. At that point, Jonah became confident that God would graciously grant him the opportunity of seeing the Temple.

One might also say that when Jonah saw the waters of the Re(e)d Sea coming over his head, he remembered the great miracle that God had done for his ancestors at the splitting of the Re(e)d Sea. He became confident that God would bring him up from the depths of the sea and grace him with the opportunity of seeing the Holy Temple, as it says, "I went down to the bottom of the mountains. The earth with her bars closed upon me forever" (Jonah 2:7). One may understand that the word "bottom" refers to a measure, that is, as high as the mountains are above the earth, so deep are the depths of the sea. The verse says, "The earth with her bars closed upon me forever." The bars refer to lines that pass to the middle of the earth to that point called *mercaz* (center) in Arabic. The line that passes through this point emerges on either side and, as it were, "bars" one side to the other. It is called a bar [since it moves in three dimensions]. It is longer than a straight line, merely passing through the earth and dividing it. The (*mercaz*) center is below all other points on earth and all lines called bars pass through it. Jonah alluded to reaching the very depth and bottom of the earth when he said, "The earth with its bars closed upon me," meaning that he was at the very middle of the earth through which all the bars pass. The phrase "upon me forever" indicates that a bar might pass through his position just as might happen were one at the center of a circle or a sphere. The verse continues, "Yet You have brought up my life from the pit, Adonai, my God" (Jonah 2:7). Note the order of the verses: "When my soul faints and weeps because of my great trouble and I mourn because of it, then I remember Adonai my God." At that moment, because of Your great mercy You will bring me up by virtue of my prayer, as it says, "And my prayer came to You, into Your Holy Temple" (Jonah 2:8). One may learn from this that God will be gracious to any person who, in great difficulty, remembers God and prays for mercy penitently and intently, involving all one's soul and might. God will have pity upon such a person, as the verse has it, "But from there [from the places of your exile] you will seek Adonai your God; and you will find God, if you search for God with all your heart and with all your soul" (Deuteronomy 4:29). In other words, 'If from the places of your exile, you will seek Adonai your God, then you will find God and will find compassion from God, if you seek God with all your heart and soul."

It is written, "I acknowledged my sin to You, and I have not hidden my iniquity. I said, 'I will confess my transgressions before Adonai.' And You forgave the iniquity of my sin, Selah" (Deuteronomy 4:32). You learn from this verse that a person is bound to confess one's sins and iniquities to God prior to one's *teshuvah*, repentance. God will then mercifully forgive them. From the verse we learn the order of confession. First, one acknowledges one's sins, which are the things that have been done, as the verse says, "I acknowledged my sin," for "acknowledged" suggests deeds done that are obvious to all. The verse continues, "I have not hidden the iniquity," meaning that the penitent is not hiding those iniquities that are evil thoughts. The phrase "I have not hidden" is used because the evil thoughts would have been hidden from everyone had the one thinking them not revealed them. The verse then states, "I will confess my transgressions" because "transgressions" refer to things said. Speech and confession are things *said* that relate to them. Statements are being discussed. The verse mentioned first sins and then iniquities. It began with the least serious and proceeded to the more serious offense. An act unaccompanied by an evil thought or an evil statement is the least serious. It cannot be called intentional. It is simply a mistake. An evil thought not acted upon or spoken of is a more serious offense than the first, for it could be a thought of idolatry, which would not be possible with an unintentional act. An evil statement might be worse than the first two, even though it be unaccompanied by an evil thought or an evil act, for it could be either blasphemy or mention of idolatry. Such a statement is worse than an evil thought, even though we might fear the thought of idolatry, because an evil statement is that thought acted upon and made audible. An evil thought per se is neither seen nor heard. Thus we find that the verse [has the penitent] confess the less serious offenses and then confess the more serious ones, even as the Rabbis taught.

At this point, we may ask why the verse mentions [God's forgiving] only the sins and iniquities, as it says, ". . . the iniquity of my sin" and did not mention the transgressions. There are two ways of interpreting this statement; one is more stringent than the other.

The less stringent explanation is that the verse, in saying "And You forgave the iniquity of my sin, Selah" joins the iniquity to the sin. Had it said "my sin" and "my iniquity," it would have meant that each was a specific offense. It did not do so because an evil thought not acted upon and an act unaccompanied by an evil thought and an evil intention is not punishable. Nor does it require repentance or confession. All that is required is that the offender be sorry for what was thought or done. Similarly, one is not punished for an unconsidered utterance. Therefore, the verse said, "the iniquity of my sin" in order to join the two, iniquity and sin, together. In other words, [whether] an act following thought or a thought dependent upon an act, both require atonement and forgiveness. It was not necessary to mention "the iniquity of transgressions" or "the transgression of iniquity" because an utterance of the mouth is an act, just as other sins are acts of other limbs. And in the same manner that the mention of "the iniquity of the sin" contained the notions of thought and act and contained within it an utterance the act of the mouth, Scripture had no need of saying more. This is the view of the one who holds a lenient position.

The more stringent position is that all offenses, whatever their severity, whether thought or act, are atoned for by repentance, regret, and confession before God. However, transgressions of the mouth are different. Whether it be the minor offense of mentioning God's name in an unseemly place or the major offense of swearing falsely, neither repentance nor confession effect atonement. Only the offender's punishment in the World to Come does. It is as the Torah states, "You should not take the name of Adonai your God in vain, for Adonai will not hold guiltless the one who takes God's name in vain" (Exodus 20:7). For that reason, those who are exceedingly pious refrain from mentioning God's name or any substitute for that name with regard to oaths or the like. They fear that otherwise they might be guilty of an iniquity that cannot be atoned for by repentance.

The psalm continues, "For this let everyone who is godly pray to You in a time when You may be found. Surely, when the great waters overflow, they will not reach him" (Psalm 32:6). The meaning is, "Let every godly person pray to You at the moment when others find mercy before You." Hence the text has "Let everyone who is godly pray" and not "Let anyone pray to You who would at the time." Not everyone who prays after confessing one's sins, iniquities, and transgressions will find that moment. Only the godly person will be able to find it. From the verse it would seem that person is the one who is careful not to sin with one's mouth. We may understand from the first verse that the person who does not refrain from mentioning the Divine Name or a substitute for it while taking an oath will not be able to fully repent. Since the second verse mentions "the one who is godly," we may deduce that anyone not extremely careful in avoiding mentioning the Divine Name cannot be called "godly."

These two verses also teach the way of reverence and repentance and the way that the prayer of the godly finds the proper moment [of acceptance]. The godly person, knowing that she has never inappropriately mentioned the Divine Name, confessing her sins, transgressions, and iniquities may then pray with assurance that her prayer will find grace and that she will be delivered from suffering, and even if all the waters in the sea were to sweep toward her, they would not touch her, as it says, ". . . the great waters overflow, they will not reach him." Jonah's words, "When my soul fainted in me, I remembered Adonai and my prayer came in to You in Your Holy Temple" (Jonah 2:6), meant, "When my soul was fainting and pouring forth prayers of supplication, then I remembered Adonai, my God, in complete innocence, with perfect devotion. I then immediately knew that my prayer was accepted," as it says, "and my prayer came to You in Your Holy Temple."

Jonah then continued, "Those who regard lying vanities forsake their own mercy, but I will make sacrifice to You with the voice of thanksgiving. What I vowed, I will pay. Salvation comes from Adonai" (Jonah 2:9, 10). Speaking to God, Jonah thought the following: "If You had compassion on these sailors who were idolaters because they had renounced their idols, and You accounted that act of renunciation as the equivalent of sacrifice and vows made to You, as it says, 'and they offered up a sacrifice and made vows,' even though they did not [really sacrifice, nor did they] believe that they would fulfill those vows, should You not have compassion upon me who, accepting Your Torah, places my prayer as a sacrifice before You? It is as the verse says: 'But I will make sacrifice to You with the voice of thanksgiving. What I have vowed, I will pay' (Jonah 2:10)." This means "May I be deemed worthy to find Your great and full salvation," even as the verse ends, "salvation comes from Adonai." God responded to Jonah's plea, accepted his prayer, and answered him immediately, as it is written, "And Adonai spoke to the fish, and it vomited out Jonah on dry land" (Jonah 2:11). We may deduce from this last verse that the fish, which had died after swallowing Jonah, was now brought back to life by God to honor Jonah. One could also say that life entered the fish because the light of salvation came to Jonah. The new life for the fish is indicated by the use again of the Hebrew word *dag* for fish. The statement ". . . it vomited out Jonah" is to indicate that the fish *immediately* vomited him out. The verse does not say "to vomit out Jonah" as the earlier verse said "to swallow Jonah" because animals are destined to serve righteous persons and not to harm them. Had the fish completed the process of swallowing Jonah, it would have harmed him. Hence, the latter act of vomiting out Jonah was to help and serve him.

As soon as Jonah reached dry land, he began to prophesy, as it says, "And the word of Adonai came to Jonah the second time, saying, 'Arise, go to Nineveh, that great city, and proclaim to it as I bid you'" (Jonah 3:1, 2). The words "the second time" may suggest another prophecy or a different prophecy. That it is the latter [a different prophecy] is indicated by the second prophecy having the possibility of repentance for the people of Nineveh, which the first lacked. The second prophecy gave that possibility with the delay of the punishment. The first prophecy said, ". . . and proclaim against it [Nineveh]; for their wickedness has come before Me." This language suggests immediate and dire punishment. It is like the description of Sodom and Gomorrah's fate, ". . . because the cry of them has greatly increased before Adonai. And God has sent us to destroy it" (Genesis 19:13). Had the first prophecy been fulfilled, the people of

Nineveh would have been destroyed. The second prophecy contains the words ". . . and proclaim to it what I bid you." One can understand the words "what I bid" to have a future sense, "what I will bid you," in order to indicate a time period in which the gates of repentance will be open. The first prophecy contains the words "Proclaim *against* it." The second contains the words "Proclaim *to* it." Proclaiming *against* has an evil connotation, as in "He has called a solemn assembly *against* me" (Lamentations 1:15). Proclaiming [or calling] *to* has a good connotation, as in "And I will call for [literally, *to*] the corn and will increase it" (Ezekiel 26:29). You will find in every aspect of the second prophecy that the words are more lenient than the words of the first. Hence, "the second time" means a different prophecy.

The verse continues, "So Jonah arose, and went to Nineveh, according to the word of Adonai" (Jonah 3:3). This means that Jonah went to complete his mission and fulfill Adonai's word, as it said, "what I bid you." The text says, "Now Nineveh was a very great city to God, of three days journey" (Jonah 3:4). "To God" suggests that its greatness could not be measured in human terms, but only in divine terms. Nineveh had three sister cities: Rechovot, Resen, and Calah. Nineveh was the largest, followed by Rechovot, and then Calah, the smallest. We learn that from the verse "Out of the land went forth Asshur, and built Nineveh, and Rehovot-ir, and Calah. And Resen between Nineveh and Calah—the same is the great city" (Genesis 10:11, 12).

"And Jonah began (*vayahel*) to enter the city a day's journey" (Jonah 3:4). We learn that Jonah was hoping (*meyahel*) and waiting for the promised word of Adonai, "And proclaim to it what I bid you." He did not know what word until he had proceeded a day's journey into the city. It was not until the beginning of the second day that it became clear to him: "And he proclaimed, and said, 'In forty days, Nineveh will be over-thrown.'" The reason for the delay was so that Jonah could reach the center of the city, so that all the people of Nineveh might know the certainty of his message. One might also say that a day's delay of the message made possible the hearing of and the telling of that message by those who might have returned to the entrance of the city to the other side. There were those on the third day who were running ahead to give the message. Thus, you find that Jonah's message was heard throughout the city, because there were people running in terror to make it known.

Jonah's preaching lasted forty days, the same number of days that the rain fell on earth in the period of the Flood. As a result, one learns that the wickedness of the people of Nineveh was as great as that of the people of the Flood. It is said of them, "And Adonai saw that human wickedness was great on the earth" (Genesis 6:5) and it is said of the people of Nineveh, "for their wickedness has come before Me" (Jonah 1:1). One can further say that the wickedness of the people of Nineveh was as great as that of the generation of the Flood because the wickedness of the latter covered the earth, as it says, "the wickedness of humans was great on earth," while the wickedness of the former extended up to heaven, as it says, "their wickedness has come before Me." Even so, God delayed punishing the people of Nineveh while immediately punishing the generation of the Flood because at the time of the Flood all flesh had corrupted its way, yet at the time of Nineveh only the people of the place had [corrupted their way]. When the people of Nineveh heard what Jonah had to say, they immediately believed it, as it says, "And the people of Nineveh believed God . . ." (Jonah 3:5).

Although their faith was not perfect, the people did believe that God could do what God said. Even heathens who have no reverence for God will call upon God in need as did the sailors,

". . . so be it that God will think about us, that we might not perish" (Jonah 1:6). When the sailors became truly reverent, it says, "Then the men feared Adonai exceedingly" (Jonah 1:16). Therefore, we may deduce that the faith of the people of Nineveh was not perfect, that it was inferior to the faith of the sailors in three different aspects:

1. Reverence [for God] is greater than the primary meaning of faith. Faith means affirming that something is true and correct. Yet it is possible that something might be neither true nor correct, as the verse has it, "The fool believes every word" (Proverbs 14:15), that is, whether it is true or false. Not everything is true. Most things are false. The fool can't distinguish between the two. For that reason, the fool believes in everything. The wise person [who can distinguish between true and false] only believes some things. From the aspect of faith, however, even with the differences between them, the fool and the wise both might be called believers. This indicates that faith comes first before reverence, for anyone who would revere something in which he or she has no faith would have an imperfect, doubtful, or conditional reverence. That might be called dread or fear or something similar, but not really reverence. It follows then that true reverence depends on a belief that precedes it. Since it is said of the ship's crew that "then the men feared Adonai exceedingly" (Jonah 1:16), we may call them reverent *and* believers, since fear of God depends upon [belief in God]. We do not call the people of Nineveh reverent even though they had a measure of belief [in God] because there are believers who are not reverent. That is the first distinction to be made between the sailors and the people of Nineveh.

2. The second distinction is that while it is said of the sailors, "the men feared Adonai exceedingly," it is said only of the people of Nineveh, "And the people of Nineveh believed God"

(Jonah 3:5). In other words, Scripture says of the sailors "the men feared Adonai," joining their great reverence and their repentance to the Divine Name [the Tetragrammaton] Adonai [YHWH] the Great and Awesome name, used when God sits upon the Throne of Steadfast Love and Mercy, Righteousness, Honor, and Sovereignty. No other being uses that [Tetragrammaton] name. Of the people of Nineveh, however, it is written that "they believed in God." Their faith was linked to the Divine Name [*Elohim*], related to God sitting upon the Throne of Justice and Law. The name *Elohim* does not only refer to God. It may [also] refer to judges and magistrates.

3. Thus you find that the people of Nineveh believed that God was able to punish them in the same manner as any king or ruler might punish one of their subjects. It was because of their fear and not because of their faith that it is said of them, "and they proclaimed a fast, and put on sackcloth, from the greatest of them even to the least of them" (Jonah 3:5). It was done to bewail and weep for their souls because of their fear of impending punishment in this world, not because of any true reverence or perfect faith. The faith of the people of Nineveh began when Jonah began to preach to them, since their faith is mentioned immediately after his preaching, as it says, "and he proclaimed, and said: 'In forty days, Nineveh will be overthrown'" (Jonah 3:4). The text continues, "And the people of Nineveh believed God. They proclaimed a fast, and put on sackcloth, from the greatest of them to the least of them" (Jonah 3:9).

All this did not reach the king that day, perhaps because the royal quarters were on the other side of the city from where Jonah had arrived. Jonah began preaching on the second day and the word came to the king on the third day, as it is written, "And the news reached the king of Nineveh. He arose from his throne, took off his robe, covered himself with sackcloth, and sat in ashes" (Jonah 3:6). The news that reached him was that the people of Nineveh had proclaimed a fast and put on sackcloth. He did the same thing that they did, as it is written, "And the news reached the king of Nineveh, and he . . . covered himself with sackcloth, and sat in ashes," that is, a summary of what he did. Moreover, we find that the king followed the views of the people of his city, as it says, "And he caused it to be proclaimed and published through Nineveh by the decree of the king and his nobles, saying . . ." (Jonah 3:7). That indicates that they acted as a result of the king's decree and the important people of the city, not out of the fear of God.

The verse continues, "Let neither human nor beast, herd nor flock, taste anything: let them not feed, nor drink water. . . ." The term "human" includes infants, sucklings, and young children who have no awareness, as is indicated by the end of the prophetic statement, ". . . which are more than sixscore thousand persons that cannot discern between their right hand and their left hand and also many cattle" (Jonah 4:11). The term *adam* ("human" in the prior verse and "person" in the latter verse) has the same sense in both verses as referring to the babies who did not know the difference between good and evil [as suggested by "right hand" and "left hand" in the latter verse]. Those who had reached the age of understanding, whether young or old, had begun fasting and putting on sackcloth on their own, as it is written ". . . they . . . put on sackcloth, from the greatest of them to the least of them." Only the babies and infants were left. It was they whom the king, following his own thinking and that of his nobles, ordered not to eat and drink, as it says, "Let them not taste anything. Let them not eat, nor drink water" (Jonah 3:7). "Taste" refers to both eating and drinking. "Anything" and "eat" refers to eating. "Nor drink" [obviously] refers to drinking. This interpretation follows the order of items given. First "don't taste" stands alone. Then "feed on nothing" and "don't drink water" come with their separate meanings. However, the verse can be interpreted in a different manner. "Don't taste" may refer to humans. "Don't feed" may refer to animals. "Don't drink" may refer to both. In this interpretation, "Don't taste" refers to food, as in the verse "Even as the palate tastes its food" (Job 12:11). Thus only the palate—and no other organ—tastes food. Scripture continues, ". . . but let them be covered with sackcloth, both human and beast" (Jonah 3:8) so that all living creatures were doing the same thing regarding food, drink, and dress. "Let them cry mightily to God" so that the children and the animals whom the king had commanded be dressed in sackcloth should cry out mightily to the Judge and Sovereign of the Universe because of the king's command, not out of faith in God. Animals and infants—lacking understanding—could hardly cry out to God on the basis of reverence, faith, or knowledge. They could weep and wail with all their might because of their distress.

You won't deduce from the verse that the people of Nineveh were crying out to God or praying to God. Rather you find that their plan was to make their innocent babies and their dumb animals suffer so that because of them God might be moved to compassion. The people prayed, but they were not accustomed to prayer. They could not depend on prayer because of their many sins. One might judge them favorably for their actions, saying that they did not pray because they were embarrassed to lift their eyes to heaven as a result of their many sins.

The end of the proclamation that the king sent throughout the city states, "but let them be covered with sackcloth, both human and beast. Let them cry mightily to God. Yes, let every one turn from his [or her individual] evil way, and from the violence that is in their hands" (Jonah 3:8). The words "every one from his [or her individual] evil way" includes the infants and the babies, all who are not adults. "From his [or her] evil way" refers to each person's customary way of life. "From the violence that is in their hands" suggests that they were to return all things acquired by theft and robbery to their rightful owners.

Scripture then comes to indicate their reason for doing this by saying, "Who knows whether God will not turn and repent, and turn away from God's fierce anger, so that we don't perish" (Jonah 3:9). They were asking not to perish. God had not made them worthy to ask for forgiveness and atonement! Even the very beginning of their request was problematic: "Who knows whether God will not turn and repent," that is, who knows whether God will or won't! They did not have faith in their repentance that it would nullify the decree against them. Nonetheless, the All Compassionate One did not hide the divine face from them, as it says, "And God saw their deeds, that they turned from their evil way. So God repented of the evil that God said God would do to them. God did not do it" (Jonah 3:10). [Note the Divine Name] *Elohim*, God, who sits [in judgment upon them] on the Throne of Justice—in the same judicial sense as [the Divine Name *Elohim*] as in ". . . both parties shall come before the God [*Elohim*]" (Exodus 22:8). So the phrase "And God saw their deeds" means that God saw their works, that is, what they had done by bringing animals upon whom it was fitting to show mercy, to cry out to God. They had turned away from their evil ways and had restored [to the rightful owners] all stolen things in their possession. And "So, God repented of the evil" means that this change by God referred to what would happen to these people by reason of the divine judgment in this world. They had repented of their deeds only for the sake of this world, not for the sake of heaven. The text does not say "And Adonai" [with the Divine Name of the Tetragrammaton], for that would indicate that they had been afforded forgiveness in the World to Come, which would follow the divine attribute of mercy [indicated by the Tetragrammaton].

Thus you find that there are two kinds of repentance, excluding the kind afforded to the righteous. There is one kind that brings life only in this world. There is another kind that brings life in this world and forgiveness and atonement in the next. Scripture speaks of the second kind of repentance when it says, "Let the wicked forsake the way, and the iniquitous person one's thoughts. Let that person return to Adonai and God will have compassion upon him, and to God, for God will abundantly pardon" (Isaiah 55:7). Repentance mentioned here has two components: one's way and one's thoughts. The former refers to the evil deeds done. The latter refers to one's inclination to do evil. Scripture says, "And let that person return to Adonai, and God will have compassion upon him, and to God, for God will abundantly pardon" to indicate that one's repentance should be for the sake of heaven and God will then have compassion upon that person. And "to our God" refers to the One who sits upon the Throne of Justice who then will pardon that person, "for God will abundantly pardon."

You find then that the repentance of a wicked person requires three things. First, [one must] turn away from the sinful acts. Second, [one must] turn the mouth and the heart from focusing on and speaking of sin. Third, both acts of turning must be for the sake of heaven. You will find these three elements in the story of the sailors. Their intentions were for the sake of heaven, as it says, "Then the men feared Adonai exceedingly" (Jonah 1:16) since the verse continues, "and they offered a sacrifice to Adonai, and made vows" you can see that there was a change in their actions. Offering a sacrifice is an action. Scripture attests that it was an action for the sake of heaven, as it says,

"Then the men feared Adonai exceedingly" (Jonah 1:16). Since the verse continues, "and they offered a sacrifice to Adonai and made vows," you can see that there was a change in their actions. Offering a sacrifice is an action. Scripture attests that it was an action for the sake of heaven, as it says, "to Adonai." Since the verse ends with "and [they] made vows" shows that both thought and mouth [deed] were involved. Thus, they were worthy of atonement.

Scripture speaks about penitence that is incomplete in the following words: "'Have I any pleasure at all that the wicked should die?' says Adonai, God. Rather, she should return from her ways and live" (Ezekiel 18:23). Were God to decree death against a sinner because of her wickedness, that death would be decreed conditionally. Were the sinner to repent, God would nullify the decree and apportion to that person those years that had been allotted from birth, as indicated by the words "that she should return from her ways and live," that is, the life that had been apportioned to her.

Another verse teaches, "As I live, says Adonai, God, I have no pleasure in the death of the wicked, rather the wicked should turn from his way and live" (Ezekiel 33:11). This verse seems like the verse quoted above. Both verses speak of the wicked of the nations. However, the second verse ends with the mention of the repentance of the wicked among the people of Israel, as it says, "Turn, turn from your evil ways. Why should you die, O house of Israel?" (Ezekiel 33:11). "Turning" [repenting] is mentioned twice in the latter verse and only once in the former verse, as indicated in the words "that he should return from his ways and live," to teach that the wicked among the people of Israel merit forgiveness and atonement in the World to Come only when they fulfill two conditions. First, they must turn from their evil ways. Second, the act of repentance must be for the sake of heaven. The fulfillment of both conditions in their act of repentance merits the World to Come. The act of repentance by the wicked among the nations will secure for them life in this world, which was the reason for their repentance. It will not serve for them life in the World to Come, because their act of repentance was not for the sake of heaven. They will have no portion at all in the World to Come. That is suggested by the words [in the verse] "Why will you die, O House of Israel" which means "Why will you die that kind of death that is punished in the life to come?" As for the repentance of the wicked, Scripture says, "The wicked should turn from his way and live," which means that she will live in this world. The verse does not say "Let him repent and not die," because for the wicked among the nations, their death is absolute destruction in both this world and the next, whether or not they repent. Note that Scripture does not say to Israel, "Turn from your way and live" because their repentance is not for the sake of the life in this world.

You should know that the life of the righteous in this world is not called "days of life" but rather, [they are called] days of sojourning and fear. The proof for this is in what Jacob said when asked by Pharaoh, "How many are the days of the years of your life?" (Genesis 47:8). He answered, "The days of the years of my sojournings are . . . few and evil" (Genesis 47:9). He did not use the word "life" used by Pharaoh in his question. Jacob used it only [at the end of the verse] when he said, ". . . they have not attained the days of the years of the life of my ancestors in the days of their sojourning." Jacob termed the days of his life and the days of the life of his ancestors as "days of sojourning" because the righteous live for this world and for the next. The World to Come is for the righteous their true life, for it is there that they will have perduration. They live in this world in order to acquire those merits and to perform those *mitzvot* that will serve as sustenance and provender for the World to Come. The righteous call life in this world "days of sojourning" because they fear that they may not have provided proper provender [for the World to Come].

You might think that the life of the people of Israel in this world is called life because of what is in the verse "'For I have no pleasure in the death of the one who dies' says Adonai, God. Instead, turn yourselves and live" (Ezekiel 18:32). You might think further that the term "the one who dies" refers to those who die, whether they are part of Israel or of the other nations. However, from the end of the verse "turn yourselves and live," you are to understand that refers to life in the World to Come for both, for Israel and for the other nations. Hence, life in this world is called the days of life for Israel. Thus, we would say to you that the term "the one who dies" refers here to a thief, as well as in similar contexts. Every transgression with the exception of theft is atoned for by the act of repentance. Theft, however, is atoned for only when the thief makes restitution, whether it be to the owner [of the stolen article] or her nearest relative or [failing the first two] to God. This has been clearly explained in the Torah. For this reason, the sinner is called "the one who dies" because he is dead in every aspect [in this world and in the next]. If he is part of Israel, his death will not bring him atonement if the stolen article remains in his possession. He will be punished for the theft after his death in the World to Come. Thus, he will be dead in this world and will be punished in the World to Come. Thus, this is the meaning of "Instead, turn," that is, [return] yourselves and live. The verse refers to the theft. It says to the thief: return the stolen article and live. Were a Jew to have stolen something and returned it, he would have fulfilled his days of sojourning in this world and would have acquired life in the World to Come when he died. He would not be punished for that transgression there. Were a non-Jew to have stolen something [and returned it], she would live out the full measure of her days in this life and would not die a premature death like others [who have stolen].

There is another verse that speaks of the thief: "Return and turn yourselves from all your transgressions" (Ezekiel 18:30). This verse teaches that there are transgressions for which repentance alone will bring atonement. These transgressions are between the individual and God. There are transgressions that require repentance and restitution, such as theft, robbery, and the like. These transgressions are between individuals. "Turn yourselves from your transgressions" may refer to wrongful speech. Theft and robbery are wrongful acts. Scripture could have said, "[Turn yourselves] from all your sins." However, it said "from all your transgressions" to include verbal assaults that rob and deeply offend a person, whether done privately or publicly. These can only be forgiven when the offender appeases the one offended. Thus, "all your transgressions" is stated to cover all kinds of robbery, whether by words or by acts. Scripture calls these deeds "transgressions" because robbery by words before God is worse than stealing money.

You may now see how great is the return of what is lost and the restoration of what was stolen, as well as how wondrous is the seeking of forgiveness for such acts. That act of restitution alone was the reason that God nullified the decree of destruction against Nineveh, which had been threatened by Jonah. Jonah was distressed that his prophecy was not fulfilled, as it is written, "But it displeased Jonah exceedingly, and he was angry" (Jonah 4:1). It was difficult for him [to accept the fact] that his prophecy was not fulfilled. The passage continues, "And he prayed to Adonai" (Jonah 4:2). Here we are to understand that the prayer was not an appeal for mercy. Rather, it was a demand for judgment, that is, he asked God, ". . . was not this my way of saying, 'when I was yet in my own country'" (Jonah 4:2). In other words, I kept talking about this all the time that I was on my own land, "for I knew that You are a gracious God, compassionate, long-suffering, and abundant in mercy and You repented of the evil" (Jonah 4:2). Because I knew this, I therefore fled from You to Tarshish. Certain of Your forbearance and compassion, I knew that You would forgive my transgressions and sins and would not punish me. "Therefore now, O Adonai, I beseech You, take my life from me. It is better for me to die than to live" (Jonah 4:3) because You have repented of the evil that You promised to the wicked people of Nineveh, who only repented for their own purposes. I am Your servant. You forced me to go to them [and preach doom to them]. Now they will think of me as a liar. Therefore, ". . . it is better for me to die than to live" (Jonah 4:3). God supported Jonah's argument, as the verse says, "You do well (*hahetev*) to be angry" (Jonah 4:4), that is, You are right to be angry. The particle *ha* in *hahetev* is not the sign of a question; rather, it is the sign of a statement. Had it been a question, Jonah would have answered affirmatively or negatively, as he does in the verse that follows (4:9).

One must say that God revealed to Jonah through the Holy Spirit the reason why God repented of the evil that God had Jonah proclaim against Nineveh. This follows what Amos said: "For Adonai will do nothing, but You reveal Your counsel to Your servants the Prophets" (Amos 3:7). This was revealed to Jonah at the beginning of the forty days that he proclaimed against Nineveh. Jonah became incensed and proceeded to argue with and demand a judgment from God. However, when God said, "You do well to be angry," Jonah was appeased, since God had accepted his argument. Jonah now hoped that perhaps the prophecy [of doom] would be fulfilled. This is the mean-

ing of the words "Then Jonah went out of the city and sat on
the east (*makedem*) side of the city" (Jonah 4:5). [The verse
should be understood as] Jonah went out from the pain that he
felt in his heart because of the wickedness of the city, which he
maintained had not changed but was as it had been (*makedem*).
"And there he made a booth, and sat under it in the shadow"
(Jonah 4:5). This means that Jonah's trust and hope in God were
to him as a booth ". . . and [he] sat under it in the shadow." This
means that he sat beneath it in the hope that he would see what
would happen to Nineveh at the end of the forty days that he
had proclaimed: whether its people would be saved from the
decree or not.

Seeing what Jonah was thinking, God revealed to him the
secret meaning of what had happened and explained to him that
what he was thinking was wrong and would not occur. He did
this through the use of symbols, as it says, "And Adonai, God,
prepared a gourd, and made it grow above Jonah so that it might
shade his head, to deliver him from his evil. So Jonah was exceptionally glad for the gourd" (Jonah 4:6). The use in the verse
of two Divine Names, "And Adonai, God," suggests that the
growth of the gourd was like the growth of the trees in the Garden of Eden, where the two Divine Names occur, "And out of
the ground Adonai, God made grow every tree that is pleasant
to the sight . . ." (Genesis 2:9). Just as the trees in the Garden of
Eden came into existence fully grown, so too the gourd [that
shaded Jonah]. As soon as God prepared it, immediately ". . . it
grew above Jonah." Just as the trees [in the garden] were created without being planted or cared for by humans, so too was
the gourd. Just as the trees were exceptionally beautiful, so was
the gourd. The verse says, "And Adonai, God . . . made it to grow
above Jonah, in order to cast a shadow on his head" (Jonah 4:6),
that is, to provide a shade for him should the shade of the booth

in which he was sitting move. The words "to deliver him from his evil" suggest that all this—to the very end—was designed to deliver Jonah from the distress that he felt. You may also say that the words "to deliver him from his evil" suggest that all this, to the very end, was designed to deliver Jonah from the distress that he felt. You may also say that the words "to deliver him from his evil" apply whether the shadow that had been prepared for Jonah's head by the booth in which he was sitting remained or whether the shadow of the gourd remained over him to save him from the heat. Thus, Jonah greatly rejoiced over the gourd. His joy was great for two reasons: the gourd was exceptionally beautiful and it provided shade for him. Jonah's joy over the gourd resembled other human joys of this world that lack permanence. These are joys about which one should neither rejoice nor be troubled about their loss.

Because of Jonah's joy about matters of this world, Scripture comes to show how little is their benefit, how vile is their pleasure, and how weak is their power. The words "But God prepared a worm when the morning rose the next day, and smote the gourd, so that it withered" (Jonah 4:7) are metaphoric. The worm stands for the days and nights that consume the lives of all living things, causing them to lose track of time, aware of that loss only when the final moment comes abruptly. The words "when the morning rose the next day" suggest that the event occurred at the appropriate time. The worm was to smite the gourd when the morning rose, because that was close to the time that people need shade, that is, when the sun rises.

The verse "And it came to pass, when the sun arose" (Jonah 4:8)—that is, when shade is beneficial—"that God prepared a vehement (*harishit*) east wind," that is, at the time of plowing (*haharish*). The word *harishit*, "vehement," is derived from the word *haharish*, "plowing." The derivation may be due to the

fact that the east wind at the season causes problems. It may be
that the derivation does not come from the time of the plowing
but rather from the action of the east wind, which plowed up
the land and raised dust and dirt into the nostrils of Jonah, shak-
ing up his booth, moving the shadow from him.

The words "And the sun beat down on the head of Jonah
so that he fainted (*vayitalaf*)" (Jonah 4:8) suggest that he was
astounded in the same way that "your children have fainted
(*ulafu*)" (Isaiah 51:20). Jonah was troubled, wondering why the
gourd had dried up, why the booth provided no shade. Therefore Scripture says, ". . . and requested for himself that he might
die, and said, 'It is better for me to die than to live'" (Jonah 4:8).
One who suffers great pain often despairs of his life and may
curse his days. Job did that when he said, "Why did I not die in
the womb? Why did I not perish at birth?" (Job 3:11).

When God saw Job's pain and anger, God began asking
him what caused him that pain, as it says, "And God said to
Jonah, 'Are you very angry at the gourd?'" (Jonah 4:9). Here the
he in *hahetev*, "Are you very," is the particle indicating a question and not the particle indicating a statement. This is different from what we said about the first use of *hahetev*. This use is
different, as indicated that Job answered the question: "I am very
angry, even to death" (Jonah 4:9). You will note that in the use
of Divine Names in this section, the name *Elohim* is used to
suggest the Holy Blessed One is sitting on the Throne of Justice and Law. Thus, "But God (*Elohim*) prepared a worm" and
"God (*Elohim*) prepared a vehement east wind" and "God
(*Elohim*) said to Jonah." Such use was due to Jonah's demand
for juridical determination why he suffered. However, when the
Holy Blessed One came to tell him the verdict, it was done with
the divine quality of mercy. He therefore mentioned the Tetragrammaton, which is used when the Holy One occupies the

Throne of Steadfast Love and Compassion, as it is written, "And Adonai said, 'You have had pity on the gourd, for which you did not labor or nurture to grow, which grew up overnight, and perished overnight'" (Jonah 4:10). That means, "You had pity on the gourd because you thought that it might provide you with some pleasure. You did not work for it. You did not grow it. It was there by chance, growing up in one night and perishing in the next. It provided no benefit and it had no permanence." "And should I not have pity on Nineveh, that great city, in which there are more than sixty thousand persons that cannot tell the difference between their right hand and their left hand, and also much cattle?" (Jonah 4:11). God says, "It is My desire for the world to be established on truth so that violence, robbery, and iniquity is removed, not because those sins affect My glory but because of My great compassion for all living things and for the work of My hands. I do not have pity on the great city of Nineveh, which has more than sixty thousand persons who cannot tell the difference between their right hand and their left hand and who therefore cannot be punished. One who lacks knowledge and understanding can neither be guilty nor innocent. Moreover, there are many cattle there that are perishing because of the wicked sins of the people of Nineveh. Is it not right that because of My great compassion on the one hand and because of My righteous judgments on the other, that when these wicked people got rid of the [gains of] violence that had been in their hands that otherwise would have caused the destruction of them, their children, and their animals, that I should be as one who has compassion upon the children and the animals to keep them alive and to keep the wicked people alive with them? The wicked will live because of the children and the animals in place of the children and the animals dying because of the sins of the wicked." When Jonah heard how correct, just, and faithful was this argument, he was appeased and understood the divine manner of judgment. He became silent for he had nothing to say but to acknowledge the truth.

When you look at this [book of] prophecy, it will become clear to you that there are three levels of repentance, and you will understand the differences between them. You will find that the reward for the first is eternal life, peace without end, and steadfast love and compassion on every side. The second level is forgiveness and atonement at the beginning and a good hope for the ultimate end. The third has the nullification of the decree [of doom] at the time of judgment for its beginning. The Holy One will extend the life of the wicked to test whether they will repent of their wickedness so that they will have no excuse when that wickedness is requited on the day of judgment. You will find that each level at the beginning has a benefit, either in principle or in appearance. The difference is what happens at the end. For some, the end is total steadfast love and truth. For others, it is terror and fear. To investigate this ultimate end and to see how it is arranged, I now return to the first part of the matter under discussion, which I will begin. I will speak with the aid of the One Who begins and the One who is complete, may God's name be praised and glorified forever and eternally.

❧ 4 ❧

Chovot Halevavot
(Duties of the Heart)

Bachya ben Joseph ibn Pakuda

Bachya was a moral philosopher and *payatan* (liturgical poet) who lived in the second half of the eleventh century in Muslim Spain, probably in Saragossa. While he composed his work originally in Arabic, its Hebrew translation by Judah ibn Tibbon is better known to the Jewish community. *Duties of the Heart* profoundly influenced subsequent pietistic writing. In it, Bachya drew on non-Jewish sources, including material from the Muslim mystical tradition and Arabic Neoplatonism.

In *Duties of the Heart* the author divides the obligations of religious persons. Those that are the responsibility of the body require overt action. Those that he considers duties (or responsibilities) of the heart, and thereby do not require overt action, reflect the inner life. He is concerned with the inner life—the spiritual life of the individual—because he believes that it has been significantly neglected by Jewish tradition and by individual Jews. Bachya considers his work to be a counterpart to halachic compendia. With *Duties of the Heart*, Bachya hopes to direct the actions of the religious person.

The writer divides his book into ten sections or gates, each of which is devoted to a particular duty of the heart that the individual must do in order to achieve spiritual perfection. Humility, repentance, and introspection are essential ingredients of the process. Borrowing the model of Muslim mystics, the author takes the individual through ascending stages of one's inner life. In this way, he intends to lead the reader toward the intended spiritual perfection and finally union, or at least communion, with God.

THE SEVENTH GATE:
THE GATE OF REPENTANCE

We have already discussed humility in the previous gate [section]. Since humility is the root of repentance and its essence, it is fitting that we join to it an exposition of the elements of repentance and the ways that it can be accomplished. I would say first that it is manifest both from reason and from what is reflected in the Torah that we are obligated to do *teshuvah* and there is a need for it. Each person fails to fulfill what is imposed upon him/her by the Creator. From the perspective of reason, we find that each person has a distinct nature: the elements of one's physical being and the qualities of one's soul. Yet, the causes of one's behavior are all different. It follows, therefore, that one's deeds will also be different. Some will be noble, while others will be reprehensible. Some will be vile, while others will be righteous. Some will be good, while others will be evil. As a result, human beings need the guidance of Torah tradition. The Torah suggests this when it states that ". . . the imagination of one's heart is evil from youth (Genesis 8:21) and ". . . every imagination of the thoughts of one's heart was continually only evil" (Genesis 6:5). The Book of Job adds, ". . . a wild ass's colt is born a human" (Job 11:12); "Behold, even the moon has no brightness. The stars are not pure in God's sight. How much less is the human who is a worm! And the human child who is a maggot!" (Job 25:5, 6); and "How can one be clean if born of a [human] woman?" (Job 25:4).

Alas, human frailties are so apparent that the Creator has given us [the opportunity to do] repentance so that we may correct our errors and be restored to God's service. In love and compassion, God has strongly urged us to repent. Through God's servants, the Prophets, God promised us that when we went astray, God would accept the many excuses that we might present on our behalf. God grants us immediate favor, even though our rebellion against God's word and our neglect of the covenant is of long duration. This has been made clear by the verse "And when the wicked turns away from wickedness and does what is lawful and right, the individual will live as a result" (Ezekiel 33:19).

There are two kinds of righteous people: those who have been spared sin and iniquity and those who have repented from sin. Most righteous people are those who have repented. Thus, the Psalmist sang, "Happy is the one whose transgression is forgiven, whose sin is pardoned" (Psalm 32:1). The Psalmist then mentions a second group who have never sinned, who stand at a higher level. Every penitent was once righteous, but not every righteous person has been a penitent. The Psalmist mentions the second group, saying, "Happy is the one unto whom Adonai does not count iniquity" (Psalm 32:2). This group is mentioned second because there are very few in any generation, even as the verse says: "If You, Adonai, should count iniquities, O God, who could stand?" (Psalm 130:3). And another verse teaches, "For there is not a righteous person on earth that does [only] good, and does not sin" (Kohelet 7:20). Still another verse says, ". . . for there is no human who does not sin" (1 Kings 8:46). For this reason, the Sages placed the benedictions dealing with repentance and forgiveness among the first petitions of the

Tefillah [the *Amidah* prayer]. Those benefactions end with the formulae "Who delights in repentance" and "Who is abundant in forgiveness."

There are ten matters dealing with the topic of *teshuvah* that we shall discuss:

1. What is repentance?
2. In what way is it divided?
3. What are the human requirements for repentance?
4. How many requirements are there?
5. Do they have any preconditions?
6. What ways can people be brought to repentance?
7. What are the impediments to repentance?
8. Is one who is penitent the equal of one who never sinned?
9. Can one achieve repentance for every sin?
10. Are there any methods that can be employed if one finds penitence difficult?

With God's help we shall complete our discussion of the elements of repentance and their requirements, and thus may we obtain forgiveness for all our transgressions.

CHAPTER ONE

I would say that the essence of *teshuvah* is in the preparation to return to the service of the Creator after having left it by sinning. In so doing, one is restored to what one has lost either by not knowing God or not knowing how God should be served. Since one's Evil Inclination overpowered one's intellect, one disregarded that which was due to God and one's association with wicked companions had enticed one to sin, as the writer of Proverbs said, "My son, if sinners entice you, do not consent" (Proverbs 1:10). He also said, "My son, fear Adonai and the king. And do not meddle with them that are given to change" (Proverbs 24:21).

One leaves the service of Adonai in one of two ways. Either one neglects or avoids doing what Adonai has instructed us to do, or one does what Adonai instructed us not to do. In either case, the intention is to rebel against God. If one has done the former, that is, not done what he should have done, then one's repentance consists of doing diligently the right thing and following closely the aspects of repentance that I will explain in this Gate. If one has done the latter, that is, what he should not have done, then one should guard oneself from doing anything like the forbidden act and diligently endeavor to do the reverse, all the while cleaving closely to the aspects and conditions of repentance that I will explain, with God's help, in this Gate.

An analogy can be drawn from nature. You can become sick because of what you eat. This can be a result of not eating what you should have, that is, what is healthy. Or you ate something that you should not have, that is, something that was harmful. In either case, you lost your health. If you did not eat the right thing, then what you have to do is to eat the right kind of food until you are healthy once again. When you reach that point, you are to eat in moderation. If you ate the wrong kind of food, then you must abstain from anything harmful and eat foods that are totally different from what you have been eating until you are healthy. When you reach that point, then you are to eat in moderation. To maintain your health, you should eat those foods that are midway between those foods that were harmful and those foods that are eaten to offset the harmful foods. The prophet compared sin to harmful food, saying, "But every person will die for his (or her) own iniquity; every person who eats sour grapes, that person's teeth will be set on edge" (Jeremiah 31:30).

CHAPTER TWO

There are three kinds of *teshuvah*. The first kind refers to the person who repents only because he is unable to sin again. He lacks the opportunity. Should he find it, his Evil Inclination would overpower his intellect and he would sin again. Having done it, he would see the shame in what he has done and he would regret it. Alas, such a person repents only with his mouth and not with his heart, with his tongue and not with his acts. Such a person deserves the punishment that God will mete out to him, as the verse has it, "Will you steal, murder, commit adultery, and swear falsely . . . and (then) come and stand before Me? Is this house where My name is called to become a den of robbers in your eyes?" (Jeremiah 7:9, 10, 11).

The second kind of repentance reflects the one who repents with mind and body, resists her Evil Inclination with her intellect, disciplines her soul to fight off her lusts in order to maintain control over herself and not to do what the Creator hates. Even so, her soul continually tries to pull her away from the service of God and to pull her panting after sin. She tries to restrain it [her soul]. Sometimes she wins; sometimes it does. This kind of repentance is not complete. It requires atoning, utter renouncing of transgressions, as the prophet wrote, "By this shall the iniquity of Jacob be expiated. And by this will the guilt of his sin be taken away. When he makes all the stones of the altar into chalkstones that are beaten in pieces, so that the Asherim and the sun-images will rise no more" (Isaiah 27:9).

The third kind of repentance involves the person who has fulfilled every requirement of repentance, whose intellect has mastered his passions, who continually reflects upon the soul, reveres the Creator, who is diffident in God's presence, and who has considered fully how great was his sin and his guilt. Such a person knows the greatness of the One against whom he had rebelled and whose word he transgressed. Continually reflecting upon his transgressions, he regrets them and asks forgiveness for them every day, even to the end of his life. This is the kind of repentance that makes one worthy of being saved by the Creator.

CHAPTER THREE

What must one do to start the process of repentance? I would say that there are seven things of which the penitent should be aware. First, one should be fully aware of how awful was the deed done. If that is not clear to the person or if there is any doubt about it or if what was done was not done on purpose but rather was done inadvertently, then there can be neither regret nor the seeking of forgiveness [and hence no repentance]. Such awareness is what the Psalmist meant when he said, "For I know my transgressions; and my sin is ever before me" (Psalm 51:5).

Second, one should know with certainty that what was done was evil and reprehensible. If that is not clear, one will neither evince regret for having done it nor accept what needs to be done to repent of it. The act will be viewed merely as a mistake and one will find excuses for having done it. Thus the Psalmist wrote, "Who can discern errors?" (Psalm 19:13).

Third, one must know with certainty that one will have to pay for what has been done. Otherwise, one will feel no need to regret having done it. Once it is clear that one will indeed suffer as a result of it, then one will regret the act and seek forgiveness for it. Thus Jeremiah wrote, ". . . after that I was turned,

I repented . . . after I was instructed . . . I was ashamed, yea confounded" (Jeremiah 31:19). The Psalmist added, "My flesh shudders in fear of You. And I am afraid of Your judgment" (Psalm 119:120).

Fourth, one should know that a record of one's transgressions is being kept, a record in which nothing is overlooked, forgotten, or omitted, even as the Torah states, "Is not this laid up in store with Me, sealed up in My treasuries?" (Deuteronomy 32:34). Another verse adds, "You seal up the hand of every human" (Job 37:7). Were one to think just because there was a delay in being punished, no notice was taken and no record was kept of one's sin, and therefore, one need not regret or seek forgiveness for having sinned, then one should reflect on the verse "Because sentence against an evil work is not executed speedily, therefore the heart of humans is fully set in them to do evil" (Ecclesiastes 8:11).

Fifth, one should truly know that repentance brings healing to one's character and is the way of remedying one's evil deeds and reprehensible acts. By it, one turns from error and retrieves what one has lost. Were this notion not clear to the would-be penitent, that person would despair of obtaining God's mercy and atonement. He would not seek forgiveness for what he has done in the past, even as the verse has it, "Thus you speak, saying: Our transgressions and our sins are upon us, and we pine away in them; how then can we live?" (Ezekiel 33:10). The prophet brought God's reply: "As I live, says Adonai, *Elohim*, I have no pleasure in the death of the wicked, only for the wicked to turn from that (wicked) way and live" (Ezekiel 33:11).

Sixth, one must think deeply about all the good things that the Creator has already given to us and, instead of being grateful, how one has rebelled. One should weigh the punishments of sin against its delights and the enjoyment of the reward of righteousness against its difficulties in this world and the next, just as the Sages said: "Compute the loss incurred in doing a *mitzvah* against its gain [in the Life to Come] and the gain involved in a transgression against its loss" (*Pirkei Avot* 2:1).

Seventh, one who would repent must expend all one's strength in order to avoid doing the wicked deed. The one to which one had become accustomed again must resolve to remove it from heart and mind, as the prophet taught, "Rend your heart and not your garments" (Joel 2:13).

When these seven notions are clearly understood by the sinner, then repentance from sin becomes possible.

CHAPTER FOUR

There are four elements of true repentance. The first is remorse. One should feel remorse for sins committed. Second, one should turn away and forsake those sins. Third, one should confess and ask forgiveness for them. Fourth, with every fiber of one's being, one should pledge never to do them again.

Remorse indicates that the deed done was reprehensible in one's sight, as it says, "The one who knows will repent and regret and leave a blessing" (Joel 2:14). The one who continues on with sin is described thus: "No person repents of wickedness" (Jeremiah 8:6). It is our experience that the remorse manifested by the sinner to the one offended is the cause of the forgiveness being offered to the sinner.

Turning from sin is a clear indication of one's belief in reward and punishment, as the prophet said, "Let the wicked forsake the way, and the person of iniquity evil thoughts; Let that person return to Adonai and God will be compassionate. And to our God, for God will abundantly pardon" (Isaiah 55:7). The prophet said about the one who continued on with sinning, "I was angry because of the iniquity of his covetousness and smote him. I was angry so I hid myself. And he went on forwardly in the way of his heart" (Isaiah 55:17). It is a common human experience that one who has stopped harming another and who has expressed regret will gain forgiveness and will have the transgression forgotten.

The seeking of forgiveness is an indication of the sinner's humility and self-abasement before God. The sinner's confession is the cause of forgiveness, as the verse teaches, ". . . whoever confesses and forsakes them [sins] shall receive mercy" (Proverbs 25:13). Of the one who will not confess, Scripture says, "Behold, I will enter into judgment with you, because you say: 'I have not sinned'" (Jeremiah 2:35). Among people, we often see that if one person sins against another and then humbly confesses that sin and the harm it caused and asks for forgiveness, the other, seeing the sinner's remorse, will speedily forgive, overlook the sin, and harbor no grudge.

Pledging not to sin again shows that the sinner has in no way changed one's understanding of the heinous quality of the act or the seriousness of the sin, even as the verse teaches, "If I have done iniquity, I will do it no more" (Job 34:32). This notion is supported by yet another verse, "Ashur shall not save us. . . . Neither will we call any more the work of our hands our gods" (Hosea 14:4). Were one to act otherwise [and not pledge to refrain from sinning], then these words would apply: "Can an Ethopian change his skin, or the leopard his spots?" (Jeremiah 13:23). It is a common experience that when a sinner pledges not to sin again, manifests regret, shows a determination not to sin again, and confesses, then that person has achieved all the requisite conditions for forgiveness, for the removal of one's guilt, and for the remission of one's punishment.

When these four elements of repentance are present along with their specifications as we shall presently explain them, then the Creator will bring atonement for the penitent's sin and will overlook the transgression. However, if the transgression is under the rubric ". . . Adonai will not hold that person guiltless" (Exodus 20:7), that is, false swearing or adultery, then the Creator will lighten the punishment in this world and will confer a benefit in the next world. Such a person will be included in the category of the righteous, as the verse has it, "And a redeemer shall come to Zion, and to those who turn from transgressions in Judah, says Adonai" (Isaiah 59:20). Two more verses teach [and convey this message of hope]: "If you will return, O Israel, says Adonai, Yea return to Me" (Jeremiah 4:1) and "[Therefore, thus says Adonai] If you return, and I bring you back, you will stand before Me" (Isaiah 15:19).

CHAPTER FIVE

Since the aspects of repentance are very numerous, I will mention only twenty of them. These are the five aspects of the four elements mentioned [in chapter four]. These aspects round out those elements.

The five aspects of remorse are: (a) the sinner should fear that divine punishment is about to befall him because of the sins that he has already committed. Such fear will intensify his remorse, as the verse has it, "Give glory to Adonai your God, before it grows dark . . . and while you look for the light, God turns it into the shadow of death" (Jeremiah 13:16).

(b) Her sin should cause her heart to be broken and should bring about her contrition before God, as taught by the verse "If My people, upon whom My name is called, will humble themselves, and pray, and seek My face, and turn from their evil ways; then I will hear from heaven, and will forgive their sin" (2 Chronicles 7:14).

(c) The would-be penitent should show his remorse in his speech, in his eating, and in everything that he does. Therefore, he should change how he dresses and take off any jewelry. Thus he would fulfill the verses "For this gird you with sackcloth, lament and wail" (Jeremiah 4:8) and "Let them be covered with sackcloth, both human and beast" (Jonah 3:8).

(d) Remorse for the sin that has been committed should be manifested by weeping, by shrieking, and by mourning in line with the verses "My eyes run down with rivers of water, because they do not observe Your law" (Psalm 119:136) and "Let the priests, the ministers of Adonai, weep between the porch and the altar" (Joel 2:13).

(e) Because the sinner failed to fulfill her duty to her Creator, she should now rebuke herself and feel deep shame, even as verse states, "And rend your heart, not your garments" (Joel 2:13).

There are five aspects in turning away from sin: (a) one must turn away from everything that the Creator has prohibited, as one verse teaches, "Hate evil and love good" (Amos 5:15) and another verse teaches, "Happy is the person who keeps his hand from doing any evil" (Isaiah 56:2) and still another teaches, "Let the wicked forsake her way" (Isaiah 55:7).

(b) One must keep away from anything that, although permitted, might bring the former sinner to do what is forbidden. Thus, the penitent should keep far from anything about which doubt exists as to its permissibility. Certain pietists of old would keep far from seventy things permitted lest they touch one thing forbidden. This follows the rule of *Pirkei Avot*, "Make a fence around the law" (*Pirkei Avot* 1:1).

(c) While one has both the capacity and the opportunity to commit transgressions, they should be avoided because of the fear of divine punishment, as the verse states, "My flesh shudders in fear of You; And I am afraid of Your judgments" (Psalm 119:120).

(d) Forsaking of sin should be due to shame in the presence of God, not shame in the presence of other human beings or fear of them or the expectation of some gain from them. One should not be like those described in the verses "And Adonai said, For as much as this people draw near, and with their mouth and their lips do honor Me, but they have removed their heart from Me, and their fear of Me is a commandment of humans learned by rote" (Isaiah 29:13) and "And Jehoash did what was right in the eyes of Adonai all his days during which Jehoida the priest instructed him" (2 Kings 12:3).

(e) Absolute and unconditional should be the forsaking of sin. Never again should the repentant sinner consider doing the particular sin. Rather one should say to oneself and to others what Elihu said: "If I have done iniquity, I will do it no more" (Job 34:32).

There are five aspects of asking forgiveness: (a) fully realizing how horrendous were one's sins, the penitent must confess them, even as the verse teaches, "For our transgressions are multiplied before You, and our sins testify against us" (Isaiah 59:12).

(b) The penitent should always remember one's sins and place them before oneself, to fulfill the verse "For I know my transgressions; and my sin is ever before me" (Psalm 51:5).

(c) Fasting by day, the penitent should pray by night when the mind is free from the matter of this world, as the verse would have it, "Arise, cry out in the night" (Lamentations 2:19). In the future, with God's help, I will discuss the high value of night prayer.

(d) At all times, the penitent should beseech God and implore God for forgiveness, the atonement of sin, and for the acceptance of repentance, as the verses teach, "I acknowledged my sin to You, and my iniquity I have not hid" (Psalm 32:5) and "For this let everyone who is godly pray to you in a time when You may be found" (Psalm 32:6).

(e) With every fiber of one's being the penitent should warn others against similar transgressions, admonish them with the punishment for such sins, and remind them of repentance, as one verse teaches, "One who knows that one has sinned will repent and God will change God's [own] mind" (Jonah 3:5), and another says, "Then I will teach transgressors Your ways" (Psalm 51:15).

There are five aspects of pledging never to do those sins that are proscribed by the Creator: (a) the penitent should weigh the faint, fleeting, and mottled pleasure of the sin against the pure, permanent, and bright bliss of the ultimate reward [for obedience to the Torah]. He should also weigh the fleeting, faint and impermanent discomfort of doing a *mitzvah* against eternal and constant pain of the ultimate punishment [for disobedience to the Torah]. Of that ultimate bliss, the prophet spoke, saying, "And when you see this, your heart shall rejoice" (Isaiah 66:14). Of that ultimate pain, the prophet spoke, saying, "And they shall go forth, and look upon the carcasses of the people who have rebelled against Me; For their worm will not die, neither will their fire be quenched" (Isaiah 66:24). It is further said, "For behold, the day comes, it burns like a furnace; and all the proud, and all those who do wickedness, will be stubble. . . . But to you who revere My name shall the sun of righteousness arise with healing in its wings" (Malachi 3:19, 20). When the one who has sinned reflects on this, that person will determine never to sin again.

(b) One should consider the day of one's death. One will have to face the Creator. God may be angry because one did not do what one should have done. The verse says, "But who may abide the day of his coming?" (Malachi 3:2). Reflecting on this, one will fear punishment and resolve never to do again anything that might arouse God's wrath.

(c) One should think about those past days when one had turned away from God and paid no attention to God's service even though one had been provided with God's beneficence. It is as the prophet said: "For, of old time I have broken Your yoke and broken Your bands; Your say, I will not pass" (Jeremiah 2:20). "I will not pass" means "I will not take on Your service," as in the verse ". . . that You should enter [lit. "pass"] into the covenant" (Deuteronomy 29:11).

(d) One should return anything stolen, refrain from any other transgressions, and refrain from harming any creature, even as the prophet wrote, ". . . the wicked [shall] restore the pledge, [and] give back what was taken by the robbery" (Ezekiel 33:15). Another verse teaches, "If iniquity is in Your hand, put it far away. . . . Surely then you will lift up your face without spot" (Job 11:14, 15).

(e) Keeping in mind the greatness of the Creator against whose word one has rebelled, from whose service and from the Torah tradition one had departed, one should rebuke oneself and be ashamed; for this is as the verse says, "Do you thus require Adonai?" (Deuteronomy 32:6). Another verse teaches, "'Do you not fear Me?' says Adonai" (Jeremiah 5:22). Here now are all the aspects of repentance concluded.

❊ 5 ❊

Shaarai Teshuvah
(Gates of Repentance)

Jonah ben Abraham Gerundi

Gerundi was a Spanish rabbi and moralist who studied in French *yeshivot*. He was born in Gerona and lived during the first half of the thirteenth century. He spent much of his adult life in Barcelona before establishing a *yeshivah* in Toledo — originally en route to *Eretz Yisrael*. Gerundi joined his teacher Solomon ben Abraham of Montpelier in his campaign against Moses Maimonides' *Guide for the Perplexed*.

When in 1240 wagon loads of Talmud volumes were burned in Paris, Gerundi took the burning as a sign of divine displeasure for his having joined the anti-Maimonist camp. It is said that he wrote *The Gates of Repentance* as a sign of remorse. He also made a pilgrimage to Tiberias to pray at Maimonides' grave. Gerundi is famous for his ethical books in which he reacts to the failure of society to respond to the *mitzvot*.

Shaarai Teshuvah is based on halachic and popular aggadic sources rather than mysticism. Its emphasis is on social justice through social action.

THE FIRST GATE

1. Repentance is one of the good things that the Holy One has provided for human creatures that they might rise up from the pit of their acts, escape the snare of their sins, save themselves from destruction, and avert divine anger. Because humankind is good and upright, You have warned them to turn to You even though they have sinned against You, for You know the inclination of their heart, as Scripture says, "Good and upright is Adonai; therefore You instruct sinners in the way" (Psalm 25:8). Were they to sin constantly and rebel continually against You, even then You would not close the gates of repentance, as the verse attests, "Turn unto God against whom you have deeply rebelled, O Children of Israel" (Isaiah 31:6) and as another verse says, "Return, you backsliding children, I will heal your backsliding" (Jeremiah 2:2).

In many places in the Torah we are charged to move to repentance. Repentance is efficacious even if it comes about because of the suffering of the sinner; how much the more so if it [repentance] came about because of the sinner's reverence for and love of God. It is as the verse teaches: "In your distress, when all these things have overwhelmed you, in the end of days, return to Adonai your God and hearken to God's voice" (Deuteronomy 4:30). It is explained in the Torah that God will help those who repent even when it is beyond their own capacity, for You will nurture within them a pure spirit that will apprehend the level of Your love, as it says, "You shall return to Adonai your God, and hearken to God's voice according to all that I instruct you today, you and your children, with all your heart, and with all your soul . . ." (Deuteronomy 30:2). In a similar manner, it is taught, "And Adonai your God will circumcise your heart and the heart of your seed . . ." (Deuteronomy 30:6) to apprehend Your love. [Just as with the Torah, so] the words of the Prophets and the Writings are filled with references to repentance. These books contain the principles of repentance, as will be explained.

2. One should know that the penalty for sin is increased daily for the one who has not yet repented. Through [divine] wrath, one's evil will increase. The Sages commented on such a matter, saying, "It is compared to a group of thieves who were imprisoned by the king. All but one dug their way out and escaped. When the jailor came to that one, the jailor began beating the remaining prisoner with a rod and saying, 'Stupid fool, you had a way out, why didn't you escape?'" (*Kohelet Rabbah* 7:32).

3. Only the ignorant delay repenting. Even when they are about to fall asleep, they don't consider [what they have done that day]. Since they lack knowledge and understanding, they are not able to save themselves [by repentance]. Some are so far from God that they don't believe their sin will be punished. [Hence they don't repent.] The Sages said, "If you see a scholar transgress at night, be assured that by morning that scholar will repent" (Babylonian Talmud, *Berachot* 19a).

4. There is something else to think about when reflecting on the great evil of delaying repentance: if someone repents, and laments [what one has done] and feels such anguish [for one's sins] that one weeps, when one's Evil Inclination tempts one a second time to sin, one will be able to conquer it. The individual will remember how bitter was remorse and hence will be unwilling to taste it again. The Psalmist alluded to such a situation, saying, "Tremble and do not sin" (Psalm 4:5), which means, "Tremble and be sorry for what you have done, so that you don't sin again." That first sin is suggested by the prior verse, "... You seek after falsehood" (Psalm 4:3).

The sense of "tremble" as indicating sorrow for what has happened or what is [still] happening is indicated by the verses "Do not tremble on the way" (Genesis 45:24) and "I tremble where I stand" (Habakkuk 3:16). Thus if one delays repentance, when one is faced with the same sin, one will again fall into its trap. One's accumulated guilt will now be so great that one's wickedness will come to God's attention.

At first, one might not have thought that the *Yetzer Hara* (Evil Inclination) would have sudden mastery over oneself. Now one sees how weak one is and how strong is the Evil Inclination. It is far stronger than the individual. One should have known how exposed one is! One needs to understand how to intensify the fear of God in one's soul so that that fear will keep oneself from the lure of the *Yetzer Hara* (Evil Inclination). About this Solomon said, "As a dog that returns to its own vomit, so is a fool who repeats one's folly" (Proverbs 26:11). That means that although a dog might detest things, spewing them up makes them even more detestable; yet the dog will eat them again. In a like manner is the fool who does something reprehensible, but doing it again makes it even more reprehensible.

5. Indeed, if someone sins again, it makes one's repentance more difficult. Sinning again makes it seem as if the [particular] sin were [somehow] permitted. Thus, one's sin is even greater, even as Jeremiah said, "Behold, you have spoken but have done evil things and [although] you were able" (Jeremiah 3:5). [The phrase] "you were able" means that those evil acts were done by you as if they were permitted and within your power. This meaning is indicated by the Aramaic translation of the verse "You are not able to eat in your gates" (Deuteronomy 12:17). The Sages said, if anyone sins and then sins again, that [forbidden activity] becomes permitted (Babylonian Talmud, *Kiddushin* 40a). Furthermore, they said that if any person sins and then

sins again and then thinks of sinning once more but somehow is prevented from doing it, the thought will count as the act. Concerning this, Jeremiah said, "Behold, I will bring evil upon this people, even the fruit of their thoughts" (Jeremiah 6:19).

7. You should know too that if anyone sins ten times, no matter how careful one may be not to commit other transgressions, one will be regarded as if one did commit them. Thus, the Sages said that if a Nazirite were told not to drink wine and he drank it and then was told again and [yet] drank it again, he would be whipped for each instance as if he had eaten [the meat] of an animal that had died [and hence was ritually unfit] or that was [ritually] impure or had eaten suet or blood (Babylonian Talmud, *Makkot* 21a).

8. Alas, the transgressions of this generation have so increased that there are many people who take it upon themselves to be wary of certain transgressions but, in fact, are not. They always act as if the prohibited behaviors were permitted. It would be bad enough, a terrible sickness of the soul, were this only one transgression. How much the worse is it when it is an accumulation of many prohibitions! Among them are many severe matters such as false swearing, using the Divine Name to curse someone else or oneself, mentioning God's name for no reason or mentioning it in an impure place or with dirty hands, avoiding helping the poor, slander, causeless hatred, arrogance, making people anxious, or looking lewdly [at another]. The worst of all [because it leads to them all] is the neglect of the study of Torah. Though there are many such sins, we have set down a few, so that this generation will remember and be wary of them. Therefore, it is fitting that a penitent make a record of all the things that have caused the individual to stumble and also of all those *mitzvot* that one has not properly fulfilled so that one might read that record each and every day.

9. As there are different levels in approaching God, so there are different levels of *teshuvah* (repentance). Though every act of repentance brings with it forgiveness, one does not become a whole person, nor are one's sins expunged, unless one purifies one's mind and prepares one's spirit, as shall be explained. Thus Scripture teaches, "Happy is the person for whom Adonai does not count iniquity, and in whose spirit there is no guile" (Psalm 32:2). A little washing may remove the surface dirt of a soiled garment; only a thorough washing will render it clean. [Therefore] Scripture teaches, "Wash me thoroughly from my transgression" (Psalm 51:4). One is cleansed from transgression as one's heart [and mind] is cleansed, as it is said, "O Jerusalem, wash your heart from wickedness so that you may be saved" (Jeremiah 4:14). Commenting on the verse "Happy is the person who fears Adonai" (Psalm 112:1), the Sages understood the word "person" to suggest that the best repentance was the mastery of Evil Inclination in one's youth while in full possession of one's faculties (Babylonian Talmud, *Avodah Zarah* 19a). All repentance, at any time, is beneficial, as it is said: "You turn humans to contrition and say: 'Return, you human beings'" (Psalm 90:3). The Sages understood this [verse] to mean that one may return even until the very end of life (Jerusalem Talmud, *Chagigah* 2:1).

THE PRINCIPLES OF REPENTANCE

10. The First Principle: Remorse. One should fully understand that leaving God is evil and bitter. One should keep in mind that there is punishment, vengeance, and recompense for sin, even as the Torah teaches, "Vengeance and recompense is Mine" (Deuteronomy 32:35). As Job stated, "Be afraid of the sword; wrath brings the punishments of the sword" (Job 19:29).

The would-be penitent should regret one's evil acts and ask oneself: What have I done? Why was not the fear of God present in my mind? Why did I not fear the reproaches of guilt and the harsh judgments? Great will be the pains of the wicked. Did I have concern for my body? Did I not care that for a momentary pleasure, I would destroy it? I am like one who would steal and rob and then eat until I am full, knowing that after eating and drinking, I would be condemned by a judge to have my teeth smashed with gravel. Proverbs puts it this way: "Bread of falsehood is sweet to a person, but afterwards one's mouth will be filled with gravel" (Proverbs 20:17). [The penitent will continue] worse yet: How cruel have I been to my precious soul, which has been contaminated by my *Yetzer Hara* (Evil Inclination). What will my soul gain if it became evil in the eyes of its Master? Why did I trade the world that will always be for this world that will pass away? Now what am I like? Like an animal! I have run after my Evil Inclination like a horse. I have been like a dumb mule. I have wandered from the path of [good] sense. The Creator breathed into my nostrils the breath of life, the wisdom of mind, the ability of intellect to recognize God and fear God to rule over the body and every act that proceeds from it in the same manner as the soul has domination over all other nonrational animals. What is precious in God's eyes is honored. I was created for that purpose. Yet the reverse has happened for me. For what purpose then do I live? Thus Scripture teaches, "The individual who strays out of the way of understanding shall rest in the congregation of the shades" (Proverbs 21:16). Indeed, I have not acted even at the level of animals, for "The ox knows his owner and the ass her master's crib" (Isaiah 1:2). But I did not know. I did not reflect. I sent forth my soul free from its Master. Tasting my honey, I forgot what would be my end. I robbed. I stole. I stepped on the poor. I did not remember that

when I die, all that will remain with my soul will be my body
and the earth [in which I lie]. What I have just explained reflects what Jeremiah spoke: "No person can repent from wickedness by [simply] saying: 'What have I done?'" (Jeremiah 8:6).

11. The Second Principle: Forsaking sin. To forsake one's
evil ways, one must resolve wholeheartedly never to return to
them again. If one has acted wickedly, one should never again
act that way, so Scripture says, "Turn, turn from your evil ways"
(Ezekiel 33:11). Another verse teaches, "Let the wicked forsake
his [or her] evil way" (Isaiah 55:7). Know that if someone sinned
by chance, simply overwhelmed by desire, the Evil Inclination
taking control before one's thoughts and senses were able to
resist, so that one could not reproach and dry up the sea of lust,
entrapped by desire and caught in its coils, and this happened
all of a sudden, while confused by Evil Inclination, not that this
was something planned or something that one thought of doing
again, then one's *teshuvah* (repentance) begins with regret and
feeling sorry in one's heart for one's sin. One should feel that
one's soul has been afflicted, that one's taste is bitter as gall. Next,
one should intensify reverence for God in one's soul, mindful
of God at all times. One's heart should be secure and feel assurance in God. Now should the Evil Inclination beset the individual as once it did and if lust beguile the individual as it had,
then one's heart will not be seduced. One will not pursue an
evil path. Scripture says, "But the one who confesses and forsakes them will receive mercy" (Proverbs 28:13). Note first, "But
the one who confesses," which means regret and confession, and
then "and forsakes them." If, however, one becomes fixed in the
wrong path, so that one keeps on pursuing the same sin and
repeating the same folly, constantly moving away from what one
should do, such a person loves doing evil. That person has set a
stumbling block before oneself. Lust and following the Evil

Inclination have become one's desire and purpose. Such a person will not be kept from doing whatever one wishes. For that person, repentance will begin in changing one's ways and one's thoughts. One has to resolve not to sin again. Then one must regret one's vile deeds and turn to God, even as it is taught, "Let the wicked forsake the [evil] way, and the one of iniquity one's [evil] thoughts. Let that person return to Adonai. And God will have compassion on that person" (Isaiah 55:7).

There is a story told of a person who wanted to ritually cleanse oneself by immersion while holding on to a contaminating reptile. To become pure, however, the person would have to let go of the reptile and then immerse oneself. Holding on to the reptile, immersion would have no effect. One would remain impure. So it is with sin and repentance. Giving up the thought of sin is letting go of the contaminating reptile; regret for having sinned, confession, and prayer are the immersion. If pain and suffering befall a wicked person who up to that moment had constantly plotted doing evil [and is now moved to repentance], let that person first accept that pain and suffering as instructive chastisement. Then let that person turn away from evil thoughts and cease evil deeds. To straighten the furrow that a calf plows, one may strike it with a goad. Likewise, to have one leave the path of death and move to the proper path, chastisement must be accepted, as it is said, "I have surely heard Ephraim bemoaning himself: 'Thou hast chastised me and I was chastised, as a calf untrained'" (Jeremiah 31:19). The meaning of these verses is, "After you chastised me, then I was chastised and I turned from my evil way. I then repented and regretted my past transgressions." These verses explain what has been discussed.

12. The Third Principle: Sorrow. Great should be the pentinent's sorrow and deep should be the anguish as one thinks

of how evil has been one's rebellion against one's Creator. One's mind should be whirling with such thoughts and one should sigh bitterly. Even so, such thought and such regret might not be enough to make recompense for them. To lose a *dinar* or an *issar* is annoying. To lose all one's wealth, to become poor, is to be reduced to mourning, to groaning, and to finding every experience bitter. To lose one's health, to suffer grievous pain, is to grieve continually and to spend one's day in sorrow. How much more should one grieve and groan for having rebelled against God? How could one have become so corrupt? How could one have become so vile? How could one have forgotten the Creator, the One who formed the individual out of nothing? You, whose steadfast love, whose hand leads the individual at all times, who at every moment guards every soul, have been forgotten! What motivated that [evil] person to provoke God? What so blinded the sinner so as to not use one's mind? That person who now would use one's mind, whose eyes are now opened, will fix these matters in the heart, so that they may enter the deepest recesses of one's being.

13. As are the levels of bitter self-reproach and sorrow for sin, so are the levels of repentance. Repentance should follow from the purity of the soul and the lucidity of the intellect. If one's intellect is discerning and if one's eyes are open, then one's thoughts relating to one's sin should be as numerous as the sins for which one would repent. Scripture says, "For I will not contend forever, neither will I be always wroth. For the spirit that wraps itself is from Me, and the souls which I have made" (Isaiah 57:16). The meaning of the verse is, "When the spirit that comes from Me, that is, from on high, wraps itself in grief, and the souls that I have made wrap themselves in grief, then I will not always contend or always be angry. How can I not be gracious and merciful to the precious soul that comes from Me and the souls

that I have made?" Thus, guilt for sin is made less like the work of groaning, for sin is made more. Grief follows from the purity of the higher soul. Guilt is more assuaged by grief than it is assuaged by the suffering of the body or its pain. To take an example: a king would more likely be kindly disposed and would act in a gracious manner to those born and educated in his household, those related to him, who were the honored princes of the land, than he would be to those who were at a distance and of a lesser status. The phrase "and the souls that I have made" suggests the closeness of the human soul to the divine, even though the human body and everything else [in the world] is the work of God's hands [so to speak]. There is a similar notion taught in the verse "And the tablets were the work of God" (Exodus 32:16). The Sages taught, "There are three partners in the creation of the human being: one's father, one's mother, and the Holy Blessed One" (Babylonian Talmud, *Niddah* 31a). Father and mother are not partners in the formation of the soul, hence the verse "and the souls which I have made." That statement relates to "the spirit that proceeds from Me," as we have interpreted the passage.

14. David sang, "Adonai, all that I desire is before You. And my sighing is not hid from You" (Psalm 38:10). That verse means, "You know that my only desire is to serve You. You know that I do not sigh for worldly or vain things. I sigh for my sins and for my inability to serve You." There is a marvelous interpretation of the verse by one who was imploring God's favor: "My sighing" refers to my fear of You. Therefore, keep such sighs far from me. "My worry" refers to my inability to serve You. Keep such worries far from me!

15. The Fourth Principle: Actual suffering. It is as the prophet says, "'Yet even now,' says Adonai, 'Turn to Me with all your heart, with fasting and with weeping, and with lamen-

tation'" (Joel 2:12). Interpreting the verse ". . . that you do not go about after your heart and your eyes, after which you used to go astray" (Numbers 15:39), the Sages said, "The heart and the eyes are both procurers of sin" (Jerusalem Talmud, *Berachot* 1:4). These procurers can be the means of atonement. To the degree that they led astray, they may lead to repentance. When sinners break their hearts with bitter lamenting, they fulfill the meaning of the verses "For the spirit that wraps itself is from Me" (Isaiah 57:16) and "A broken and contrite heart, O God, You will not despise" (Psalm 51:19). Unclean vessels are broken and thus purified from their contamination, as the Torah teaches, ". . . whether oven, or range for pots, it shall be broken into pieces" (Leviticus 11:35), [likewise is a broken heart purified]. Tears atone for the sins brought on by the eyes, as it is said, "My eyes run down with rivers of water, because they do not observe Your law" (Psalm 119:136). Note that the text did not say "because I did not observe" but rather "because they [my eyes] did not observe Your law." They [my eyes] caused me to sin; therefore, I have shed "rivers of water."

16. The Fifth Principle: Worry. The would-be penitent should worry about and fear the results of transgressions. There are transgressions for which repentance merely makes atonement possible but suffering makes it actual. Thus the Psalmist said, "For I do declare my iniquity; I am full of worry because of my sin" (Psalm 38:19). One grieves about the past; one worries about the future. One must also worry whether one has repented enough, suffered enough, has felt the bitterness [of remorse] enough, whether one has fasted enough, and whether one has wept enough. No matter how much one has suffered and wept, one should fear and tremble that one has not sufficiently paid for one's sins. Reflecting that for each human being the service of God is exceedingly important while rebellion

against God is infinitely evil, one should consider that however one may increase one's acts of service or one's ways of repentance, they are insignificant [compared to the one] and minute [compared to the other]. Solomon wrote, "A wise person fears and [therefore] departs from evil" (Proverbs 14:16). The meaning of the verse is that the wise person still fears that one has not met one's obligations and that one has not been sufficiently careful to do what one should, although one has turned from evil with all of one's powers. There is another verse, "Than one who is perverse in one's ways, though one be rich" (Proverbs 28:6), that is taken to mean "although one is rich." The Sages interpreted the verse above, "A wise person fears and [therefore] departs from sin" (Proverbs 14:16), as "A wise person departs from sin and fears" (*Tanchuma Lech Lecha* 15). Their interpretation is correct, as is suggested by the continuation of the verse, "But the fool behaves overbearingly and is confident" (Proverbs 14:16). The nature of a fool is the reverse of the nature of a wise person. The fool may become angry but is sure that neither sin nor harm will befall him [or her], even though angry people are prone to sins and open to harm, as it is taught in Proverbs: "And a wrathful person abounds in transgression" (Proverbs 29:22) and "Like a city broken down and without a wall, such is the one whose spirit is without restraint" (Proverbs 25:28).

17. The would-be penitent must constantly worry that one's Evil Inclination may yet conquer the self, even as the Sages said, "Don't trust yourself until the day of your death" (*Pirkei Avot* 2:4). How much more does this apply to one whose Evil Inclination has conquered the self in the past, lying in wait at every moment. How careful one must be to daily intensify one's reverence for God so that it may be one's fortress when the Evil Inclination attacks the self in the future.

18. When Solomon spoke of repentance, he dealt with the

notion of worry. He said, "When the righteous exult, there is great glory, but when the wicked rise, people must be sought for" (Proverbs 28:12). The meaning of this statement is that righteous people glorify and honor others for every good quality that they have; wicked people seek out every blemish and every fault that others may have in order to bring them low, even if such persons have given up their sins and become penitents. Solomon continued, "The one who covers transgressions will not prosper, but the one who confesses and forsakes them shall obtain mercy" (Proverbs 28:13). The penitent need not reveal one's sins to other people, as may be deduced from the verse "but when the wicked rise, people must be sought for" (Proverbs 28:12). Still one must confess one's sins, as it is said, "I acknowledged my sin to You, and my iniquity I have not hid" (Psalm 32:5). Another verse states, "Behold, I will enter in judgment with you, because you say: 'I have not sinned'" (Jeremiah 2:35). The Sages have interpreted "The one who covers one's sins will not prosper" as referring to one who has covered over sins committed against another human being (Babylonian Talmud, *Yoma* 86b). Such sins can gain no atonement until the one who has harmed the other by stealing, robbing, or filching has returned what was taken. Or the one who has harmed the other by offense, insult, or slander has asked forgiveness for doing so. The verse may also be applied to those sins against God of which people have become aware. If one transgresses publicly and desecrates the name of God, in order to sanctify the name of God, that person must lament and mourn publicly, as it is written, "Surely after that I was turned, I repented, and after that I was instructed. I smote upon my thigh" (Jeremiah 31:19). "I repented" refers to regret and suffering. As we have explained, the very essence of repentance is bitterness of heart [of the penitent caused by regret and suffering]. "And after that I was instructed, I smote upon my thigh" means after what I did became public knowledge, I mourned for my sins by public acts, as indicated by "Smite therefore upon your thigh" (Ezekiel 21:17) and "One comes before people, and says: 'I have sinned, and perverted what was right'" (Job 33:27).

19. "But whoever confesses and forsakes them [one's sins] will obtain mercy" (Proverbs 28:13). The verse indicates that there are three elements in repentance: regret, confession, and the forsaking of the sin. Regret is included in confession; to confess is to regret. Still, repentance requires all three elements. Were one to regret and confess but not forsake one's sin, one would be like the one who holding a contaminating reptile went into the ritual bath. Such immersion would not avail! Only one who confesses and forsakes sin can obtain mercy, for then the person is a true penitent. We have explained, however, that there are various levels of repentance.

20. The passage in Proverbs continued, "Happy is the person that always fears; but one that hardens one's heart will fall into evil" (Proverbs 28:14). Because there are various levels of repentance, the penitent should always fear that even though one has confessed and foresworn doing further wrong, one may not have done enough to fully repent. Every day one must exert oneself fully to proceed along the levels [of *teshuvah*]. One need also fear the renewal of one's Evil Inclination. Against that, one must guard oneself at all times. One should constantly intensify the fear of God within one's soul and continually pray that God help the individual to attain repentance and to save the person from one's inclination. The part of the verse "but one that hardens one's heart will fall to evil" refers to the would-be penitent who says to oneself, "I have already fulfilled what repentance requires." Such a person will not constantly strive to reach new levels of repentance, nor to increase the level of rev-

erence within the self. That person will be punished for this. [Such behavior indicates that] one is arrogant and does not understand one's inner faults. One does not recognize how great is one's obligation to correct one's ways in every possible manner before God. Such a heedless person will fall under the control of one's Evil Inclination, which is always lurking.

21. The Sixth Principle: Shame. Jeremiah said, "I was ashamed, yea, even confounded, because I did not bear the reproach of my youth" (Jeremiah 31:19). One who might sin would be very ashamed to transgress in the presence of others. One would be abashed if others had a full awareness of the sins that one had committed. Yet how is it that one is not ashamed in the presence of God? It can only be if God is not present in one's thoughts! Thus one may be ashamed of those who are created and not ashamed of the Creator! The Sages relate that when Rabban Yochanan ben Zakkai was about to die, he told his disciples who asked for his blessing, "May the fear of heaven be to you as the fear of flesh and blood." Astounded, his students asked, "Only that far?" He answered, "Would that you did that! Know that a person transgresses in secret saying, 'May no one see me!'" (Babylonian Talmud, *Berachot* 28b).

22. The worst shame that one can experience is to be confounded by the realization that one has sinned before God. Being so confounded, one feels a shame marked by a change in one's appearance, even as the Psalmist said, "Confusion has covered my face" (Psalm 69:8). This kind of confusion is always mentioned after shame because it is so intense, as in "Be ashamed and confounded in your ways, O house of Israel" (Ezekiel 36:32) and in "I was ashamed, yea, even confounded" (Jeremiah 31:19). When the [now penitent] sinner sees that God does not treat her according to her sins nor punish her according to her transgression, but rather with forbearance forgives

them, she will become even more ashamed. Had she been for-given by an earthly ruler whom she had betrayed, would she not feel shame in that king's presence? [How much the more for the Divine Sovereign], as Ezekiel wrote, "So you may remem-ber, and be confounded, and never open your mouth anymore, because of your shame; when I have forgiven you all that you have done; says Adonai, God" (Ezekiel 16:63). The Sages said, "All transgressions are forgiven for the one who is ashamed be-cause of something he did" (Babylonian Talmud, *Berachot* 12b). We find that Saul said, ". . . God . . . answers me no more, nei-ther by prophets, nor by dreams" (1 Samuel 28:15), but said nothing of the *Urim* and *Tummim* since he was ashamed to mention them. He had slain the people of Nob, the city of the priests [who wore the *Urim* and *Tummim*]. In response [to Saul's expression of shame], Samuel said, "And tomorrow you and your sons will be with me" (1 Samuel 28:19). "With me" means "in my camp" (namely, I have accepted you). One may attain the highest level of shame by reflecting in solitude upon the great-ness of God and of the evil of rebelling against God's word and by always remembering that God sees one's deeds, examines the depths of one's being, and observes one's thoughts.

23. The Seventh Principle: Wholehearted humility. One who recognizes one's Creator knows how debased, lowly, and deficient is the one who would transgress God's word. Thus the Psalmist said that the ideal person was one "in whose eyes a vile person is despised" (Psalm 15:4). [Vile people are described in] another verse: "How much less one who is abominable and impure, a human who drinks iniquity like water" (Job 15:16). They are described in yet another verse: "Refuse silver shall people call them" (Jeremiah 6:30). Therefore, one should be humble and subservient in one's own eyes. In the confession of sin that David made after being approached by Nathan the

prophet, he concluded, "The sacrifices of God are a broken spirit; a broken and contrite heart, O God, you will not despise" (Psalms 51:19). "A broken spirit" refers to a humble spirit. From this we learn that humility is one of the essential elements of repentance. This psalm is a model for the process of *teshuvah*. Humility enables a person to achieve divine favor, as it is written, "But on this person will I look, even on the one who is poor and contrite of spirit" (Isaiah 66:2). It is written concerning repentance, "Cast up, cast up, clear the way. Take up the stumbling block out of the way of My people. For thus says the High and Lofty One, who inhabits eternity, whose name is Holy: I dwell in the high and holy place, with the one also who is of a contrite and humble spirit, to revive the spirit of the humble, and to revive the heart of the contrite ones" (Isaiah 57:14–15). We learn from this verse as well that humility is one of the essential elements of repentance. The rest of the passage also deals with repentance: "For I will not be content forever. . . . For the iniquity of your covetousness was I angry. . . . I have seen your ways, and will heal you; I will also lead you" (Isaiah 57:16–18). "I have seen your ways" refers to humility, as it is said, "For the spirit that wraps itself is from Me" (verse 16). "And I will heal you" means "I will forgive your transgression," just as one verse says, "I will heal their backsliding" (Hosea 14:5), and another says, "Return and be healed" (Isaiah 6:10). "And I will also lead you" (Isaiah 57:16) means "I will help you to forsake sin and I will make you triumph over your Evil Inclination."

24. There are many levels of humility, as will be explained in the [section called] Gates of Humility. The highest [humility] follows necessarily from the notion of repentance, specifically that one should intensify and glorify the service of God. In so doing, one should not ascribe merit to oneself but rather one should view everything as minimal in comparison to what

is maximally attributed to God. Hence, one should serve God in the most humble fashion. Let that person not seek after honor or praise. Let that person conceal as far as is possible from the knowledge of others the fact that one is the author [of those acts].

25. This idea is stated as an essential element of repentance, even as the prophet taught, "How shall I come before Adonai, and bow myself before God on high?" (Micah 6:6). The meaning of the verse is, "How shall I come before Adonai for God's many kindnesses," since the passage contains mention of such kindnesses, and "How shall I bow myself before God on high?" for my many sins? Mention of "God on high" is to teach one who has rebelled against God on high how lowly and insignificant is the individual. The continuation of the passage, "Shall I come before God with burnt offerings, with calves of a year old? Will Adonai be pleased with thousands of rams, with ten thousands of rivers of oil?" means "Can I offer them for the many kindnesses that God has done for me?" "Shall I myself bow before God on high?" The meaning is, "Shall I give my firstborn" to indicate my subjugation and my humility for my many sins, recognizing that they are so severe that my firstborn might well be a sacrificial offering for their remission? "The fruit of my body for the sin of my soul" suggests that "the firstborn" [in the prior verse] refers to offense while "the fruit of body" [in this verse] refers to a sin. An offense, as the rabbis understood it, means rebellion and is hence worse than a mere sin.

The answer given to the questions of the prophet, namely, "It has been told you, O man [O woman], what is good, and what Adonai requires of you; only to do justly, to love mercy, and to walk humbly with your God" (Micah 6:8) teaches that such acts are offerings that are superior to burnt-offerings and meal-offerings and are to be presented to God in response for all kindnesses. "To walk humbly with your God" indicates that humility means one should not seek honor for good deeds. How much more one should not desire distinction for those qualities that God does not desire for God's creatures. Therefore, one should not take pride in wealth, power, or in the knowledge of the various sciences, but only in the knowing and understanding of God, even as the prophet taught, "Let not the wise person glory in wisdom . . ." (Jeremiah 9:22).

26. Furthermore, as an aspect of humility, one is required to attempt to remove from oneself those qualities that lead to sin, that cause acts of rebellion.

27. Pride is the cause of many transgressions. It magnifies the power of the Evil Inclination upon a person, even as the Torah states, "Then your heart will be lifted up, and you will forget Adonai, your God" (Deuteronomy 8:14). Proverbs adds, "A haughty look and a proud heart—the tillage of the wicked is sin" (Proverbs 21:4). Pride is "the tillage of the wicked" because sins sprout from it. [The prior verse taught] "Then your heart will be lifted up, and you will forget." The Psalmist said, "Through the pride of the wicked, the poor is hotly pursued" (Psalm 10:2) and "Which speak arrogantly against the righteous, with price . . ." (Psalm 31:19). Another verse adds, ". . . because they caused their terror in the land of the living" (Ezekiel 32:26). Just as one puts a furrow in a field so that seeds will sprout and a fine harvest may be realized, so the wicked make pride the furrow within their hearts so that they may set down the seeds of evil thoughts from which they may produce those transgressions that are the fruit of those thoughts. The prophet said by way of parable, "Thus judgment springs up as the hemlock in the furrows of the field" (Hosea 10:4). "Sin," mentioned in relation to "the tillage of the wicked" (Proverbs 21:4), includes many kinds of sins, as does the [singular] "sin" in "the sin of Judah" (Jeremiah 17:1). There is another possible interpretation

of the word "sin." It may be understood as "and sin" even though it lacks the copula *vav*, in the same manner that "moon" is understood as "and moon" in "The sun and moon" (Habakkuk 3:11). The meaning then would be: not only does pride cause sin, [but] it [pride] is a sin in itself! This interpretation finds support in "Everyone that is proud in heart is an abomination to Adonai" (Proverbs 16:5). This suggests that a proud person is handed over to one's Evil Inclination because, being "an abomination to Adonai," one can gain no assistance from God.

28. The would-be penitent should take a lead from the Sages with regard to humble behavior. They said, "And be lowly of spirit before all people" (*Pirkei Avot* 4:10). From this one may deduce that one should neither become angry nor deal strictly with one's associates. One should pay no mind to anything one hears spoken against oneself. One should view any personal injury caused by others as an atonement for one's sins. Such action would confirm what the Sages said: "Were one to overlook injuries, one's sins would be forgiven" (Babylonian Talmud, *Rosh Hashanah* 17a). This would be a kind of measure for measure. As one overlooks what others did to you, God will overlook what you did to God, so to speak. This is a significant opportunity for hope. Even the verse teaches, "Let them put their mouths in the dust. If they do so, there may be hope. Let them give their cheek to those who smite them. Let them be filled full with reproach" (Lamentations 3:29, 30).

29. The Eighth Principle: Humility in deed. One should accustom oneself to give soft answers, as the verse has it, "A soft answer turns away wrath" (Proverbs 15:1). One must speak softly. Such is the way of humility, as the verse has it, "And brought down you shall speak out of the ground. And your speech shall be low out of the dust" (Isaiah 29:4). Such humble speech is the reverse of the rich and proud person described in Proverbs:

". . . but the rich answers impudently" (Proverbs 18:23). The one who intends to repent should dress modestly and not wear beautiful clothes or ornaments. The Torah teaches, "Therefore now take off your ornaments from you" (Exodus 33:5) and the Book of Kings says about Ahab, ". . . and he fasted and lay in sackcloth and went softly" (1 Kings 21:27). About this God said, "Do you see how Ahab humbles himself before Me?" (1 Kings 21:29). The phrase "and went softly" means that Ahab's behavior was unlike all other kings who go about well attended and in crowds. The would-be penitent should also go about with lowered eyes, as the verse has it, "You will deliver the one whose eyes are lowered" (Job 22:29).

The signs of humility are a soft answer, a low voice, and lowered eyes. All these will remind the penitent that one's heart should be humbled.

30. The Ninth Principle: The diminishing of physical desire. The would-be pentinent should realize that such desire causes the body to sin and drags along transgression with the bonds of falsehood. One, therefore, should set a boundary to guard the path of repentance and separate oneself from all pleasures, even from those that are licit. One must conduct oneself in an ascetic manner. One should eat only to meet one's need and to preserve one's body, even as it is written, "The righteous eat [only] to the satisfying of desire" (Proverbs 25:13). One should be involved with sex only for reproduction or to fulfill the requirement of marital intercourse. So long as one follows desire, one is drawn to the processes of matter, and one is kept from the way of the rational soul. One's Evil Inclination will be increased, as the Torah teaches, "But Yeshurun grew fat, and kicked" (Deuteronomy 32:15) and "unless you eat and are satisfied . . . then your heart will be lifted up" (Deuteronomy 8:12, 14). Proverbs adds, "Unless I become full, and deny" (Proverbs

30:9). The Sages stated, "There is a quality in the human being that if satisfied, begins to hunger and that if made to hunger, begins to be satisfied" (Babylonian Talmud, *Sukkah* 52b).

31. The desire that is set in the human heart is the source of all of one's actions. Therefore, were one to set one's desire in order, instead of having one's body in all of its aspects serving it, it would have those elements serve and be joined to the intellect. All one's actions would then be properly directed, as indicated by the verse "But as for the pure, this person's work is right" (Proverbs 21:8). It seems to me that "but as for the pure" refers to those who are free of desire and "this person's work is right" refers to those whose deeds are fit and right. This interpretation is supported by the context, "The soul of the wicked desires evil; the neighbor finds no favor in her eyes" (Proverbs 21:10), which states the reverse. Another verse says, "Desire is sweet to the soul" (Proverbs 13:19). The word *nihiyeh* here translated as "is" may be understood as "fainted," as in the verse "I fainted [*nehayti*] and became sick" (Daniel 8:27). When one breaks one's desire with regard to licit matters, one's soul shall succeed. This quality shall be pleasant for one's soul, for in this manner shall one's intellect gain mastery.

". . . And it is an abomination to fools to depart from evil" (Proverbs 13:19). Fools who do not weaken their desire constantly pursue human pleasures, even when that desire leads them on the way to sin; they do not turn away from anything that is evil. Because of their pursuit of pleasure, they are called fools, even as the verse has it, "But a foolish person swallows it up" (Proverbs 21:20). Other verses teach, "Woe to them who rise up early in the morning, that they may follow strong drink" and "And the harp and the psaltery, the tabret and the pipe, and wine are in their feasts; but they do not regard the work of Adonai" (Isaiah 5:11, 12). Still others teach, "But the belly of the wicked shall want" (Proverbs 12:25), and "And I will spread dung on your faces, even the dung of your sacrifices" (Malachi 2:3). The last verse was taken by the Sages to refer to those who would treat every day as if it were a festival (Babylonian Talmud, *Shabbat* 151b). Another verse says, "The one who separates oneself seeks one's own desire. And snarls against all sound wisdom" (Proverbs 18:1). Its meaning is that if one only pursues one's own desire, in the end that person will be separated from every friend and associate. Friends and neighbors will keep their distance precisely because every person's desire differs one from another. What one wants, another does not. If, however, one pursues the way of the intellect, then people will join together with such a person and will have many friends. It is as one learns in ethics: "Were one to improve one's character traits, one would find many eager to join that person."

The quoted verse can be interpreted in a different manner: "One who separates oneself seeks one's own desire" may refer to one who, bereft of relatives and friends, can only pursue one's own desire. Because one follows only what one wants, one becomes separated even further from any possible human association, in the same sense as "But as for the poor, her friend separates herself from her" (Proverbs 19:4). "And one snarls against all sound wisdom" (Proverbs 18:1) suggests that one who follows one's own desire will end up not only committing one sin but will snarl at everything that the Torah contains. This interpretation is confirmed by the verse "But every fool will be snarling" (Proverbs 20:3).

32. There is another benefit to be gained by diminishing physical desire. If one is tempted by one's desire to do something vile and sinful, one can say to oneself, if I give in to the desire that is licit, how will I reach out to what is illicit?

33. Breaking the power of physical desire has an extremely

great benefit, for it shows that one's mind and desire are properly directed toward repentance and that aspect of one's nature that caused the sin has been rejected. The would-be penitent, therefore, will be accepted by God and will find grace in God's eyes. Thus Scripture teaches, "The sacrifices of God are a broken spirit. A broken and a contrite heart, O God, You will not despise" (Psalm 51:19). "A broken spirit" refers to a lowly and submissive spirit. "A broken heart" refers to the breaking of the power of physical desire, for such desire is said to be in the heart, as in the verse "You have given him his heart's desire" (Psalm 21:3). Since the psalm (51) speaks of repentance and contains the verse "A broken and contrite heart, O God, You will not despise," we may conclude that the would-be penitent becomes acceptable to God through the breaking of the power of physical desire. Indeed, this is one of the principles of repentance. Furthermore, it is stated with regard to penitence ". . . to revive the spirit of the humble, and to revive the heart of the contrite ones" (Isaiah 57:15).

34. The Sages said, "Whoever possesses the following three qualities of a good eye, a humble spirit, and a restricted desire is a disciple of Abraham our ancestor" (*Pirkei Avot* 5:19). "Restricted desire" means that one does not follow after physical desire even in matters that are licit, as we find that Abraham said [to Sarah], "'Behold now, I know that you are an attractive woman to look at'" (Genesis 12:11). Until that day he had not noticed the quality of her beauty. Concerning the verse "So were they shut up in widowhood until the day of their death with their husband still alive" (2 Samuel 20:3), the Sages taught that David ordered that these women should have their hair done and provided with their cosmetics daily so that their beauty might be enhanced. He did this in order to first arouse his lust and then control it. Thus he would conquer his Evil Inclination and so

atone for his sin with Batsheva (Jerusalem Talmud, *Sanhedrin* 2:3).

35. The Tenth Principle: The improvement of one's acts related to one's sins. Thus if one has been guilty of looking lewdly, let one then go about with downcast eyes. If one has sinned with slander, let her study Torah. With whatever part of the body one has sinned, let one use the same part to do *mitzvot*. Thus the Sages taught, "Those who would be righteous will be reconciled by the same that they have sinned." They also said, "If you have piled up transgressions, pile up even more *mitzvot* against them." If you have "feet running to do evil," let those feet run to fulfill a *mitzvah*. If you have "a lying tongue," let truth be in your throat, let your mouth be open to help your poor brother or sister. If you have had "haughty eyes," be humble with eyes that are lowered. If you have had "a heart devising evil thoughts," then store up words of Torah and understanding thoughts in your heart. If you have been one "sowing discord among brethren," be one to seek peace and pursue it (*Leviticus Rabbah* 21:4 on Proverbs 24:6 and 6:17–19).

36. The Eleventh Principle: Searching one's ways. It is said, "Let us search and try our ways, and return to Adonai" (Lamentations 3:30). There are three reasons for doing so. First, one should remember all the things related to one's sinning so that confession may be made for all (confession being one of the principles of [seeking] atonement). Second, knowing how many are the transgressions and sins committed, one becomes even more humble. Third, even though one has determined to forsake every kind of sin, one should be mindful of all things related to one's [past] sins so that they may serve as barriers and guard one's soul from the onslaught of the Evil Inclination. One may succumb to such things because, having gained control over one's Evil Inclination, one may think that they [no longer]

have any significance. Such a person's soul has been sickened by these things. Whenever an ill person begins to get better, one needs to be cautious in order to prevent a relapse.

37. The Twelfth Principle: One must make a full investigation of each punishment for every transgression. One should know which are punished by stripes, which by excision, and which by judicial death penalties. Thus, one may realize how great is the guilt to be confessed. One should bitterly bewail one's vicious provocations so that one will become humble and will fear sin even more. As far as the serious transgressions are concerned, repentance suspends their atonement while punishment wipes them away, as the verse teaches, "See your way in the valley. Know what you have done" (Jeremiah 2:23). This principle will be [further] explained in the Third Gate.

38. The Thirteenth Principle: There are four reasons to regard the minor transgressions as seriously as the major transgressions. First, one should not look at how small was the infraction but how great was the One who directed that it not be done. Second, the Evil Inclination has power over minor infractions. This might be the reason that one has persisted in doing them. If piled up long enough, minor transgressions take on the character of major transgressions. It is like a silk thread which, although thin and weak, if doubled and redoubled becomes as strong as a rope. Third, if one keeps committing the same transgression, it seems after a while to be permitted. Once the yoke [of its prohibition] is broken, one no longer guards oneself from it. Then one may be considered to be one of those who are "yoke breakers" and apostates related to a particular matter. Fourth, if the Evil Inclination can conquer you with regard to a minor matter today, it will conquer you with regard to a major matter tomorrow. It is as the Rabbis taught: "Anyone who breaks pots in anger should be viewed as if worshiping idols. This is the way

the Evil Inclination operates. Today it says, 'Break pots.' Tomorrow it will say, 'Worship idols!'" (Babylonian Talmud, *Shabbat* 105b). The Torah taught, "If you do well, will it not be lifted up?" (Genesis 4:7). This relates to [the prior verse] "Why has your disposition taken a downturn?" (Genesis 4:6), which means "If you improve your acts and return to Me, there will be lifting up." This last [section of verse] is to be understood as "you will lift up your face," as in the interpretation of "Surely then you will lift up your face without damage" (Job 11:15). "Lifting up" may also be understood as forgiveness. The verse continues, "And if you do not do well, sin couches at the door" (Genesis 4:7). It means that, having sinned, if you do not now repent, not only will the guilt rest with you but the Evil Inclination rests at your door to cause you to sin wherever you go. Having won once, it will continue to win against you. It will ensnare you. You will be caught because you have not repented. The continuation of the verse, "and to you is its desire" (Genesis 4:7), means that it will lead you astray because it lies in wait for you every moment. The end of the verse, "but you may rule over it" (Genesis 4:7), means that you can conquer it if you want to do so. Since I have given you the power to control your Evil Inclination, you will be punished for having committed your sin.

39. Solomon said, "Whoever despises the word will suffer as a result of it. But the one who fears the *mitzvot* will be rewarded" (Proverbs 13:13). His words refer to that person who disregards minor infractions. Such a person will suffer consequences of all that we have already mentioned. "But the one who fears the *mitzvot*" refers to that person who does not fear performing the least of *mitzvot* as that person fears committing the severest transgression. Such a person "shall be rewarded." That person is destined to receive a full reward. The Sages said, "Be as careful in the performance of a minor *mitzvah* as a ma-

jor one" (*Pirkei Avot* 2:1) and ". . . a *mitzvah* pulls along a *mitzvah* and a transgression pulls along a transgression. The reward of a *mitzvah* is a *mitzvah* and the reward of a transgression is a transgression" (*Pirkei Avot* 4:2).

40. The Fourteenth Principle: Confession. As the Torah teaches, ". . . one should confess in what one has sinned" (Leviticus 5:5). The would-be penitent should mention one's own sins and the sins of one's ancestors if one has continued their practices and is to be punished for their sins and one's own, even as the Torah teaches, "And they will confess their iniquity and the iniquity of their ancestors" (Leviticus 26:40).

41. The Fifteenth Principle: Prayer. The would-be penitent should pray to God and ask for God's mercy for the atonement of all of one's sins, even as the prophet taught, "Take with you words, and return to Adonai. Say to God: 'Forgive all iniquity and accept what is good. So will we render for bullocks the offering of our lips'" (Hosea 14:3). "Take with you words" refers to confession. "Say to God: 'Forgive all iniquity and accept that which is good'" refers to prayer. "And accept what is good" refers to the good deeds that we have done. The Sages taught that a transgression extinguishes [the light of a] *mitzvah* (Babylonian Talmud, *Sotah* 21a). When one repents, atonement is made for transgressions. One now becomes aware of the worth of the *mitzvah*. That light that had been dimmed [by sin] now becomes brighter because of *teshuvah*. Thus it is written, "If you had been pure and upright, surely now God would awake for you and make your righteous precinct prosperous" (Job 8:6). The Sages understood the verse not as "If you had been pure" but rather as "If you are pure" and commented that by repentance, Job *would be* pure (Jerusalem Talmud, *Rosh Hashanah* 1:30). They understood the continuation of the verse, "Surely now God would awake for you," to mean that after repentance, God would

bring for review all the acts of righteousness that Job had done. For example, Job had kept his house wide open [so that the poor might enter]. He had provided for many, as the verse has it, "[I opened] my doors to the roadside" (Job 31:32). [Job is told] before you repented, your acts of righteousness could not protect you; after your repentance and after the departure of your transgression, God will be awake to your merit and will make prosperous your righteous precincts. The prophetic words "So will we render for bullocks the offerings of our lips" (Hosea 14:3) ask that God consider our confessions sin-offerings presented to God. Bullocks are mentioned, because the sin-offering of a bullock was offered on the inner part of the Temple. The blood of the offering was sprinkled on the curtain and the altar of gold.

42. The would-be penitent should pray to God that God may blot out with a thick cloud all of one's prior transgressions and all of one's sins and that God should favor her, accept her and accept her pleas as if she had not sinned. This is as Elihu said with regard to the penitent who had endured affliction, "You pray to God, and God is favorable to you" (Job 33:26). After all, it is possible that one's transgression may be forgiven, redeemed through suffering and the enduring of harsh decrees. Still God might find no favor in the individual and one's offering may not be acceptable. What the righteous desire most is to receive favor from God and that God desire them. To receive God's favor means to have true eternal life and to bask in the great light that encompasses all delights, as the verse teaches, "Adonai Tzevaot, restore us. Cause Your face to shine, and we will be saved" (Psalm 80:20). The Sages commented on that verse, "All that we have is the shining of Your face" (*Midrash Tehillim* 80), that is, God's favor. Of this we have already spoken. You will find that David prayed when he repented, "Wash me thoroughly from my iniquity, and cleanse me from my sin" (Psalm 51:4).

Then [David] prayed for that favor from God that he had experienced prior to his sin: "Do not cast me away from Your presence. Do not take Your holy spirit from me" (Psalm 51:13). Next he prayed, "Restore to me the joy of Your salvation" (Psalm 51:14), by which he meant that the divine miracles and God's salvation should be with him, that the spirit of God should descend upon him as it had previously. David then said, "And let a willing spirit hold me up" (Psalm 51:14). By this he meant, "I have become diminished because of my sins. I am not worthy of Your miracles or the manifestation of Your holy power. Even if You have forgiven the guilt of my sin, I am not worthy to be loved or accepted as I once was. However, let a willing spirit hold me up, for there is no limit to Your grace or goodness." The word *varuach*, "and a spirit," is to be homiletically understood as *uvevaruach*, "and with a spirit" (a similar usage is in "*vedagan vetirosh semachtiv*—and with corn and wine have I sustained him" [Genesis 27:37]). The prophet Hosea suggested the same notion, as did David when he said, "I will heal their backsliding, I will love them freely" (Hosea 14:5). "Freely" (*nedavah*) is similar to "willing" (*nedivah*), as in, "And with a willing spirit hold me up."

43. The would-be penitent should pray continually to God and ask for divine help in one's *teshuvah*, even as the prophet taught, "Turn me and I shall be turned, for You are Adonai my God" (Jeremiah 31:18).

44. The Sixteenth Principle: The repair—as far as is possible—of the misdeed. The text teaches, "And God saw their works, that they had turned from their evil way" (Jonah 3:10), and "Yea, let them turn every one from the way of evil, and from the violence that is in their hands" (Jonah 3:8). In transgressions between persons, such as theft or robbery, the sin is not atoned for until the stolen object is returned. If someone has harmed a

neighbor or oppressed, insulted, or slandered that neighbor, atonement can only occur when the sinner asks pardon from the injured party. Our Sages said that though one may have paid compensation for the shame caused another or paid compensation for the pain of an injury done to another, that shame and that pain are not atoned for until one asks forgiveness from the injured party. As the Torah teaches, "Now, therefore, restore the man's wife; for he is a prophet and he shall pray for you, and you will live" (Genesis 20:7/Babylonian Talmud, *Kiddushin* 92a).

45. The would-be penitent should ask forgiveness from the person wronged before confessing so that one's confession will be acceptable. King David did this when he repented. He said, "Against You, You alone have I sinned, and done what is evil in Your sight. So that You may be justified when You speak and be in the right when You judge" (Psalm 51:6). He meant, "To You alone am I considered a sinner. I need no one else to receive Your forgiveness. If I have sinned against someone, I have already asked for that person's forgiveness and received atonement from that person." It is as the Torah states: "Then I will bear blame to my father forever" (Genesis 44:32). That means, "For this sin, I will be considered by my father to be a sinner all my days and he will not forgive me for this [sin]." The *Targum* renders the verse thus: "And I will be a sinner to my father." There is another interpretation of the verse in Psalms: "Against You, You alone have I sinned." "I have not sinned against anyone, I have not spoken badly against anyone, I have not taken anything from anyone that I should have to return it to gain that person's forgiveness. My atonement is dependent only on Your forgiveness." "That You may be justified when You speak, and be in the right when You judge." That means, "in order to show the nations Your righteousness and the greatness of Your for-

giveness on the day when You speak and judge me." The use of "that" in the phrase "That You may" is to show the greatness of the righteousness in forgiving the greatness of the sin. It is as if the origin of the sin was that the steadfast love of God might be revealed and God's righteousness in forgiveness on the day of judgment. There is a similar usage in the verse "Of their silver and gold have they made idols, that they may be cut off" (Hosea 8:4), where the making of the idols is the reason for the cutting off of their silver and gold. Thus it is suggested that they made the idols in order to be cut off. There is another possible interpretation: "That You may be righteous when you speak" may refer to the visitation and the payment, that is, David accepted God's judgment and punishment upon himself. "That they may be cut off" (in Hosea 8:4) may therefore mean "because of this they will be cut off."

46. The Sages understood (in *Midrash Tehillim* 51) the verse (Psalms 51:6) following the first interpretation and compared it to a surgeon who saw a wound and said, "This is a serious wound!" The patient responded, "I received such a wound to show off your excellent ability and marvelous skill as a physician!" We will discuss this principle further in the Fourth Gate.

47. The Seventeenth Principle: To pursue works of steadfast love and truth. It is as stated in the verse "By steadfast love and truth iniquity is expiated. And by the fear of Adonai people depart from evil" (Proverbs 16:6). If you now reflect on the inner meaning of the verse, you will understand that if the sinner does not return to God, no act of divine steadfast love will provide atonement for one's sin. It is as stated in the Torah, "For Adonai your God . . . does not regard persons, nor take rewards" (Deuteronomy 10:17). The Sages interpreted "nor take rewards" to mean that God does not take the sinner's performance of a *mitzvah* as a kind of bribe to forgive or neglect the other trans-

gressions one has committed. (*Yalkut Shimoni Proverbs* 11 No. 947). The Sages further said that "whoever thinks that the Holy Blessed One is indifferent will have his life treated indifferently" (Babylonian Talmud, *Bava Kamma* 50a). God is patient, but if sinners still will not hearken, God will measure out their recompense straight to their heart. Solomon said, "By steadfast love and truth iniquity is expiated" applies only to the person who repents. There are transgressions that repentance and the Day of Atonement cause to be held in abeyance until suffering scours out their traces. This was explained in the Fourth Gate. Steadfast love will protect the sinner who repents and will keep that repentant sinner from suffering and indeed will deliver that person from death, as it is written, "But [God's] righteousness will deliver from death" (Proverbs 10:2). There is one kind of transgression—the profanation of the Divine Name— that repentance and suffering hold in abeyance and death scours out its traces, as it is said, "Surely this iniquity will not be expiated by you until you die" (Isaiah 22:14). If one holds on to the truth, supports it, is motivated by its words, and causes its light to shine forth that people can see it, and sustains and honors those who are people of truth, and if [while doing so] one casts down even to the dust those groups who support falsehood, then that person is following the ways of sanctifying the Divine Name. One brings honor and glory to the divine word and work in the world and strength and beauty to the sanctuary of God's Torah. It is in the multiplication of actions to sanctify the Divine Name and to awaken [others] to the truth, to prepare it and sustain it, that one's guilt with regard to the profanation of the name is forgiven. One's repentance consists of balancing the truth against the guilt of the profanation, as it were, the measure of one's repentance against the measure of one's going astray. This is the explanation of the verse "By steadfast love and truth iniquity is expiated."

48. The Eighteenth Principle: One's sin should ever be present in mind. It is fitting that the sinning soul remember its transgressions continually and never forget them—even to the end of time. If one's thought of transgression leaves one's mind, another should take its place. It is as the verse teaches: "For I know my transgressions and my sin is ever before me" (Psalm 51:5). This principle will be explained in the Third Gate.

49. The Nineteenth Principle: Not to sin even if one has the opportunity and the strong desire to sin. The Sages taught, "Who is that penitent whose repentance rises up even to the Throne of Glory? That one who could be tested and emerge innocent of wrong even though he is in the same period [of his original sin] and in the same place [where he had sinned] and in proximity to the same woman [with whom he had sinned]" (Babylonian Talmud, *Yoma* 86b). By their statement, the Sages meant that the penitent had the same opportunity to sin as before, the same lust as before, and the same physical ability as before, yet had conquered his Evil Inclination and was delivered from sin by the strength of his reverence for God and the power of his awe. That person who had not had all these opportunities for sin should increase the reverence for God in his soul daily so that reverence for God will conquer his Evil Inclination and will rule over the power of his lust. God, who is the Searcher of hearts and the Guardian of the soul, will understand and will know that should such a person be tempted and an occasion for sin be presented, the individual will deliver one's soul from the Evil Inclination. Such a person will stand before God on the highest level of repentance. This is what Solomon intended in the verse "By steadfast love and truth iniquity is expiated, and

by the fear of Adonai people depart from evil" (Proverbs 16:6). The sense of the verse is ". . . and by the fear of Adonai *to* depart from evil when it presents itself." "Depart" here is an infinitive, as indicated that the word [*sur* in Hebrew] is not found joined with the conjunctive *vav* (and). [The same sense is indicated in the infinitive and participial forms], as stated in "Depart from evil and do good" (Psalm 34:15) and "One who fears God and departs from evil and do good" (Psalm 34:15) and "One who fears God and departs from evil" (Job 1:8). All these refer to the turning away from evil when one comes upon it. One cannot speak of turning away from doing a deed unless one has come close to doing it. One should understand in a similar manner the statement of the Sages, "The one who merely sits and does not transgress will receive the reward of one performing a *mitzvah*" (Babylonian Talmud, *Kiddushin* 39b). It refers to one who had the opportunity to sin and delivered oneself from it.

50. The Twentieth Principle: To move others from transgression. The verse teaches, "Return and turn yourselves from all your transgressions" (Ezekiel 18:30). We learn from the verse the aforementioned principle of repentance. The verse ". . . you should surely rebuke your neighbor, and not bear sin because of him" (Leviticus 19:17) teaches us that if we don't rebuke our neighbor we will be punished for our neighbor's sins. David said in his psalm of repentance, "Then I will teach transgressors Your ways and sinners shall return to You" (Psalm 51:15).

51. We have now finished our presentation of the principles of repentance. Now one should pay attention to those things that impede repentance. Thus if one casts off the yoke and is continually trapped by one of them, one will find repentance to be difficult. If you have stumbled with one of them, be strong and of courage to pour out your prayers and supplications. Gather your strength to fulfill the principles of repentance. You

will learn more about them in the discussion presented in the Fourth Gate. May you find mercy and gain compassion.

52. I will now mention what the Sages said concerning this. They said that there were twenty-three impediments to repentance. They are: talebearing; slander; anger; dwelling on evil; being the buddy of a wicked person; always being the guest at meals of those who haven't enough for themselves; wanton gazing at women; being the partner of a thief; saying, "I will sin and repent" for the *Mishnah* states, "One who says, I will sin and repent, will have no chance to repent. I will sin and the Day of Atonement will effect atonement, then the Day of Atonement will not effect atonement" (*Yoma* 8:9); glorying in another's shame; separating oneself from the community; despising one's parents; despising one's teachers; cursing the masses; delaying them from doing something that is instructed; beguiling one's neighbor from the right path to the wrong path; making use of a poor person's pledge; receiving a bribe to pervert justice; finding something and not returning it to its owner; seeing one's child going astray and doing nothing about it; suspecting the innocent; hating reproaches; and mocking the *mitzvot* (*Yoma* 8).

❋ 6 ❋

Hilchot Teshuvah
(Laws of Repentance)

Moses Maimonides

Perhaps the best-known of all Jewish thinkers, Moses Maimonides (1135–1204)—alternatively Moses ben Maimon, also
known by the acronym RaMBaM—lived in Cordoba, Spain,
then Fez. *Hilchot Teshuvah* is included here in its entirety
because in it the author claims to have collected all of Jewish
law relevant to the process of *teshuvah*. This selection is from
Maimonides' *Mishneh Torah*, his massive codification of Jewish
law. In the entire collection from which these selections are
taken, RaMBaM claims to take no personal view unless he finds
no talmudic authority with an opinion on a particular law. At
the end of his commentary on the *Mishnah*, he claims the reason for his work: "my mind was troubled . . . amid divinely
ordained exiles, [I was] on journeys by land and [felt] tossed
on the tempest of the seas."

———— ❖ ————

CHAPTER ONE

If anyone transgresses any instruction of Torah, whether a positive or negative *mitzvah*, whether inadvertently or intentionally,
when that person repents and turns from that particular sin, the

individual must confess before God, the Holy Blessed One, as it says, "If any man or woman do . . . then they shall confess the sin that they did" (Numbers 5:6, 7). This refers to a confession in words. Such a confession is a positive *mitzvah*.

1. How should people confess? One should say, "Adonai, I have sinned before You. I have transgressed. I have acted perversely. I have done all these things. I now regret it! I am ashamed of what I have done and I will never do it again." This is the essence of confession. The one who confesses freely and in detail is to be praised. Thus did those who [in ancient times] brought sacrifices for their sin and for their guilt when they brought their offerings for their inadvertent or intended sins. For they did not achieve atonement until they repented and confessed aloud, as it says, "And one will confess that which one sinned" (Leviticus 5:5). Thus, all those who were condemned by the court to death, or to whipping, received atonement. But it was not by reason of their death or by their being whipped but only as a result of their repentance and confession. Similarly, one who injures a neighbor physically or monetarily, even though the individual has made restitution for what had happened, the person does not gain atonement until that person confesses and swears not to ever again do such a thing, as it says, "From any human sin" (Numbers 5:6).

2. The priest must confess all the transgressions of the Israelites upon the goat that is to be sent forth because it is an atonement for all of Israel. If one has repented, that goat atones for all transgressions of all the *mitzvot* whether major or minor, intentional or inadvertent, brought to consciousness or not. However, if one does not repent, the goat atones only for the minor sins. The major sins are those for which the court may decree death [and the Heavenly Court may decree *karet*, life cut off before its time]. False swearing and lying are among

the major sins, even though they do not incur *karet*. The major sins relate to those positive or negative *mitzvot* that do not incur *karet*.

3. Repentance is all that we have, now that the Temple does not exist and we do not have its altar to effect atonement. Repentance atones for all kinds of transgressions. Were a person to be wicked throughout life and yet finally repent, that person's wickedness would not be mentioned, for it says, "The wickedness of the wicked shall not cause the individual to stumble on the day that the individual turns from wickedness" (Ezekiel 33:12). Yom Kippur by its very nature brings atonement to those who repent, as it is written, "For on *the* day shall atonement be made for you" (Leviticus 16:30).

4. Although repentance atones for everything and Yom Kippur brings atonement, there are transgressions that are atoned for only after some time. For example, were one to transgress a positive *mitzvah* that did not have *karet* as its punishment, and then repent, that person would be forgiven on the spot, as it says [in such cases], "Repent, you mischievous children, and I will heal your mischief" (Jeremiah 3:22). Were one to transgress the kind of negative *mitzvah* that does not carry *karet* as punishment or the death penalty and then repent, then the effect of that repentance would be suspended until Yom Kippur, which then would provide atonement. It is written [concerning such cases], "For on *that* day, atonement shall be made for you" (Leviticus 16:30). Were one to violate those *mitzvot* that do carry *karet* and the death penalty as punishment, and then repent, then the effect of that repentance and the effect of Yom Kippur would be suspended. The suffering of the individual would instead complete the process of atonement. Such a person would never achieve complete atonement until the individual suffered, as it says [in such cases], "And I will visit their

transgressions with the rod and their iniquity with strokes" (Psalm 89:33). To what do these words apply? To the case of one who did not profane the Divine Name while sinning. However, if one did, even if that individual were to repent and even if Yom Kippur came and the person remained steadfast in repentance and suffered, that person would not achieve full atonement until death. For this individual, repentance, Yom Kippur, and suffering, all three of them, would be suspended. Death alone would bring atonement, as it says, "And it was revealed in the ears of Adonai that your transgression will not be atoned for until you die, says Adonai Tzevaot" (Isaiah 22:14).

CHAPTER TWO

1. What is true repentance? If the repentant individual has the opportunity and the ability to sin and refrains because the individual has repented rather than because the individual is afraid or because that person lacks the capacity to sin, then that is true and complete repentance. For example, were a man to have sinned sexually with a woman, and after a period of time, having repented, he is alone with her in the same context where previously he had sinned and still desiring her, physically able to sin again, he does not, such a person has truly repented. King Solomon alluded to such a case when he wrote, "Remember your Creator in the days of your youth" (Ecclesiastes 12:1). However, were a person to repent in old age at a time when the repetition of the sin would be physically impossible, even such a deficient act of penitence would be efficacious. Such a person would indeed be considered having done *teshuvah*. Were a person to have been a sinner all her life and yet repent on the day of her death, and to have died while still repenting, all her sins would be forgiven. This is suggested by the verse "Before

the sun and the light and the moon and the stars are darkened, and the clouds return after the rain" (Ecclesiastes 12:2). From this we learn that if one remembered the Creator (Ecclesiastes 12:1) and repented before death, that person would be forgiven.

2. What is repentance? It is that the sinner should leave sin and turn from (evil) thought and conclude never do that sin again, as it says, "Let the wicked leave that way and so on" (Isaiah 55:7). The individual will then be remorseful for transgressing, as it says, "After I repented, I had remorse" (Jeremiah 31:18). The One that knows the secret things will attest that the individual will never again return to that particular sin, as it says, "We will not call the work of our hands our God" (Hosea 14:4). All these matters that the penitent has already decided in the heart should be confessed with the lips.

3. However, whoever confesses merely with words but has not decided to stop sinning is like one who immerses oneself in a ritual bath still holding a [contaminating] reptile. The immersion will not be effective until the person who "confesses and forsakes sin shall gain compassion" (Proverbs 28:13). The penitent should confess one's sin in detail, as it says, "Oh, this people have sinned a great sin, and have made them a god of gold" (Exodus 32:31).

4. One of the ways of repentance is for the penitent to cry out weeping and in supplication continually before God and give *tzedakah* charity according to one's ability, keeping far from the context in which the person has sinned. The person should change one's name as if to say, "I am a different person. I am not the one who did those things." That person should endeavor to change all of one's ways in order to do good and go the proper way. That person may even go into exile, since exile atones for guilt. It causes one to humble oneself, to become meek and humble of spirit.

5. It is extremely praiseworthy to confess publicly and to make known one's sins to all, to reveal one's transgressions between oneself and others and say to all, "Indeed, I have sinned against so-and-so and I did thus and such. Today, I have repented and shown remorse. Whoever arrogantly hides one's sins and will not make them known will not achieve full repentance, as it says, "The one who hides one's sins will not succeed" (Proverbs 38:13). To what do these words refer? To those transgressions between person and person. However, with regard to transgressions between persons and God, one need not publicize them. It would indeed be arrogant to reveal them. Rather let such a person repent before God and detail the sins before God. A simple undetailed public confession is sufficient. Such simplicity is better than not revealing the transgression, as it says, "Happy is the one whose transgression is forgiven, whose sin is hidden" (Psalm 32:1).

6. Although it is always good to repent and to cry out [to God], it is even better to do so on the ten days between Rosh Hashanah and Yom Kippur. At that time, such acts are instantly accepted, as it says, "Seek Adonai where God may be found" (Isaiah 55:6).

7. Yom Kippur is a time of *teshuvah* for all, for individuals and for communities. It is also a time of forgiveness and compassion for Israel. Therefore, all [Jews] are obligated to repent and confess on Yom Kippur. The obligation of confession on Yom Kippur begins on *Erev* Yom Kippur before the person eats [the final meal] in order to preclude the possibility of choking and prevent the person from confessing. However, even though one has confessed prior to eating, the individual must confess again on *Erev* Yom Kippur during the Evening Service and confess again during the Morning Service, and again during the Afternoon Service and yet again during *Neilah* [closing]

Service. The individual worshiper should confess after reciting the *Amidah*. The *Shaliach Tzeebor* confesses in the midst of the *Amidah* after the fourth benediction.

8. The essence of the customary Jewish confession is contained in the words "But we have sinned." The transgressions for which one has confessed on one Yom Kippur may be confessed on the next, even if one has remained steadfast in one's *teshuvah*, as it says, "I know my transgressions and my sin is always before me" (Psalm 51:5).

9. *Teshuvah* and Yom Kippur bring atonement only for transgression between individuals and God. Such is the case for one who ate something forbidden or engaged in forbidden sexual relations and similar matters. However, in transgressions between individuals, such as in the case of one who injured one's neighbor or who cursed one's neighbor or who robbed that person and similar matters, one is not forgiven until one restores [whatever is necessary] to the injured party and gains that person's favor once again. For example, if one paid back the money owed to another, that person would still have to gain that person's favor by asking for forgiveness. Even were one to provoke another with words alone, such a person would still have to appease the other, entreating forgiveness. If the other were not willing to forgive, then the one [asking for forgiveness] should bring three individuals to shout, to entreat, and to request the other person to indeed forgive. If that person (the injured party) remains adamant and is unwilling to forgive, then the person asking for forgiveness should bring a second and a third group of people. If the person still refuses, then the person asking for forgiveness should leave and go on his or her way. The one who would not forgive is now the sinner! If, however, the affronted party were the other individual's teacher, then the student must come and go even a thousand times until forgiven.

10. It is forbidden for a person to be cruel and unwilling to be appeased; rather one should be easy to appease and hard to provoke. When the sinner asks to be forgiven, it should be done with a whole heart and with a willing soul. Even if one has provoked and sinned against another a number of times, the individual should not be vengeful or carry a grudge. This is the way of the descendents of Israel whose heart is proper. It is different for idolaters, these uncircumcised of heart, who hold a grudge forever. Thus Scripture describes the Gibeonites who, because they were unwilling to forgive or become appeased, were ". . . not [part] of the children of Israel" (2 Samuel 21:2).

11. The one who sins against a person who dies before one can ask forgiveness should bring a *minyan* [ten individuals] to that person's grave and say in their presence, "I have sinned against Adonai the God of Israel and against this person. I did thus and so." If the individual were obligated to pay money to the deceased, that person should pay that money to that person's heirs. If the individual does not know who the heirs are, the individual should leave that money with the court and confess.

CHAPTER THREE

1. [As a result of his or her actions], every human being is merited with both strengths and weaknesses. The one whose strengths are greater is considered righteous. [On the other hand], the one whose weaknesses are greater is considered wicked. The one whose actions are equally good and bad, that person is considered mediocre (ordinary). The same is true with regard to a city; if the meritorious actions of its inhabitants are greater, then it is considered righteous. If the evil activity is greater, then it is considered wicked. The same holds true for the entire world.

2. Should one's vices be much greater than one's virtues, then that person should immediately die, as Scripture says, ". . . for the multitude of your transgressions" (Jeremiah 30:14). The same is true for a city whose vices greatly outnumber its virtues. It would immediately perish, as the Torah states, ". . . the cry of Sodom and Gomorrah is great" (Genesis 18:20). The same would be true for the entire world. Were its vices to greatly outnumber its virtues, it would be destroyed immediately. The Torah states, "And Adonai saw that the wickedness of human-kind was great on the earth . . ." (Genesis 6:5). The evaluation (of vices and virtues) is not according to quantity but rather quality, since there are virtues that may overbalance many vices, as it states, "Because there is found in him some good thing" (1 Kings 14:13). Likewise, there are vices that may overbalance many virtues, as it states, "But one sinner destroys much good" (Ecclesiastes 9:18). This evaluation is done only by the God of all knowledge, who knows how virtues are evaluated against vices.

3. Whoever regrets performing the *mitzvot* and wonders about all the virtues, and then says to oneself, "What benefit have I gained in doing them, would that I had not done them," such a person has destroyed [the value of] all of them. No merit may be mentioned on their behalf in this world, as it says, "The righteousness of the righteous shall not deliver a person in the day of his [or her] transgression" (Ezekiel 33:12). This [day of transgression] refers to one who wonders about one's prior acts. Just as a person's virtues and vices are evaluated on the day of death, thus in each and every year the moral strengths and character weaknesses of each inhabitant of this world are evaluated on Rosh Hashanah. Whoever is judged innocent receives the verdict of life. Whoever is judged guilty receives the verdict of death. Whoever is judged ordinary has the verdict suspended until Yom

Kippur. If one repents, one receives the verdict of life. If not, that person receives the verdict of death.

4. Although the sounding of the *shofar* on Rosh Hashanah is in response to a scriptural instruction, it also suggests further meaning, as if to say: "Wake up, you who sleep. Arise, you who slumber. Examine your deeds and repent. Remember your Creator, you who forget the truth amid the vanities of the moment, who follow foolishly that which is least valuable and that which will neither benefit nor save. Look to your souls. Improve your ways and your deeds! Let every one of you leave the wicked path of evil thoughts. Let everyone see oneself throughout the year as if one were semiinnocent and semiguilty. So too is the entire world balanced, half-guilty and half-innocent. One sin affects the balance moving the sinner and the world toward being guilty, thus causing the destruction of both. However, performance of one *mitzvah* moves the balance in the other direction toward innocence, bringing salvation and redemption to the performer of the deed and to the world, as Scripture states, "The righteous person is the foundation of the world" (Proverbs 10:25). This means that righteousness has overbalanced the entire world to the side of virtue and has saved it.

As a result, it was customary for the entire household of Israel to increase the number of charitable acts and good deeds in the period between Rosh Hashanah and Yom Kippur more than the rest of the year. It was also the custom during the Ten Days of Repentance to arise while it was still dark and go to the synagogue and, saying *selichot* (special penitential texts), pray until daybreak.

5. At the moment when an individual's transgressions are weighed against one's virtues, the first or second transgression is not counted. Rather the third and those that follow are counted. If one's virtues are greater than one's transgressions,

counting from the third transgression, then one's transgressions are pardoned one by one. The third transgression is considered the first, since the first two are forgiven. Thus, the fourth is treated as the first, since the third is forgiven. Thus is the case with all of one's transgressions. These words refer to an individual, as it says, "All these things does God work, twice, even three times with a person" (Job 33:29). However, with a community, the first three transgressions are suspended, as it is written, "For three transgressions of Israel and for the fourth, I will not let a person repent" (Amos 2:6). When transgressions of a community are computed, they are counted from the fourth on. Those who are ordinary folks (whose sins are balanced), if the totality of one's sins was tantamount to never putting on *tefillin*, then that person is judged according to one's personal level of sin. That individual has a share in the World to Come. The wicked whose sins overbalance (virtues) are judged according to their sins. They too have a portion in the World to Come even though they sinned, as it says, "Your people are all righteous. They shall eternally possess the earth" (Isaiah 60:21). [Here "the earth" is a metaphor, as if to say, "the land of life," which is the World to Come.]

6. The following have no portion in the World to Come and are cut off and destroyed as judged. Their wickedness and sin is great: the heretics; the Epicureans; those who deny the Torah; those who deny the resurrection of the dead; those who deny the coming of the redeemer; those who rebel and those who cause the multitude to sin; those who separated themselves from the ways of the community; and the one who proudly and publicly transgresses like Yehoiakim; those who inform; those who for no religious reason cause the community to fear; those who shed blood; those who slander; and those who change the physical mark of the covenant.

7. These are the five who are called heretics: the one who says that there is no God and the world has no ruler; the one who says that the world has a ruler but there are two or more; the one who says that there is a master (of the universe) but that the master has a body and a shape; and thus the one who says that God is not the first and only cause; and thus too the one who worships a star or constellation or something else that that thing should be an intermediary between an individual and the Master of the Universe. Every one of these five is a heretic.

8. Three are termed *apikursim* (heretics, literally, Epicureans): the one who says that there is no prophecy at all and no information at all extends from the Creator to the heart of humankind; the one who denies the prophecy of Moses, our teacher; and the one who says that the Creator does not know the actions of individual people. Every one of the three is an *apikuros*. There are three [kinds of people] who deny the Torah. First is one who says that the Torah does not come from God. Were one to say that a verse, a word, or even a letter came from Moses and not from God, such a person would be called a denier of the Torah. So too would be a person who denied its interpretation, [the Oral Law] and who, like Zadok and Boethius, contradicted its interpreters. Likewise would be the view of one who, like the *Hagarim* (Arabs), held that the Torah came from God but thought that the Creator had changed one particular commandment for another. Such a view nullifies the Torah. All three of these deny the Torah.

9. The following two are apostates of Israel: an apostate with regard to one transgression or an apostate with regard to one entire Torah. The apostate with regard to the transgression is the one who intentionally, customarily, and publicly performs one transgression, even were that transgression a minor one, such as the one who continually wears *shatnez* [clothing made with

mingled threads (Leviticus 19:19] or the one who has his hair cut in a particular manner [transgressing the commandment against cutting the "corners" of the hair (Leviticus 19:24)]. Such a transgression makes it seem that that particular commandment could never be fulfilled. Such a person is an apostate with regard to that particular *mitzvah*. That person's action is a provocation [to God]. The apostate to the entire Torah is one who in a time of persecution takes on the religion of the idolaters, saying to oneself, "What benefit is it to remain a Jew when we are subjugated and persecuted, while others are powerful?" Such a person is an apostate to the entire Torah. [The commentator RABAD objects to this comment, "At least such person affirms one's view of God. Hence, that person is not a heretic!"]

10. Those who mislead in sins, great or small, cause the masses to sin. Great are the cases of Jeroboam, Zadok, and Boethius. Small is the case of one who merely nullifies a positive commandment. One who compels others to sin is like the case of Menasseh who, on pain of death, forced the Israelites to worship idols. One who simply causes others to err has them fall away (from the Torah).

11. Even if one has not committed a transgression, that person has turned away from the congregation of Israel. That person has not fulfilled commandments on their behalf, has not entered into their difficulties, nor (even) participated in their fasts. That one has turned away from the practices of the community. Rather, that person has gone one's own way, as if that person were one of the nations and not a member of the Jewish community. Such a person has no portion in the World to Come. The one who is termed a misinterpreter of the Torah is so called because that person dares to reveal oneself as unashamed of [transgressing] the words of the Torah.

12. There are two kinds of *moserim* ("one who hands Jews

over"). The first one hands one's fellow (Jew) to be beaten or killed. The other is the one who will hand over the money belonging to a Jew to a non-Jew (in some nonviolent manner) or who hands over that money to a violent person who is not Jewish. Neither kind of *moser* has a portion in the World to Come.

13. "Those who without religious reason cause the community to fear" refers to the one who like a pagan king would rule with such force that his people would be frightened and terrified, even though his intent [in instilling such fear] is for his own glory, his own needs, and not for the glory of God.

14. Each of the twenty-four people that we have detailed have no portion in the World to Come, even though they are Jews. There are also some lesser transgressions regarding which the Sages said that anyone who becomes accustomed to perform them would have no portion in the World to Come. One should be warned to keep far from them. They are the following: the one who gives an [insulting] nickname to one's fellow and calls that person by that name even though that person is publicly humiliated; the one who glories in the shame of one's fellow; the one who scorns the disciples of the wise, who disdains one's teachers; the one who treats the festivals disdainfully; and the one who desecrates the holy. To what do these words refer? Each and every one of them has no portion in the World to Come, should that person die without making *teshuvah*. However, if one repents of one's wickedness and then dies while repenting, then that person will be among those in the World to Come since there is nothing that can stand in the way of *teshuvah*. Even were a person to be an atheist all his life and at the very end repent, that person would have a portion in the World to Come, as it says, "Peace, peace to those far off and those near, says Adonai, and I will heal you" (Isaiah 57:19). All the wicked and all the apostates and all similar people, were they to repent

whether in public or in private, they would be accepted, as Scripture has it, "Return O mischievous children" (Jeremiah 3:14). Even if the individual were still mischievous [and made *teshuvah* in private and not in public], that person would still be accepted as a repentant sinner.

CHAPTER FOUR

1. There are twenty-four acts that impact negatively on repentance. [Among them,] four are such major transgressions that if one does them, due to the severity of the sin, the Holy Blessed One will not allow the person to do *teshuvah*. The transgressions: (a) one who causes the multitude to sin; in that category of transgression is the one who would prevent the multitude from doing a *mitzvah*; (b) one who would move one's fellow from the right path to the wrong one, like one who incites or seduces; (c) one who sees one's own child going astray but does not reprove the child when able to do so (and such discipline would help the child to grow); here the parent acts as the one who causes others to sin; and (d) one who says, "I will sin and Yom Kippur will provide me with necessary atonement."

2. These five acts close off the path of *teshuvah*: (a) were one to separate from the community, for when they repent, that person would not be among them, nor would that person share in their merit; (b) were one to disagree with the words of the Sages, the ensuing controversy would separate that person from the community and keep the individual from knowing the ways of *teshuvah*; (c) were one to mock the *mitzvot*, then seeing that they were of little personal value, that person would neither pursue them nor do them; how then could the individual gain merit?; (d) were one to despise one's teachers, that person would be bereft and rejected, like Gehazi (2 Kings 5:20ff), that person

would be unable to find a teacher or a [spiritual] guide to bring the individual to the path of truth; (e) were one to hate moral criticism, then that person would have left no path for *teshuvah*. Such reproof makes for *teshuvah*, for when one is told of one's sins and is shamed as a result, one becomes penitent, even as it is written in the Torah, "Remember, do not forget . . . you were rebels" (Deuteronomy 9:24, 27) "and Adonai gave you heart" (Deuteronomy 29:3), "O people foolish and unwise" (Deuteronomy 32:6). Thus Isaiah criticizes Israel, "Ah, sinful nation" (Isaiah 1:4). "An ox knows the master's crib" (Isaiah 1:3). "Because I knew that you are obstinate" (Isaiah 48:4). Indeed, God instructed Isaiah to criticize sinners, as it is said, "Cry aloud, spare not" (Isaiah 58:1). Thus all the Prophets reproved Israel in order to encourage them to make *teshuvah*. Therefore, in each and every Jewish congregation, someone should be appointed to morally critique [or reprove] the others and encourage them to do *teshuvah*. Such a person should be a great scholar, advanced in years, reverent from one's youth, yet beloved by all one's people. Yet, the one who hates such reproach will hardly come to one who would offer such criticism, nor listen to such advice. That person will continue to sin since it seems good to do.

3. There are five things for which the individual cannot do complete *teshuvah*. They are sins between an individual and one's fellow. In such sins, one does not know against whom one has sinned. Thus, the individual cannot turn to one's fellow and ask to be forgiven. They are the following: (a) one who curses the community without designating any particular person from whom one could ask atonement; (b) one who divides up the spoil of a thief, because one does not know from whom the particular article was stolen; all that person knows is that the thief stole from the community and brought it forward. So the indi-

vidual just took it. Indeed, that person supports the thief and causes the thief to sin; (c) one who finds something lost and does not announce the find so that it might be restored to its owner. Afterward, having repented, the finder no longer knows to whom the article should be restored; (d) one who consumes the ox belonging to the poor, to orphans, or to widows. These are unfortunate people who are not well known, who wander from city to city. There is none to recognize the ox [and therefore its owner] in order to restore it to its owner; (e) one who receives a bribe to pervert justice may not know how far the perversion of justice may go and what its power would be to be reversed. The matter develops its own impetus. Indeed, such an act sustains the sinner and causes that person to sin further.

4. There are five things that are considered trivial. Thus, one may presume that most people will not repent of them because they are regarded as minor matters and are not regarded as sin. They are: (a) one who eats from a meal that is insufficient for those who tendered the invitation — there is a touch of theft here. One who does such a thing will imagine that nothing was done wrong, saying to oneself, "I only ate at their invitation"; (b) the one who makes use of the item pledged by a poor person. Even were the item an adze or a plow, one might say to oneself, "They will not lose anything. After all, I did not steal it from them"; (c) one who looks lewdly at another and says to oneself, "There is nothing wrong with it. After all, did I make love to her? Did I even come close to him?" Such a person does not realize that the very act of covetous looking is a great sin since it leads to the majority of sexual sins, as the Torah states, "Do not go after your hearts and after your eyes" (Numbers 15:39); (d) one who glories in one's friend's disgrace and says to oneself, "Look, my friend is not here. No shame has reached my friend. I have not shamed my friend" — all the individual has

done is compare one's own good deeds and one's wisdom to another's deeds and wisdom so that the comparison will make the individual seem honorable and the friend held in contempt; (e) one who suspects the upright, saying to oneself, "There is no sin in doing this. After all, I have not done anything to that person. There is only suspicion. Maybe that person did do something wrong, maybe not." Such a person does not realize that it is a transgression to consider an innocent person guilty.

5. There are five things that are so seductive that the sinner, once started, continually does them and has great difficulty not doing them. Therefore, a person should keep far from them in order not to be ensnared by them. They are all evil qualities: (a) talebearing; (b) gossip (*lashon hara*); (c) a choleric nature; (d) continually thinking evil thoughts; and (e) being the companion of a wicked person. The individual learns the evil person's acts and is impressed by them. It is as Solomon said: "But the companion of fools shall smart for it" (Proverbs 13:20). We have already explained in *Hilchot Deot* (laws relating to psychic dispositions) that every person should be careful about such qualities. How much more should one who has made *teshuvah* be careful.

6. All these and similar things impede *teshuvah* but don't prevent it. Were a person to fully repent of these things, that person would be a penitent and would therefore have a portion in the life to come.

CHAPTER FIVE

1. Free will is given to everyone. If one wishes to follow a path of goodness and be righteous, one can. If one wishes to follow a path of evil and be wicked, one can. That is what Scripture meant when it said, "Behold, Adam is unique; by his own

nature he knows good and evil" (Genesis 3:22) [this translation follows rabbinic interpretation]. In other words, the human species is unique in the world. No other species resembles it by being able by its nature, by mind and by thought, to know good and evil, able to do what we wish and with none to prevent us from doing good or evil. Because it is so, Scripture says, "Lest one stretch out one's hand . . ." (Genesis 3:22).

2. Let not what gentile fools and ignorant Jews think pass through your mind that God decrees from conception that any person will be righteous or wicked. The matter is simply not so. Each person has the ability to be as righteous as Moses our teacher or as wicked as Jereboam, to be wise or to be foolish, to be compassionate or cruel, to be a miser or a spendthrift, or any other inclination of character. There is no one who compels, decrees, or attracts the individual to do one thing or the other. Rather, the individual by oneself with one's own mind inclines to whatever way that person wishes to follow. Thus Jeremiah stated, "Evil and good do not proceed out of the mouth of the Most High" (Lamentations 3:38). In other words, the Creator does not ordain that any human being be righteous or wicked. Any one who sins has destroyed oneself. Therefore, it is fitting that such a person should weep and lament over one's sins. What that person has done to one's own soul caused it to suffer evil. Therefore, Scripture continued, "Why should a living human complain, a strong person because of sins" (Lamentations 3:39). Such a person should do *teshuvah* and say, "Since the choice was in our hands and with our minds we did all these evils, it is fitting for us to repent and to leave our wickedness. Once again the choice is ours, even as Scripture says, 'Let us search and try our ways and return to Adonai' (Lamentations 3:40)."

3. This is a great principle. Indeed it is a pillar of the Torah and the *mitzvot*. As the Torah states, "See, I have set before you

this day life and good and death and evil . . ." (Deuteronomy 30:15). Another verse says, "Behold, I have set before you this day a blessing and a curse . . ." (Deuteronomy 11:26). It is as if to say, "You have the choice. Whatever a person wishes to do as a human being, that person may do, whether good or bad." Because of this [human capacity] Scripture says, [for God] "Would that their heart were such as to fear Me and to keep My *mitzvot*" (Deuteronomy 5:26). In other words, the Creator neither decrees nor compels human beings to do good or do evil. Rather, everything is up to them.

4. Were God to decree that an individual be righteous or wicked or were there something that attracted a person by one's very nature to follow one path or another, whether it be knowledge or a notion or any particular act, as those fools scanning the heavens imagine, how then could God instruct us through the Prophets: "Do this, don't do that?" [How could God say] "Improve your ways. Don't follow after your own evil," if from one's very conception one was destined or one's physical makeup so moved the individual to something from which one could not budge? Indeed, what place would there be for such a situation? By what kind of justice and by what kind of law could the guilty be punished or the innocent rewarded? "Shall not the Judge of all the earth do justly?" (Genesis 18:25). Don't you wonder and say, "Well then, how can the individual do all that one wants and have all of one's acts under one's own control, if all that one does is under the control and desire of God, one's Possessor, even as Scripture says, "Whatever pleases Adonai, that has God done, in heaven and earth . . ." (Psalm 135:6). Know that all God wishes, God does. Even so, our acts are under our control. How? Just as the Creator wishes that fire and air ascend and water and earth descend and the sun sphere moves in a circular fashion and all other creatures follow the pattern that

God desires, so God wishes that the human person be free, able to choose, and all of our acts are under our own control. There is none to compel us or to attract us, but rather we ourselves with our own minds and our own understanding that God has given us are able to do all that a human being can do. Therefore, we are judged by our own acts. If we have done good, we receive good. If we have done evil, we receive evil. It is as the prophet said, "This has been of your own doing" (Malachi 1:9). [Another text says:] "Indeed, they have chosen their ways" (Isaiah 66:3). Concerning this matter, Solomon said, "Rejoice, young person, in your youth . . . but know that for all these things God will bring you into judgment" (Ecclesiastes 12:9). In other words, know that you have the power to do as you wish, but know that in the future you will be judged.

5. [This is all to keep you from] saying that God knows what will be seen before it happens and God knows who will be righteous and who will be wicked or God does not. If God does know who will be righteous, then it is impossible for that person not to be righteous; and if you say that God does know but that it is impossible for that person not to be righteous, then God really does not know! Know that the answer to this question is "longer than the measure of the earth and broader than the sea" (Job 11:9). Many important principles and great doctrines depend upon it, but you should know and understand what I am about to say. We have already explained in the second chapter of *Hilchot Yesodei Torah* (Laws of the Foundations of the Torah) that God does not know by knowledge that is exterior to God as people do, whose knowledge and being are different. Rather God, may God's name be praised, and God's knowledge are one. No human being can fully understand this, just as no human being can fully understand the true nature of the Creator, even as the Torah teaches, "No human shall see

Me and live" (Exodus 33:20). Similarly, it is not within the capacity of human beings to understand and comprehend divine knowledge. Thus the prophet said, "For My thoughts are not your thoughts, nor are your ways My ways, says Adonai" (Isaiah 55:8). As a result, we are not able to understand how God knows all created things and all [human] actions. But this we do know, without any doubt: each human being controls one's individual activity. The Holy Blessed One neither ordains [that one should do something] nor attracts anyone to do anything. It is not merely as a matter of religion that we know this. We know it as well by clear proofs from philosophy. Hence it is said in the prophetic literature that one is judged by one's acts, whether the acts are good or bad. All the words of prophecy depend on this principle.

CHAPTER SIX

1. There are many verses in the Torah and in the words of the Prophets that seem to contradict this principle [of free will]. As a result, many have stumbled and thought that the Holy Blessed One decrees that a person should do good or evil, that a person is unable to use one's mind to do otherwise. I, therefore, will explain this great principle since you will not know how to interpret those verses. When any individual or the members of any community sin (and the sinner intentionally, voluntarily sins as we have suggested), then that sinner should be punished. The Holy Blessed One knows how to punish. There are sins for which the sinner ought to be punished in this world through body, or wealth, or through one's minor children. Minor children do not yet understand. They have not reached the age of maturity, the age which they are obligated to fulfill the *mitzvot*. They are considered "possessions" of one's parents. The verse suggests, "Every person shall be put to death for one's

own sin" (Deuteronomy 24:16), in other words, when one becomes an adult. [An adult dies for one's own sin, yet a child may die for the sin of one's parents!] There are sins for which the sinner should be punished in the World to Come and not suffer at all in this world. There are also sins for which the sinner may be punished in this world and in the next world as well.

2. How can we apply these words? To the case of one who has not done *teshuvah*. If, however, one has repented, *teshuvah* is a shield against punishment. Just as one sinned intentionally, and willingly, so one should do *teshuvah* intentionally and willingly.

3. It is possible that the sin that one commits may be so great (or the sins may be so many) that the True Judge should properly punish that sinner for the sins committed freely, with intention. In such a case, *teshuvah* is withheld from that sinner and that person is not given the opportunity to turn away from wickedness so that one may die and be destroyed by the sin one committed. This is what the Holy Blessed One meant, speaking through the prophet Isaiah, "Make the heart of this people fat so that they do not . . . return and be healed" (Isaiah 6:10). [With a similar message], another verse states, ". . . they mocked the messengers of God, and despised Your words, and scoffed at Your prophets, until divine wrath arose against Your people, until there was no remedy" (2 Chronicles 36:16). In other words, they sinned so willingly and transgressed so frequently that the healing of *teshuvah* was withheld from them. For that reason, we have a verse in Torah, "I will harden Pharaoh's heart" (Exodus 4:21). Pharaoh first sinned on his own, harming the Israelites who were living in Egypt, as it says, "Come, let us deal wisely with them" (Exodus 1:10). It was appropriate that *teshuvah* was withheld from him so that he could be punished. Thus, the Holy Blessed One hardened his heart. [One might wonder then] why

God sent [a message] to Pharaoh through Moses to repent and
send out [the Israelites] when God had already said to him, "I
know that you will not send them out," as the verse suggests,
"But as for you and your servants, I know that you will not yet
fear Adonai as God" (Exodus 9:30). [The answer is indicated]
by the verse "But for this result have I made you stand, to show
you My power, so that My reputation could be declared throughout all the earth" (Exodus 9:16). This teaches to all who are in
this world that when the Holy Blessed One withholds *teshuvah*
from a sinner, that sinner will be unable to turn from sin. Instead, that person will die in that wickedness that first was done
willingly. The same is true with Sihon, who, because of his many
sins, had *teshuvah* withheld from him, as it says, ". . . for Adonai
your God hardened his spirit, and made his heart obstinate, that
you could deliver him into your hand . . ." (Deuteronomy 2:30).
In the same way, because of their abominations, God kept the
Canaanites from *teshuvah* so that they would wage war against
Israel, as it says, "For it was Adonai who hardened their hearts,
to come against Israel in battle, that they might be utterly destroyed, that they might have no favor, that they be destroyed as
Adonai commanded Moses" (Joshua 11:20). The same is true
with Israel in the time of Elijah. They had sinned so often that
God prevented those who were accustomed to sin from repenting, as it says, ". . . for You turned their hearts backward" (1 Kings
18:37). In other words, "You have withheld *teshuvah* from
them." It follows that God did not decree that Pharaoh should
harm Israel or that Sihon should sin in his land or that the
Canaanites should act abominably or that Israel should worship
idolatry. All of them sinned on their own. All were punished by
being kept from being able to do *teshuvah*.

4. There is something similar [about withholding *teshuvah*] to what the righteous and the Prophets do when they ask

in their prayers to God for aid in their pursuit of truth. When David wrote, "Teach me, O Adonai, Your way, so that I may walk in Your truth" (Psalm 86:11), he meant, "Do not let my sins block the path of truth through which I may know Your ways and the uniqueness of Your reputation." Thus when David said, "And let a willing spirit uphold me" (Psalm 51:14), he meant, "Let my spirit do Your will. Do not let my sins keep me from repentance. Rather let the choice be mine until I return, knowing and understanding the way of the truth." These verses can be understood in a similar manner.

5. What then is the meaning of David's words: "Good and upright is Adonai. Thus does God instruct sinners in the way. You guide the humble in justice and You teach the humble Your way" (Psalm 25:8). It means that God has sent prophets to inform people of God's ways so that God may move them to *teshuvah*. It further means that God has given them the power to learn and understand. That quality is in every person as long as people follow the ways of wisdom so that justice becomes attractive to them and [as it were] pursues them. This is what the Rabbis meant when they said, "The one who comes to purify will receive aid [from on high]." In other words, that person will be assisted in the task. [Were one to respond] it is written in the Torah, ". . . [they] shall serve them and they shall afflict them" (Genesis 15:13), [remember it was] God who decreed that the Egyptians do evil! Is it not written, ". . . and this people will rise up, and go astray after the foreign gods of the land . . ." (Deuteronomy 31:16). Behold, God decreed that Israel would worship idols! Why then did God punish them? [The answer is that] God did not decree that any one individual be the one to go astray. Each and every one of those individuals, had they wished, could have refrained from worshiping the idols. What the Creator did was to inform Moses of what might be the general course of

events. It is as if one would say of a particular people that it would include righteous and wicked persons. No wicked person can say that just because God informed Moses that there would be wicked persons in Israel that it was therefore ordained that one should be wicked. In the same manner the verse "The poor shall never cease from the land" (Deuteronomy 15:11) [does not require that any particular individual be poor]. The same is the case with the Egyptians. Each one of those afflicting Israel had the ability to refrain had he or she wished to do so. God does not decree the actions of any individual. God merely informed Abraham that his offspring would be slaves in a foreign land. We have already stated that it is not within human capacity to understand how the Holy Blessed One knows the things that will occur in the future.

CHAPTER SEVEN

1. Every person has free will, as has been explained. Hence, let each person endeavor to repent, confess one's sins aloud, and cleanse oneself of one's sins. In this way, one may die as one who has repented and, as a result, merit life in the World to Come.

2. Each person should always view oneself as if one were about to die. Therefore, one should always repent on the chance that a person might die any moment and remain tied to one's sins. Let no one say, "I will repent when I become old." That person may not live long enough to become old. This is what Solomon meant when he wisely wrote, "Let your garments be always white. And let your head lack no oil" (Ecclesiastes 9:8).

3. Don't say [to yourself] that repentance relates only to sins that involve an action, such as illicit sex, cheating, or theft. Just as one should repent for such acts, so should one search

oneself for such evil dispositions as anger, enmity, mockery, the pursuit of money, the pursuit of glory, gluttony, or similar inclinations. For these things, one must repent. [In a way,] they are more serious than those that involve an action, for were a person given over to them, that person would have difficulty separating from them. For that reason, Scripture states, "Let the wicked forsake the [evil] way. And the person of iniquity, one's thoughts. And let that person return to Adonai" (Isaiah 55:9).

4. Let no repentant sinner imagine that he or she is far from the level of the righteous because of the transgressions and sins that they committed. Indeed, the matter is not so. That person [the sinner] is beloved and desirable to our Creator as if he or she had never sinned. More than that, the individual's reward is great, for that person had tasted sin and yet separated from it. Thereby the individual controlled the inclination [to do evil]. The Sages have said that where the penitent stand, no completely righteous person can stand. They meant that the level of those who are penitent is higher than the level of those who have never sinned because they [those who sinned and repented] have controlled their inclinations more than the others.

5. All the Prophets exhorted [the people] to do *teshuvah*. Israel can only be redeemed through *teshuvah*. The Torah has already guaranteed that Israel will repent at the end of its exile. At that moment, [Israel] will be redeemed, as the Torah states, "And it will come to pass, when all these things have come upon you, the blessing and the curse, which I have set before you, and you will think yourself among all the nations, where Adonai your God has driven you. You will return to Adonai your God and hearken to God's voice according to all that I instruct you today, you and your children, with all your heart and with all your soul. Then Adonai your God will turn your captivity and have compassion on you and will return and gather you from

[among] all the peoples, where Adonai your God has scattered you" (Deuteronomy 30:1–3).

6. Great is *teshuvah*, for it brings the individual closer to the *Shechinah*, as the Scripture states, "Return, O Israel, to Adonai your God" (Hosea 14:2). Another verse teaches, "'You have not returned to Me,' says Adonai" (Amos 4:6). Yet another verse says, "If you would return to Me, O Israel, you would re-turn" (Jeremiah 4:1). The verse means that if you return in *teshuvah* to Me [says God] you would [therefore] cleave [to Me]. *Teshuvah* brings near those who are far off. The person who was recently hateful to God, abhorrent, distant, an abomination, the same person today is beloved, desired, near, a close friend. [The difference is *teshuvah*!] You will note that the same expressions by which the Holy Blessed One keeps sinners at a distance, God brings those who do *teshuvah* close [to God]. This is true whether the penitents are individuals or an entire people. Thus, the prophet speaks [for God], "And it will come to pass that, instead of what was said to them, 'You are not my people,' it will be said to them, 'You are the children of the living God' (Hosea 2:1). When Yeconiah was wicked, it was said of him, "Write that this man will be childless, a man that shall not prosper in his days" (Jeremiah 22:30) and ". . . were Coniah, the son of Yehoiakim, king of Judah, the signet upon My right hand, I would pluck you out anyway" (Jeremiah 22:24). Yet it was said of his son Zerubbabel, when exiled, he repented, "'On that day,' says Adonai Tzevaot, 'will I take you, O Zerubbabel, the son of Shealtiel. My servant,' says Adonai, 'I will make you as a signet, for I have chosen you,' says Adonai Tzevaot" (Haggai 2:23).

7. How marvelous is *teshuvah*! Recently, this person was separated from Adonai, the God of Israel, as it says, "But your iniquities have separated you from your God" (Isaiah 59:2). That person might have called out but was not answered, as it says,

". . . when you make many prayers, I will not hear" (Isaiah 1:15).
Though that person may observe the *mitzvot*, they are thrown
into his or her face, as it is said, "Who told you to do this, to
trample My courts?" (Isaiah 1:12). And "'Oh, that there were
even one among you that would shut My doors, that you might
not kindle fire on My altar in vain! I have no pleasure in you,'
says Adonai Tzevaot. 'Neither will I accept an offering at your
hand . . .'" (Malachi 1:10). Another verse says, "Add your burnt-
offerings to your sacrifices, and eat flesh" (Jeremiah 7:21). Today,
the same person [having done *teshuvah*] cleaves to the *Shechinah*,
as the Torah states, "You who cleaved to Adonai your God are
alive today, every one of you" (Deuteronomy 4:4). Now should
that person cry out, that person will be immediately answered,
as Scripture states, "And it will come to pass, that before they
call, I will answer. While they are still speaking, I will respond"
(Isaiah 65:24). Should that person now perform a *mitzvah*, it
will be readily and joyously accepted, as it is said, "For God has
already accepted your works" (Ecclesiastes 9:7). Not only that,
such acts are desired [by God] as the text has it, "Then will the
offering of Judah and Jerusalem be pleasant to Adonai, as in the
days of old, as in ancient days" (Malachi 3:4).

8. Penitents should be exceedingly meek and humble.
Should fools berate them concerning their former deeds, saying, "But last night you did such and such," the penitents should
not be upset. Rather, they should listen with joy knowing that
[such mocking] constitutes merit for them. Indeed, the more
that they are embarrassed and ashamed because of what they
have done in the past, the more their merit is increased and their
status improved. However, it is a great sin to say to a penitent,
"Remember your former deeds" or to remind the individual of
them [past sins] in order to cause embarrassment or to mention
similar matters so that the person who did *teshuvah* will remem-

ber past sins. All of this is forbidden. Such acts come under the category of wronging someone with words, something prohibited by the Torah, as it says, "And you will not wrong one another. Rather, you will fear Adonai your God, for I am Adonai your God" (Leviticus 25:17).

CHAPTER EIGHT

1. Life in the World to Come is [full of] that goodness that is stored up for the righteous. It is a life in which death does not intrude. It is goodness without any evil mixed in. It is that [life] to which Torah refers, "That it may be well with you and that you may prolong your days" (Deuteronomy 22:7). [Jewish] tradition understood those words thus: "That it may be well with you" — in a world that is totally good; "that you may prolong your days" — in a world that is without end, that is, in the World to Come. As a reward, the righteous will merit this joy and be in this goodness. The wicked will be punished so that they will not merit that life. Rather, they will be cut off and die. Whoever will not merit that [eternal] life will die and never again live. Rather, that person will be cut off as a result of his/her sin and will be destroyed like an animal. That is the meaning of *karet*, literally "cut off," to which the Torah refers, as in ". . . that soul will be utterly cut off, its iniquity will be upon him or her" (Numbers 15:31). The tradition interpreted the verse to mean that the individuals who sin will be cut off in this world *and* in the World to Come. It is as if to say that the soul of the one who sins when it separates from the body in this world will not merit entering the World to Come. Rather, it will be cut off from that world.

2. In the World to Come, there are no physical bodies at all. Instead, the souls of the righteous exist without bodies, like the ministering angels. Since there are no bodies, there is no

eating or drinking, nothing that humans might need in this world. There is no sitting, standing, sleeping, death, sadness, joy, nor anything similar. Thus, the ancient Sages said that in the World to Come there would be neither eating, drinking, nor sexual intercourse. Instead, the righteous would sit with crowns on their heads and bask in the light of the *Shechinah*. It is therefore clear to you that if there are no bodies, there can be no eating or drinking. Even the statement that the righteous would sit has to be understood as a metaphor. The sitting of the righteous means that they exist there [in the World to Come] without labor, without toil. What is said about their crowns is also a metaphor. It means that the knowledge that merited their life in the World to Come remains with them there. It is their own crown, just like what Solomon meant when he said, ". . . the crown with which his mother crowned him . . ." (Song of Songs 3:11). The "joy" in the verse "And everlasting joy will be upon their heads" (Isaiah 35:11) is not something physical that could rest on one's head. Likewise, the "crown" of which the Sages spoke [is also not physical]. It is a metaphor for knowledge. When the Sages spoke about basking in the light of *Shechinah*, they spoke in a metaphor. It means that the righteous will apprehend and understand something about the true nature of the Holy Blessed One, which they could not do while confirmed by in their lowly, opaque bodies.

3. The soul spoken of here is not that kind of soul that needs the body. Rather, it is the form of the soul. It is that knowledge of the Creator, of the abstract notions and other matters that it apprehends, according to its ability. It is the form that we discussed in chapter four of the "Laws regarding the Principles of the Torah." In this context, it [the soul] is called *nefesh*. A life that is without death is a life without a body, because death is an accident of [mortal] bodies. Since in the World to Come

there are no bodies, there can be no death. Such a life is called "the bundle of life," as it is said, ". . . the soul of my lord shall be bound in the bundle of life with Adonai your God" (1 Samuel 25:29). This is the greatest possible reward and the greatest possible good. It is this that every prophet desired.

4. Metaphorically, it has been called by a number of names, specifically, the mountain of Adonai, God's holy place, the way of holiness, the courts of Adonai, the pleasantness of Adonai, the tent of Adonai, the temple of Adonai, the house of Adonai, and the gate of Adonai. The Sages referred metaphorically to that good that was destined for the righteous as a banquet. They generally called it the World to Come.

5. The greatest possible punishment is that the soul gets cut off so that it does not merit that life [in the World to Come], just as the verse states, "That soul shall be utterly cut off, its iniquity shall be upon it" (Numbers 15:31). This is what the Prophets called "the pit of destruction," "extinction," "*tofet*" [hell], and "leech." They applied [to *karet*] terms of annihilation and destruction because the extinction of the soul is a loss that cannot be restored, a damage that cannot be repaired.

6. Perhaps this [notion of] good may seem trifling to you. You may imagine that the proper reward to a person [performing] the *mitzvot* and being perfect in the ways of truth should be to drink and eat good food, have [wonderful] sex with beautiful people, dress in embroidered garments of linen, dwell in ivory residences, use silver and gold vessels and other similar [material] things. That [conception] would be like the kind that the foolish, stupid, and sexually obsessed Arabs imagine. The Sages and people of knowledge, however, know that such a view is foolish and meaningless, without any purpose. In this world, we have bodies. Since such things [like food and sex] are necessary for the body, the soul might passionately desire them for

the health and well-being of the body. When there is no body, all these things would be useless. In this world, there is no way to apprehend or know the [kind of] great good that the soul will have in the World to Come. In this world, all we know is what is good for the body, what we desire. However, this world provides no comparison to that exceedingly great good [for the soul] except by way of the metaphor of eating and drinking. In truth, there is no way to compare that [ultimate] benefit of soul in the World to Come with the benefits of the body in this world. That great good is unimaginable and incomparable. It is the kind that David spoke of, saying, "How abundant is the goodness that You have stored up for the one who reveres You" (Psalm 31:20).

7. How much did David desire the World to Come! Even as it is written, "If I had not believed [enough] to look upon the goodness of Adonai in the land of the living!" (Psalm 27:13). The ancient Sages have already informed us that no human being has the ability to fully comprehend the goodness of the World to Come nor have a sense of its nature, its greatness, or its beauty. The Holy Blessed One alone has that ability. All the benefits about which the Prophets foretold regarding Israel were only physical things that Israel would enjoy during Messianic Time when dominion would return to Israel. The goodness of the life in the World to Come has no comparison or likeness. The Prophets never likened it to anything else in order to prevent themselves from diminishing it. It is what Isaiah said: "No eye has seen, O God, other than You, what You will do for the one who waits for You" (Isaiah 64:3). The verse means that the good God has prepared for the one who waits for God is known only by God and is seen by no one else, not even by a prophet. The Sages said [to confirm this view] that the Prophets prophesied only with regard to Messianic Time, but with regard to the World to Come, "No eye has seen, O God, other than You."

8. The World to Come was not so named by the Sages, because [they held that] that world does not presently exist or that it will arrive when this world disappears. No way! That world presently exists, reflected in the verse "Oh, how abundant is Your goodness, which You have stored up for those who revere you" (Psalm 31:20). They named it [the World to Come] because of the life that comes to a person after this world in which we exist as body and soul, the way that every person first exists.

CHAPTER NINE

1. It is known that the reward for the performance of the *mitzvot* and the good that we will merit if we keep the way of Adonai as written in the Torah is life in the World to Come, as it says, "So that it may be well with you so that you may prolong your days" (Deuteronomy 22:7). The punishment meted out for those who have forsaken the paths of righteousness that is written in the Torah as *karet* (being cut off) is as the Torah states, "That soul shall certainly be cut off, its iniquity will be in it" (Numbers 15:31). Thus, what then is the meaning of those statements found throughout the Torah: "If you hearken, such and such will come to you" and "If you don't hearken, such and such will happen to you." Examples of such promises and threats include: war and peace, domination and degradation, dwelling in the Land [of Israel] and exile [from it], success and failure, and the other words of the *Brit* (Covenant). All these things are true. They have been and they will be. When we perform all the *mitzvot* of the Torah, we will receive all the benefits of this world. When we transgress those *mitzvot*, then all the evils written in the Torah will happen to us. Even so, all those benefits are not the end of the reward for [those who observe] the *mitzvot*. This is the pattern: the Holy Blessed One has given us the Torah.

It is a tree of life. Whoever does all that is written in it, knows it properly and completely, will merit life in the World to Come. That merit will depend on the number of deeds and the level of knowledge. God has promised us through the Torah that if we do [the *mitzvot*] in a good spirit, with joy, and continually enjoy its wisdom, God will keep from us things such as sickness, war, famine, and the like that prevent our [future] doing [of the *mitzvot*]. God will shower upon us good [things] such as prosperity, peace, and wealth. This strengthens our hands to do [the *mitzvot* of] the Torah. We will not have to spend our days pursuing those things that the body needs. Instead, we will be free to study wisdom and pursue the *mitzvot* through which we may merit life in the World to Come. Thus, God says in the Torah after promising good in this world, "and it will be righteousness for us, if we observe to do all the *mitzvot* before Adonai our God, as God has instructed us" (Deuteronomy 6:25). God has also informed us through the Torah that if we consciously forsake the Torah and occupy ourselves with the vanities of the time as the Torah states, "But Yeshurun got fat and kicked" (Deuteronomy 32:15), then the True Judge will remove from those who forsake [the Torah] all the benefits of this world that enabled them to kick. And [God] will bring upon them all the evils that will impede them from acquiring the World to Come so that they may be destroyed in their wickedness. This is what the Torah meant when it said, "Because you did not serve Adonai your God joyfully, with gladness of heart, by reason of the abundance of all things. Therefore, you will serve your enemy whom Adonai will send against you, in hunger, and in thirst, and in nakedness, and in want of all things . . ." (Deuteronomy 28:47–48). You will serve your enemies whom Adonai will send against you. The explanation of all the blessings and curses is that if you serve Adonai joyfully and keep God's way, then God will shower you with blessings and keep curses far away from you. Thus, you will be free to become wiser through the Torah and be occupied with it so that you will merit life in the World to Come. God will do good for you in the life in the world that is entirely good and you will extend your days in a world that is endless. Thus, you will merit two worlds: a good life in this world, which will bring you to the life in the World to Come. If one does not acquire wisdom and good deeds in this life, how then will one gain merit [for the World to Come]? It is as the verse teaches, ". . . for there is no work, device, knowledge, nor wisdom in the grave" (Ecclesiastes 9:10). If you have forsaken Adonai, and erred through food, drink, sex, and the like, God will bring upon you all these curses and will remove all the blessings. Your days will be spent in terror and fear so that you will not have a free mind or a healthy body to perform the *mitzvot* and you will lose the World to Come. Thus, you will lose both worlds. When a person suffers sickness, war, and famine in this world, that person will not engage in the gaining of wisdom or the performing of the *mitzvot* by which one merits life in the World to Come.

2. Therefore, all Israel, its Prophets, and its Sages, yearned for Messianic Time, which would release them from the power of the kingdoms that did not permit them to properly engage in the study of the Torah and the performance of the *mitzvot*. Then they would find the leisure that would enable them to gain wisdom and so merit the life in the World to Come. In those [messianic] days, knowledge, wisdom, and truth would increase, as foretold in the verses "For the earth will be full of knowledge of Adonai. As the waters cover the sea" (Isaiah 11:9) and ". . . they will teach no more every person, one's neighbor, and every person, one's siblings, saying, 'Know Adonai, for they will all know Me' . . ." (Jeremiah 31:34) and "I will take away the stony heart out of your flesh and I will give you a heart of flesh"

(Ezekiel 36:26). The leader from the seed of David who will arise at that time will be a wiser person even than Solomon. A prophet almost as great as Moses our Teacher, who, therefore, will teach all of the people and guide them to the way of Adonai. All the nations will come to hear him, as the verse says, "And it will come to pass at the end of the days that the mountain of Adonai's house will be established as the top of the mountains. And it will be exalted above the hills. All nations shall flow unto it. And many peoples will say: 'Come you, and let us go up to the mountain of Adonai to the house of the God of Jacob.' And you will teach us your ways, and we will walk in your paths" (Isaiah 2:2; Micah 4:1). Life in the World to Come is the ultimate reward, [the enjoyment of] absolute goodness without interruption or deficiency. Messianic days, however, are in this world operating in its usual way with the difference that dominion has returned to Israel. The Sages of old already stated that the only difference between this world and Messianic Time would be that imperial power [over Israel] would be removed.

CHAPTER TEN

1. Let no one say, "I will perform the *mitzvot* of the Torah and will engage in the study of its wisdom so that I can receive all of its blessings or so that I can merit life in the World to Come." [Let no one say], "I will keep far from the transgressions that the Torah warns against so that I will be saved from the curses listed in the Torah or that I may not be cut off from the life in the World to Come." It is not fitting to serve Adonai in this manner. That would be serving Adonai out of fear. That would not be the way of the Prophets or the Sages. Only the ignorant serve God out of fear since they are not yet educated to serve Adonai out of love.

2. The one who serves God out of love, studies the Torah, does the *mitzvot*, and walks in the paths of wisdom does so for no worldly reason. [This person does not serve God] out of fear of evil or because of a hope to inherit what is good. Rather, the individual simply wishes to engage the truth because it is the truth. Also [because of] our ancestor Abraham, whom the Holy Blessed One called "my friend," because Abraham served only out of love. It is the level that the Holy Blessed One instructed us through Moses, saying, "you should love Adonai your God" (Deuteronomy 6:5). When one loves Adonai with a proper love, that person will immediately do all the *mitzvot* out of love.

3. What is that proper love? It is when one will love Adonai with such an exceedingly great love, so strong that a person's soul will be bound up with the love of Adonai, so utterly engrossed that a person will seem lovesick, like a man who can't keep his mind off a particular woman [or a woman's mind off a man], continually thinking of the other person, whether sitting, eating, or drinking. The love of Adonai should be even greater than this in the hearts of those who would love God. They should be thinking of God continually, as God has instructed us, "with all your heart and with all your soul" (Deuteronomy 6:5). It is what Solomon meant when he said in a parable, "For I am lovesick" (Songs 2:5). Indeed, all of the Song of Songs is a parable about this [kind of love].

4. The Sages of old said, "You might say, 'I will study Torah in order to become rich or so that I may be called Rabbi or that I may receive reward in the World to Come,' therefore Scripture teaches 'Love Adonai your God' (Deuteronomy 19:9; 30:6; 16:20)." All that you do should be done only for love. The Sages continued this notion when they commented on the verses "Happy is the person who delights greatly in your *mitzvot*" (Psalm 112:1, 2). They said [it says] "your *mitzvot*" and not "the

reward for your *mitzvot.*" Thus, the greatest of the Sages would charge the most intelligent and understanding among their students: "Do not be like servants who serve their master in order to receive a reward" (*Pirkei Avot* 2:3). Because God is *the* master, it is fitting to serve God out of love.

5. Whoever studies the Torah in order to receive a reward or in order to avoid punishment is not studying the Torah for its own sake. Whoever studies the Torah out of love instead of fear and not to receive a reward, the Master of all the earth who instructed it [the Torah] is the one studying Torah for its own sake. The Sages said that one should always study the Torah even if not for its own sake. Therefore, when one teaches children, and the majority of unlearned people, one teaches them to serve out of fear and to receive a reward. As their understanding improves and they become wiser, one then reveals little by little the secret [of serving God out of love] until they become accustomed to know and understand it so that they may serve out of love.

6. It is perfectly clear that the love of God can be linked to a person's heart only when that person is properly and continually engrossed in it. [As a result,] that person will forsake everything else in the world. It is as God instructed and said, "With all your heart and with all your soul" (Deuteronomy 6:5). One loves God only through the knowledge that one possesses. According to the [level of] knowledge, so [comes] the love: if little [knowledge], then little [love]; if much [knowledge], then much [love]. Everyone, therefore, should dedicate oneself to understand and comprehend the scientific concepts that will lead one to know one's Master as far as it is humanly possible to know and to comprehend. We have already explained this in *Hilchot Yesodei Torah* (Laws of the Foundations of the Torah).

❈ 7 ❈

Hilchot Deot
(Laws of Disposition)

Moses Maimonides

This selection, like the one that precedes it, was taken from the massive collection of Jewish law collected by Moses Maimonides (1135–1204) under the name *Mishneh Torah*. This small section is from a larger part of the collection called *Hilchot Deot*, material that is relevant to personal growth and development. In a sense, therefore, it is designed to enhance the path of *teshuvah* of the individual as directed in *Hilchot Teshuvah*. All of the material is compiled in such a way as to help the individual organize and reorient his or her life to a righteous life.

CHAPTER ONE

1. There is a vast range of personality traits to be found among people. One person may be hostile and continually enraged. Another may be placid and hardly ever angry. One person may be exceedingly proud, while another may be exceedingly humble. One person may be so desirous that he is never satisfied, while another is so pure-hearted that he/she does not desire even inconsequential things that the body may need. One

person may be so greedy that no amount of money can satisfy him [or her], as Scripture says, "the one who loves silver will not be satisfied with silver" (Ecclesiastes 5:9). Another may be so frugal, satisfied with something that really is not sufficient but will not expend the effort to get what is needed. One person will afflict the self with famine while gathering funds. Only after great tribulation will a penny be spent. Another will consciously squander all one's wealth. All of these people reflect personality traits: manic and melancholic, miserly and spendthrift, cruel and compassionate, tenderhearted and hard-hearted.

2. Within each trait are extremes, but there is also middle ground. Some of these traits are genetic, grounded within a person's physical constitution. Some are physical dispositions that make a particular trait more easily acquired, and some have no physical basis but are the learned result of habit.

3. The ultimate extremes of any particular trait are not the proper path for anyone to follow. No one should set them as a goal, nor teach them to oneself. If one finds oneself attracted to one or disposed to one, it has already become a habit. Thus, let one change oneself to the better. Model the ways of good people. Follow the proper path.

4. The proper path is the mean in any human trait. It is that which is midway between extremes, equally far from and close to each. The Sages of old, therefore, charged everyone to reflect upon and evaluate one's own traits and direct them toward a middle path. As a result, each person might be completely healthy. Thus, a person should not be so irascible to be easily provoked and, fittingly so, to prevent the reoccurrence of a heinous matter. Therefore, let a person desire only those things that the body absolutely requires, as taught by the verse "The righteous eat [only] until satisfied of desire" (Proverbs 13:25). Therefore let a person be engaged in business only to acquire what is

needed at any particular moment, as the verse has it, "A little is good [enough] for the righteous" (Psalm 37:16). A person should neither be tight fisted nor spendthrift. One should give charity according to one's means and grant loans to whomever is in need. Let a person not go about ridiculously happy or consistently depressed. Instead, let that cheerful person rejoice quietly throughout life. So it is with all traits: one should follow the teaching of the Sages in order to find the middle road, without extremes. A person who follows this path is called wise [*chacham*].

5. One who is punctilious about one's own behavior, who would move only a slight distance to one side or the other of the middle path, is considered pious. If one were to simply become humble, the middle ground, such as a move, would be the mark of wisdom. Such a person would be called wise. It is the same with all traits. The pious of old would move their traits from the mean toward either extreme; some would move in one direction and others would move in another. This is going beyond the letter of the law, for we are instructed to follow the middle paths, which are the appropriate ways, as taught by the verse ". . . you should walk in God's ways" (Deuteronomy 28:9).

6. They [the Sages] explained the *mitzvah* [in the verse above] thus: As God is gracious, so should you be; as God is compassionate, so should you be; as God is called holy, so should you be. In the same manner, the Prophets described God as "long-suffering," "full of mercy," "righteous and upright," "perfect," "mighty," and "powerful," and others to make known that these are appropriate characteristics that a person should emulate. By doing so, one might imitate God, as far as it is humanly [and individually] possible.

7. How does a person train oneself in these [proper] traits until they become part of oneself? Do them once, then again, and then a third time! One should keep doing these things to

reach the middle path until they seem easy and no bother. In so doing, one will fix them on the soul. By these terms, the Creator is known. They are the middle path that we are obliged to follow. This way is called the "way of Adonai." It is that which Abraham [and Sarah] our ancestors taught their children, as the Torah teaches, "For I have known them so that they may command their children and their household after them, that they may keep the way of Adonai to do righteousness and justice" (Genesis 18:19). Whoever goes in this path brings blessed goodness to oneself, as the verse continues, "to the end that Adonai may bring upon Abraham, as God has spoken of him" (Genesis 18:19).

CHAPTER TWO

1. Some physically ill people taste bitter as sweet and sweet as bitter. Other sick people, depending on the severity of their illness, have an implacable desire to eat things that are not edible, such as dirt and charcoal, while they hate eating good food, such as bread and meat. Similarly, people who are soul-sick, depending on the severity of their illness, will desire evil traits and reject the proper path [in life], either because they are too lazy to follow it or because they find it too difficult. About such people Isaiah said, "Woe to them that call evil good and good evil, that change darkness into light, and light into darkness, that change bitter into sweet, and sweet into bitter!" (Isaiah 5:20). How is such soul-sickness treated? Those afflicted should go to those who are aware of their evil traits, and those who do not seek help to be cured by the wise are described by Solomon's words, ". . . the foolish despise wisdom and discipline" (Proverbs 1:7).

2. How is the treatment [for soul-sickness] carried out? The one who is always angry is told to conduct oneself so that even if beaten or cursed one does not respond at all. That person is to continue in this manner for as long as it takes to eradicate anger from the heart. If one is arrogant, then let that person endure contempt. Let that individual sit at the lowest level and dress in the kind of rags that bring contempt to whoever wears them. [Let that person] do such things until the trait of arrogance is removed so that the individual may return to the middle way, which is the proper path. Having reached that middle ground, let that person remain there throughout life. In this manner, let the individual deal with all one's traits. If one is far from one extreme, let one move to the other and remain there for an appreciable amount of time until one can return to the middle way, which is the proper path for each and every trait.

3. There are traits regarding which it is forbidden to remain in the middle. Rather, [in such cases] one should move from one extreme to the other. Arrogance would be such a trait. Being humble is not enough. One should be exceptionally lowly in spirit. It is said of Moses our Master that he was "exceedingly humble" (Numbers 12:3) and *not* merely that he was humble! Therefore, the Sages instruct each person to be exceedingly humble. They further said that whoever is haughty rejects God, even as the Torah states, "When your heart will be lifted up, you forget Adonai your God" (Deuteronomy 8:14). The Sages added that the possessor of any measure of pride, however small, should be placed under the ban. Anger is equally an especially evil trait. An individual should keep as far as possible from it. One should teach oneself not to get angry even when anger is appropriate to a particular situation. One may pretend to be angry in order to improve the behavior of one's children,

household, or community, if one can be a leader by eliciting fear in them. One may appear to be outwardly angry, but one must be inwardly calm. One simply pretends to be angry; one does not [actually] become angry. The Sages of old said that the angry person was like one who was an idolater. They further said that if one becomes angry, if a sage, wisdom will be taken from that person. If a prophet, prophecy will be taken from that person. The life of those who are continually angry is no [real] life. For that reason, the Sages taught that the best way to deal with anger is to condition oneself not to react to things that ordinarily would cause one to be angry. The pattern of the righteous is to accept being insulted, not to insult others, to listen to reproaches directed at them and not respond. Acting out of love, they rejoiced in their suffering. Scripture speaks of them in these words: "But they that love You should be as the sun when it goes forth in its strength" (Judges 5:31).

4. One should practice being silent. One should speak only about matters of wisdom or about those matters that are necessary for physical survival. It was said of Rav, the student of Rabbi Judah the Prince, that he, unlike the majority of other people, never engaged in idle conversation. Even concerning the needs of the body, one should limit one's speech. To this end, the Sages stated, "The one who multiplies words occasions sin" (*Pirkei Avot* 1:17). They also said, "I have found nothing better for a person than silence" (*Pirkei Avot* 1:17). Even discussing matters of Torah and matters of wisdom, one's words should be few and full of meaning. That is what the Sages meant when suggesting that in teaching one's student, one should do so concisely. Folly occurs when words are many and meanings are few. This is what Scripture meant when it said, "For a dream comes through a multitude of business. And a fool's voice [comes] through a multitude of words" (Ecclesiastes 5:2).

5. "A fence around wisdom is silence" (*Pirkei Avot* 3:14). Therefore, one should not answer too quickly or speak too much. One should teach one's students calmly and quietly, without shouting, without speaking too long. That is what Solomon meant when he said, "The words of the wise spoken quietly are heard" (Ecclesiastes 9:17).

6. It is forbidden to get used to being persuaded through flattery. One should not be one thing in the mouth and another in the mind. One should be a person with integrity. What is in the heart should be what is [also] in the mouth. It is forbidden to mislead anyone, including a non-Jew. For example, one should not sell to a non-Jew meat from an animal that died while the [non-Jewish] individual thinks that it is meat from an animal that was slaughtered. Nor should one sell [the non-Jewish] individual a sandal made from [the hide of] an animal that died while [the non-Jewish] person thinks that it was made from [the hide of an] animal that was slaughtered. One should not press a friend to [accept an invitation to] dine knowing that the friend will refuse. One should not ply another with gifts knowing that the other will not accept [them]. One should not open up a barrel of wine as if to honor a friend when in fact one would have had to open it in order to sell it. In these and in similar cases, even one word of false claims or deception is forbidden. Honest speech, a proper spirit, and a pure heart are to be preferred over practiced deceit.

7. One should neither be one who jokes or makes mockery. One should neither be melancholy nor mournful. One should be happy. The Sages said, "Jesting and levity accustom a person to lewdness" (*Pirkei Avot* 3:14). The Sages ordered that one should neither laugh all the time nor be continually sad and mournful. Rather, one should receive every person cheerfully. One should not want too much so that one chases after wealth,

nor should one be so complacent that one does not work. One should be contented, engaging little in business but much in Torah. One should rejoice in the little that one does have. One should not be contentious, jealous, lustful, or in pursuit of glory. The Sages said, "Jealousy, lust, and ambition put a person out of this world" (*Pirkei Avot* 4:21). In summary, let every person walk a middle path with regard to each and every trait, so that all traits are directed toward a mean. This is what Solomon meant when he said, "Balance your steps, so that your ways may be firmly established" (Proverbs 4:26).

CHAPTER THREE

1. Were one to say, "Since envy, lust, ambition, and similar things are an evil path leading one out of this world, I will keep far from them," avoiding them to the extreme so that one would not eat meat, drink wine, marry, live in a nice house, wear nice clothing, and instead [wear] only sackcloth and rough wool like priests of other religions, then [I would say that] this too is an evil way that one is forbidden to pursue. Anyone who does so is called a sinner. As the Torah states, ". . . [the priest] shall make atonement for him [the sinner] because he sinned against the soul" (Numbers 6:31). The Sages said that if the Nazirite who only abstained from wine [was called a sinner and] required atonement, then how much more should anyone who abstained from any [permitted] thing! The Sages, therefore, stated that one should only abstain from those things that the Torah proscribed. One should not prohibit oneself through oaths and vows the enjoyment of permitted things. The Sages asked, "Was it not enough for you that the Torah prohibited [some things] that you had to add others?" In this category [of those who add additional burdens] fall those who continually fast. This is not a good path

to follow. The Sages prohibited the affliction of oneself by fasting. Concerning all such matters, Solomon wrote, "Be not overly righteous; neither make yourself overly wise. Why should you destroy yourself?" (Ecclesiastes 7:16).

2. One should concentrate one's mind and [direct] all of one's actions to know God. Whether lying down or rising up or simply speaking, one should be directed to this goal. Thus, when involved in business or engaged in labor that produces a wage, one should not view this as merely the amassing of money but rather the achieving of the means by which one deals with bodily needs such as food, drink, housing, and [even] marriage. When one eats and drinks and has sexual intercourse, one should not view these as mere bodily pleasures, so that one does not eat and drink only what is delicious and have sex only for its pleasure. Rather, one should view these activities as the means by which the body is maintained. Therefore, one should not, like a dog or a donkey, eat only on the basis of taste. One should eat things that are beneficial for the body, whether they are bitter or sweet. [Likewise] one should not eat things harmful for the body, just because they taste good. Thus, if one had fever, one should not eat meat or honey, nor should one drink wine. This is what Solomon meant when he said, "It is not good to eat much honey" (Proverbs 25:27). Health considerations should be the basis of one's eating and drinking [and not taste], so that one may drink [if it is necessary] an infusion of endives even if it is bitter. While it is not possible to live without eating and drinking, they present a model for sex. It [sex] is not to be undertaken [merely] for pleasure. Rather [sex is to be enjoyed] only for physical health, to maintain the species. One should not have sexual relations merely because one wants to do so. Rather, one should have sex [literally, emit semen] for health reasons, to maintain the species.

3. One would not be following the right way if one merely
lived by the rules of hygiene, concentrated on having a healthy
and strong body, had children to do one's necessary work, [and
left it at that]. Rather, one should concentrate on having one's
body healthy and strong so that one's soul is prepared to know
God. It is impossible to fully comprehend the sciences while
being sick or in pain. Similarly, while having sex, one should
concentrate on having a child who will become wise and a great
sage in Israel. One who always acts in such a manner will continually serve Adonai, even when such a person is engaged in
business, even when such a person is engaged in sex. This is the
case because one is always directed to meeting one's physical
needs, making sure that the body is healthy in order to serve God.
Even when a person sleeps, one should sleep with the purpose
that the mind be refreshed and the body be rested to prevent
one from becoming ill and unable to serve Adonai. Such sleep
becomes a [kind of] divine service. This is what the Sages meant
when they said, "Let all your deeds be for the sake of heaven."
It is what Solomon meant when he said in his wisdom, "In all
your ways, acknowledge God, and God will direct your paths"
(Proverbs 3:6).

Glossary

Aggadah   Nonlegal material in rabbinic literature.

Cheshbon hanefesh   Introspection, an accounting of the soul.

Halachah   Jewish law.

Midrash   Rabbinic parables, stories that explain gaps in the Bible.

Mitzvot   Commandments, divine instructions.

Teshuvah   Repentance, return.

Yetzer Hara   Evil Inclination, natural drives and urges.

Yetzer tov   The inclination to do good.

Index

ABOUT THE EDITORS

Leonard S. Kravitz is professor of Midrash and Homiletics at Hebrew Union College-Jewish Institute of Religion, New York, where he was ordained and received his Ph.D. He has been an army chaplain and a congregational rabbi. He is the author of *The Hidden Doctrine of Maimonides' Guide for the Perplexed* and was one of the editors of the *JWB Prayer Book for Jewish Personnel in the Armed Forces of the United States*. With Dr. Kerry M. Olitzky, he wrote *Pirke Avot: A Modern Commentary on Jewish Ethics*. Rabbi Kravitz is married and the father of two daughters.

Rabbi Kerry M. Olitzky, D. H. L., is director of the School of Education at Hebrew Union College-Jewish Institute of Religion, New York, where he also directs its graduate studies program. He writes and lectures widely on topics related to innovative religious education and spiritual renewal. He is the author or editor of 25 books and over 100 articles. Rabbi Olitzky's recent works include *The How To Handbook for Jewish Living*, volume 2, and *Sacred Moments: Tales from the Jewish Life Cycle*, both coauthored with Rabbi Ronald H. Isaacs. As the leading contributor to Jewish Twelve Step spirituality, Rabbi Olitzky is the coauthor of *Twelve Jewish Steps to Recovery* and author of *One Hundred Blessings a Day*, a book of daily meditations and affirmations based on the calendar and holiday cycle. He also prepared *Sparks beneath the Surface: A Spiritual Commentary on the Torah* with Rabbi Lawrence S. Kushner. Rabbi Olitzky and his wife, Sheryl, live in suburban New Jersey with their two children.